How George Rogers Clark Won the Northwest

Also from Westphalia Press

westphaliapress.org

The Idea of the Digital University

Bulwarks Against Poverty in America

Treasures of London

Avate Garde Politician

L'Enfant and the Freemasons

Baronial Bedrooms

Making Trouble for Muslims

Philippine Masonic Directory ~ 1918

Paddle Your Own Canoe

Opportunity and Horatio Alger

Careers in the Face of Challenge

Bookplates of the Kings

The Boy Chums Cruising in Florida Waters

Freemasonry in Old Buffalo

Original Cables from the Pearl Harbor Attack

Social Satire and the Modern Novel

The Essence of Harvard

The Genius of Freemasonry

A Definitive Commentary on Bookplates

James Martineau and Rebuilding Theology

No Bird Lacks Feathers

Gems of Song for the Eastern Star

Crime 3.0

Anti-Masonry and the Murder of Morgan

Understanding Art

Spies I Knew

Lodge "Himalayan Brotherhood" No. 459 C.E.

Ancient Masonic Mysteries

Collecting Old Books

Masonic Secret Signs and Passwords

Death Valley in '49

Lariats and Lassos

Mr. Garfield of Ohio

The Wisdom of Thomas Starr King

The French Foreign Legion

War in Syria

Naturism Comes to the United States

New Sources on Women and Freemasonry

Designing, Adapting, Strategizing in Online Education

Gunboat and Gun-runner

Meeting Minutes of Naval Lodge No. 4 F.A.A.M ~ 1812 & 1813

How George Rogers Clark Won the Northwest

and Other Essays in Western History

by Reuben Gold Thwaites

WESTPHALIA PRESS
An imprint of Policy Studies Organization

Westphalia Press
An imprint of Policy Studies Organization
1527 New Hampshire Ave., NW
Washington, D.C. 20036
info@ipsonet.org

**ISBN-13: 978-1-633910416
ISBN-10: 1633910415**

Cover design by Taillefer Long at Illuminated Stories:
www.illuminatedstories.com

Daniel Gutierrez-Sandoval, Executive Director
PSO and Westphalia Press

Devin Proctor, Director of Media and Publications
PSO and Westphalia Press

Updated material and comments on this edition
can be found at the Westphalia Press website:
www.westphaliapress.org

How George Rogers Clark Won the Northwest

And

Other Essays in Western History

By

Reuben Gold Thwaites

Author of "Down Historic Waterways," "On the Storied
Ohio," "Daniel Boone," etc. ; Editor of "The
Jesuit Relations," "Hennepin's Travels," etc.

Second Edition

Chicago
A. C. McClurg & Co.
1915

GEORGE ROGERS CLARK

From a copy by Edwards of Jarvis's portrait; the copy being in possession of the Wisconsin Historical Society

TO

MY COLLEAGUES AND FRIENDS

THE STAFF OF THE

WISCONSIN HISTORICAL LIBRARY

Preface

THE majority of the eight papers contained in this volume were first delivered as lectures; and later, in a modified form, were printed either in popular magazines or in the *Wisconsin Historical Collections*. For the present publication they have been radically revised and brought down to date — indeed, some of them, especially the opening article, have been entirely rewritten and bear small resemblance to the originals. Owing to the different occasions for which they were prepared, there is lacking a uniformity of treatment; it is hoped, however, that this variety of form, as well as the somewhat wide range of topics, may be found acceptable.

There is more cohesion in this collection than may at first appear. The stories of Mackinac and La Pointe and the account of Early Lead Mining give us glimpses of the old French régime, the idyllic period in the history of what we now know as the Middle

Preface

West.   Upon Braddock's Road, we witness an
incident in the march of the British in their
fateful onslaught upon French possessions in
the continental interior.   In their turn the
British army were ousted by American colonists through the Winning of the Northwest
by George Rogers Clark.   The Division of
the Northwest into States of the Republic
followed in due course, the story of their re-
spective boundaries being a curious chapter in
our history.   The Black Hawk War was the
last serious Indian uprising in the Middle
West; and its close marked the beginning of
extensive immigration into both Illinois and
Wisconsin.   Some account of that gentle
scholar, Lyman Copeland Draper, and the
now famous Draper Manuscripts — the richest
collection extant of original sources for the
study of Western history — would seem fitting
conclusion for a series like the present.

R. G. THWAITES.

MADISON, WIS., September 1, 1903.

Contents

I

How George Rogers Clark won the North-
WEST   PAGE
A vast hunting-ground 3
The king's pleasure ignored 5
The inrush of settlers 6
Lord Dunmore's War 6
Kentucky settled 7
Lieutenant-Governor Hamilton 8
"The hair-buying general" 9
Kentucky raided 10
George Rogers Clark 10
French hamlets 12
Frontier forts 13
Creole militiamen 14
Life among the Creoles 14
Centres of British influence 17
Clark's project 18
Raising volunteers 19
The backwoodsmen 20
The flotilla 22
At the Falls of the Ohio 23
Desertion 24
A picked company 24

Contents

HOW GEORGE ROGERS CLARK WON THE NORTH-
WEST (*continued*)   PAGE

The march to Kaskaskia 25
A picturesque Hero Tale 28
The capture of Kaskaskia 30
"An excess of joy" 32
Father Gibault 33
Cahokia 34
A new difficulty 35
Drilling recruits 36
"Our friends the Spanyards" 37
The tribesmen confused 38
Savage friends 39
Hamilton's war-party 40
Vincennes taken by Hamilton 40
A scare at Kaskaskia 42
Clark uneasy 44
Vigo's information 45
Forestalling the enemy 46
"Inward assurance of success" 47
A difficult march 48
The "drowned lands" 48
Fatigue and hunger 49
Wallowing through the bog 50
"Hard fortune!" 51
The man of iron 52
A frightful crossing 53
Hamilton still unconscious 54
Clark's letter to the villagers 54
A ruse 56
The attack on Vincennes 57
Clark's warning 59
Terrorizing the enemy 59

Contents

How George Rogers Clark won the North-
    west (*continued*)   Page

Clark demands unconditional surrender . . 60
The surrender 61
An heroic achievement 62
Illinois a Virginian county 64
Belated reinforcements 64
Results achieved 65
The Detroit project 66
Clark's power wanes 67
Jefferson's interesting proposition 67
Clark and Genet 69
Clark's later years 70
Importance of the conquest 71
Effect on the treaty of peace 71

II

The Division of the Northwest into States

Washington's suggestion 75
Jefferson's plan 77
Ordinance of 1787 79
The famous boundary article 80
Erection of Indiana Territory 82
Admission of Ohio 84
Erection of Michigan Territory 86
Michigan-Ohio boundary 89
Erection of Illinois Territory 93
No Man's Land 94
Illinois's northern boundary 95
Michigan spreads westward 96
Dissatisfaction west of Lake Michigan . . 97
Protracted agitation 99

Contents

THE DIVISION OF THE NORTHWEST INTO STATES
(*continued*) PAGE

Erection of Wisconsin Territory 102
Wisconsin's southern boundary 105
Iowa detached from Wisconsin 108
Wisconsin's northwest boundary 108
An international dispute 110

III

THE BLACK HAWK WAR

Partisan misrepresentations 115
Treaty of 1804 116
The old Sauk village 118
Black Hawk 119
Aids Tecumseh 122
Bitterness against Americans 123
Encroachment of squatters 123
Black Hawk stubborn 125
White Cloud, the Prophet 127
The whites threatened 129
The Hawk coerced 130
The Menominee massacre 131
Bad advice 132
British Band recruited 134
Early trails 134
Frontier settlements 136
Character of settlers 137
Ready for an Indian war 138
Illinois invaded 139
Shaubena's services 140
Troops called out 141
Stockade forts 142

Contents

THE BLACK HAWK WAR (*continued*)   PAGE

Atkinson organizes the army 143
Volunteers mobilized 144
The army sets out 145
Stillman's scouts 147
Tribesmen in council 148
Stillman's defeat 151
The Hawk at Koshkonong 153
A reign of terror 154
The army disbanded 156
A fresh levy 158
Irregular hostilities 159
Notable skirmishes 160
The lead-mine district 162
Dodge's Rough Riders 164
The new army 165
The advance to Koshkonong 165
Fruitless scouting 167
Black Hawk's camp 169
Illinois men discouraged 170
At Fort Winnebago 171
Mutinous conduct 173
A hot trail 174
The pursuit 175
At Madison 177
Battle of Wisconsin Heights 179
An unsuccessful appeal 181
Preparing for the pursuit 183
A forbidding path 185
The Mississippi, at last 186
The battle of the Bad Axe 187
A dishonorable chapter 192
The cost 193

Contents

THE BLACK HAWK WAR (*continued*) PAGE

Black Hawk a prisoner 193
Death of the Hawk 195
His character 196
What was accomplished 198

IV

THE STORY OF MACKINAC

A struggle for mastery 203
Three Mackinacs 204
Champlain hears of Lake Superior 205
Jean Nicolet 206
The earliest French 207
Flight of the Hurons 208
At Chequamegon Bay 209
Hurons return to Mackinac 210
Removal to St. Ignace 211
Jolliet and Marquette 212
Marquette's Journal 213
A French outpost 214
Establishment of Detroit 216
"Old Mackinaw" 217
The English 218
The island reoccupied 219
Arrival of Americans 220
English capture the island 221
Americans regain their footing 223
Centre of the fur-trade 224
The Creoles 226
Modern life 227

Contents

V

THE STORY OF LA POINTE	PAGE
Jean Nicolet	231
Topographical significance of Wisconsin	232
Radisson and Groseilliers on the Fox	234
At Chequamegon Bay	235
First habitation of white men	238
A gloomy winter	239
Ingratitude	241
Father Ménard	242
Father Allouez	243
Father Marquette	245
Lords of the fur-trade	247
The Indian and the trader	250
Fur-trade stockades	252
A copper nugget	254
The first bark	254
Allies of the French	256
A tragic tale	257
Alexander Henry	258
John Johnston	259
The Cadottes	260
The Warrens	263
First Protestant missionaries	265
A denominational controversy	267
An early Western book	269
Father Baraga	270
Changes in location	273

Contents

VI

A Day on Braddock's Road   Page
Brownsville 277
Redstone Old Fort 278
Nemacolin's Path 279
Redstone Creek 280
The National Road 281
A coaching tavern 284
Where Braddock fell 284
Great Meadows 286
The first shot 288
Siege of Fort Necessity 288
Remains of the fort 290
Jumonville's Camp 293
Dunbar's Camp 294
The meaning of it 295

VII

Early Lead Mining on the Upper Mississippi
Aboriginal use of lead 299
Taught by whites 300
Early traffic in ore 300
Perrot's mines 302
Le Sueur's operations 303
Crozat's monopoly 305
De Renault's discoveries 306
Primitive methods 308
France and Spain 309
A considerable industry 310

Contents

EARLY LEAD MINING ON THE UPPER MISSISSIPPI
  (*continued*)   PAGE
    Duralde's grant 311
    A notable market 312
    Dubuque's mines 313
    Aboriginal smelting 315
    Aboriginal mining 317
    Dubuque's Indian prospectors 318
    "The Mines of Spain" 319
    Dubuque's statement 320
    Opening of American régime 320
    A shot tower 322
    The Buck lead 322
    French-Canadians ousted 324
    Lead a currency 324
    A general movement 326
    An enormous nugget 327
    The lease system 328
    A horde of squatters 329
    The great "boom" 330
    Spanish claimants ejected 331

VIII

THE DRAPER MANUSCRIPTS
    The collector 335
    A youthful passion 336
    A patron of learning 338
    At college 338
    Doctors disagree 339
    Notable correspondents 340
    An itinerant interviewer 341
    Pioneer hospitality 341

Contents

THE DRAPER MANUSCRIPTS (*continued*)   PAGE

Important interviews 342
A rich harvest 344
A Mississippi episode 347
In a haven of refuge 348
Alone in his specialty 349
Co-partnership with Lossing 350
Fearing to " go to press " 351
Practically founds the Wisconsin Historical
    Society 352
King's Mountain 354
Material beyond his control 355
The end 356
The man himself 356
An eminently useful career 357
An enduring monument 358

INDEX 361

List of Illustrations

FULL PAGE

                                                Page

George Rogers Clark . . . . *Frontispiece*

A Kentucky Fort 14

Clark's Route 26

Clark's Letter to Hamilton 60

Black Hawk 120

Fort Winnebago in 1834 172

Scene of the Battle of the Bad Axe 186

Lahontan's Map of Mackinac Strait, 1741 . . 214

Village of La Pointe, Madelaine Island . . . 262

TEXT

Division of the Northwest, I. 77

      "   "   "   II. 79

      "   "   "   III. 83

      "   "   "   IV. 87

      "   "   "   V. 88

      "   "   "   VI. 92

      "   "   "   VII. 94

List of Illustrations

				Page
Division of the Northwest, VIII.				98
,, ,, ,, IX.				100
,, ,, ,, X.				103
,, ,, ,, XI.				109
Seat of Black Hawk War				117
Chequamegon Bay				237
Plan of Battle at Fort Necessity				287

I

HOW GEORGE ROGERS CLARK WON THE NORTHWEST

ESSAYS

WESTERN HISTORY

I

HOW GEORGE ROGERS CLARK WON THE NORTHWEST

UPON the eve of the Revolutionary War, the vast stretch of country northwest of the river Ohio — later divided into the States of Ohio, Indiana, Illinois, Michigan, and

A vast hunting-ground Wisconsin — was a part of the British Province of Quebec. As a result of Wolfe's victory on the Plains of Abraham, Great Britain had acquired it from France by the treaty of 1763. Like the French, the British ministry designed keeping the region as an enormous hunting-ground for the benefit of the Indians and the fur-traders. In adopting this policy, the government were influenced by three considerations: first, the enormous profits reaped by English merchants from the commerce of the forest; again, the apprehension that should colonial settlement spread beyond the Alleghanies, these merchants could not supply the people as easily as before, and colonial trade would be correspondingly hampered; third, the fear that if allowed to intrench themselves behind the mountain wall, American borderers might become bolder and more impudent than ever. Selfish and short-sighted, they endeavored arbitrarily to hem in their colonists to the Atlantic Slope, thus adding a fresh cause for colonial uneasiness, already assuming ominous proportions.

A proclamation issued (October 7, 1763) in the name of King George III., declared [1] " it to be our royal will and pleasure . . . to reserve under our sovereignty, protection, and dominion, for the use of the said Indians, . . . all the lands and territories lying to the westward of the sources of the rivers which fall into the sea from the West and North West. . . . And we do hereby strictly forbid, on pain of our displeasure, all our loving subjects from making any purchases or settlements whatever, or taking possession of any of the lands above reserved, without our especial leave and license."

[1] Full text in *Gentleman's Magazine*, xxxiii., pp. 477-479; reprinted in *Wisconsin Historical Collections*, xi., pp. 46-52.

But King George's proclamation could no more keep American frontiersmen from crossing the Alleghanies and taking possession of the fertile valleys and plains drained by the west-flowing waters, than Mrs. Partington with her broom could sweep the Atlantic Ocean from her door-sill. Despite this attempt to obstruct the tide of Western settlement, the Northwest came soon to be conquered and held by Americans, until the happy result of the Revolution made it the national domain of the young Republic.

Apparently, the royal proclamation was as completely ignored by the colonists and offi- *The king's* cials of Virginia and Pennsylvania. *pleasure* as though never penned. Under the *ignored* vague terms of their charters, both these colonies claimed the country north of the Ohio. Virginia held the advantage, for Fort Pitt, at the " Forks of the Ohio," — our modern Pittsburg, — was governed by her militia, and Pennsylvania protested in vain. By this time, settlers were flocking into the Alleghany and Monongahela valleys, divided in loyalty according to the district whence they came; but the majority of them, especially upon the Monongahela, were of Virginia origin.

After a few years of comparative peace upon the border, the Indians were becoming alarmed at these formidable inroads on their hunting-grounds. The settlers were cutting down the forests, destroying the game, opening up farms, and giving every evidence of an intention to monopolize the country. Streams of borderers were also pouring into Kentucky overland, by way of Boone's road through Cumberland Gap; or down the Ohio in all manner of curious craft, laden with their families, flocks, tools, and weapons, ready to take armed possession of that bountiful land. The white army of Western occupation was not over-nice in its methods of overriding whatever lay in its path. Aside from the loss of soil, the tribesmen had much to suffer at the hands of the borderers. Small wonder, then, that in 1774 they combined to contest this wholesale invasion, and after the manner of their kind harried the entire length of the border from Lake Erie to Cumberland Gap, with fire, rapine, and human slaughter.

The inrush of settlers

Lord Dunmore, Governor of Virginia, led an army against them. As usual, the Indians were defeated; although their leader, Cornstalk, a Shawnee chief, in whom there was much to admire, fought

Lord Dunmore's war

with rare valor in the decisive battle of Point Pleasant, at the junction of the Great Kanawha and the Ohio. In this campaign, called in history Lord Dunmore's War, were engaged George Rogers Clark and many other Virginia frontiersmen who either were, or were soon destined to become, famous among the Western pioneers.

Peace was soon after declared in a great council on the Pickaway Plains in Ohio, wherein the Northern Indians surrendered to the whites what slender interests they held in the neutral hunting-grounds of Kentucky. This concession, empty though it was, combined with the discreet neutrality observed by the vanquished tribes during the first two years of the Revolutionary struggle, rendered possible the settlement of Kentucky; thus forging the first link in the chain of events on which the colonists based their claim to the country beyond the Alleghanies.

ʌAlthough the Revolution, which soon followed Dunmore's War, hampered progress upon *Kentucky* the Atlantic Slope, trans-Alleghany *settled* development progressed apace. For a time practically unhindered by the savages, settlers in goodly number came straggling into the Western country. Numerous small

communities sprang up along the Ohio and
many of its feeders, and in Kentucky there
soon were several log forts, around each of
which were grouped the rude cabins of frontiersmen, who were half farmers, half hunters,
— tall, stalwart fellows, as courageous as lions,
and ever on the watch for the crouching Indian
foe, who, although now absent, might appear
when least expected.

This quasi-peace on the Western border —
it was well towards the close of the century
Lieutenant- before there was secured absolute
Governor freedom from Indian forays — was
Hamilton soon broken. Naturally, the sympa-
thies of the Indians were stronger for the
British fur-traders than for the Americans,
who were turning the hunting-grounds into
farms, and took small pains to ingratiate themselves with the aborigines. The British post
of Detroit was commanded by Lieutenant-Governor Henry Hamilton — a bold, brave, untiring man, but unscrupulous. During the winter
of 1776–77, acting under orders from his superiors, he gathered there the Northwest Indians
in large numbers. Among his strange guests
were long-haired Sioux from Northwest Wisconsin and the Minnesota plains; sharp-faced
Chippewas, from the south shore of Lake Supe-

rior; sleek and oily Sauks and Foxes from the Mississippi, below Prairie du Chien; broad-visaged, flat-nosed, swarthy Winnebagoes from the Rock River, the Wisconsin, and the Green Bay country; Potawatomis, with open countenance and feminine cast of features, from Milwaukee River and all along the west shore of Lake Michigan; and Menominees or wild-rice eaters, from west of Green Bay and around Lake Shawano.

With the various bands, repugnant in their filth, squalor, and savagery, this cultured Eng-

" The hair-buying general " lishman held council after council, himself joining in their wild songs and dances; and, amid yelps of applause, with skilful throw planting the hatchet in the war-post, which was smeared with blood and hung with the scalps of American borderers. It is not certain to what extent Hamilton deserved the opprobrious epithet, " the hair-buying general," which the backwoodsmen fastened upón him; but we know that in the warfare which he induced the savages to undertake against the Americans, those warriors who, as evidence of their prowess, brought most scalps to Detroit, received the largest rewards. Hamilton always claimed that he made endeavors to curb the ferocity of his savage allies, but he

must have known how impossible was this feat. In judging him, however, we must remember that the ethics of warfare were not in that day as humane as in ours.

In the early spring of 1777, Hamilton's Indians began crossing the Ohio to raid the *Kentucky* Kentucky settlements. Militiamen *raided* were ambushed, several of the block-house forts were burned, prisoners were submitted to nameless horrors; it seemed as if pandemonium had suddenly broken loose upon the border. In the numerous sieges which ensued, there were performed feats of individual prowess on the part of the backwoodsmen and their wives, that are unsurpassed in the records of heroism. By the close of the year, so general had been the rush of settlers back to their old homes east of the mountains, but five or six hundred remained in all Kentucky. These were liable, on call, to garrison duty in the four remaining stations of Boonesborough, Harrodsburg, Price's, and Logan's.

Prominent among the defenders of Kentucky during this fateful year, was George Rogers *George* Clark. He had come from a good *Rogers* family in Virginia, was but twenty-five *Clark* years of age, and, for his day, had acquired a fair education, but from childhood

had been a rover of the woods.   Full six feet
in height, stout of frame, possessed of "red
hair, and a black, penetrating, sparkling eye,"
he was courageous even to audacity, and exhibited strong, often unbridled passions.   Clark
early became a backwoods surveyor, such as
Washington was, and many another young
colonial gentleman of superior antecedents and
training.   With chain and compass, axe and
rifle, he had in the employ of land speculators
wandered far and wide through the border
region, learning its trails, its fords, its mountain
passes, and its aborigines, better than his
books.   In many ways Clark was a marked
character in a community of strongly accent-
uated types — heroes and desperadoes, saints
and sinners.   At the age of twenty-one he had
served in the Dunmore War, and then settled
as a Kentucky farmer at the mouth of Fish
Creek, only again to be called out by an Indian
uprising and obliged thereafter to take a leading part in the protracted defence of the "Dark
and Bloody Ground."   Almost from the first,
Clark ranked with Boone, Benjamin Logan, and
others of his associates whose names are prominent in the bead-roll of American border
heroes; he was soon to surpass them all.

When France surrendered her American

possessions to England, the French Creoles
for the most part remained in their old haunts,
French and simply transferred their politi-
hamlets cal allegiance to King George.   In
the year 1777, of which we have spoken, there
were several little French hamlets in the country
to the north of the Ohio River, the outgrowth
either of early Jesuit missions or the needs of
the fur-trade, or of both combined.   Detroit,
commanding the straits between Lakes Erie
and Huron, was the largest of these.   The important post of Mackinac guarded the gateway
between Lakes Huron, Michigan, and Superior.   Vincennes, on the Wabash, was another
strategic point occupied by the French Canadians.   Over on the Mississippi, Kaskaskia
and Cahokia were centres of French commerce
in the West.   At Green Bay were a few fur-
traders' cabins, chief among them the establishment of Charles Langlade, first permanent
settler of Wisconsin.   At Prairie du Chien
there was as yet no village, although several
traders frequently made their headquarters
there.   In the records of the time, we have
hints of trading stations near Ashland, on
Lakes Chetek, Flambeau, Courte Oreille, and
on the eastern edge of the Wisconsin forest, at
Milwaukee Bay and the port of Two Rivers.

At Detroit, Mackinac, Vincennes, Kaskaskia, and Cahokia, were small forts built of logs. *Frontier forts* These structures had originally been erected by the French fur-traders to protect their stocks of goods, and in times of danger served as rallying-points. When the English took possession they were considerably strengthened, and under this remodelling some of them came to be formidable fastnesses in a wilderness where besiegers were chiefly savages, without artillery. As a rule, the curtains were guarded at the four corners by solidly built blockhouses, serving as bastions, these houses being generally two stories in height and pierced for rifles and cannon. One or more of the curtains were formed by the rear walls of a row of log-cabins, the others being composed of palisades, great logs standing on end, the bottoms well buried in the ground and the tops sharp-pointed; around the inner edge of these wooden ramparts, the roofs of the cabins formed a gallery, on which crouched those of the defenders who were not already engaged in the blockhouses. The heavy-timbered gate, with its massive forged hinges and bolts, was guarded with particular tenacity. In the event of the enemy forcing this, or making a breach in the curtains by burning or scaling the palisades, the block-houses were the last towers of refuge, around which the contest was waged to the bitter end.

At the time of which we are speaking, these frontier forts were generally commanded by *Creole* British captains, with a few regular *militiamen* officers and privates to form the nucleus of the garrison, the remainder of the force being composed of French-Canadian volunteers; although we shall find in charge at Kaskaskia a French officer in the English service. At Detroit and Mackinac, throughout the Revolutionary War, these Creole militiamen remained firm to the British cause; but farther south, — at Vincennes, Kaskaskia, and Cahokia, — the English were to discover in them but fair-weather allies. Sometimes the fort, as at Kaskaskia, was the centre of the little French village which had grown up around it; in other cases, as at Vincennes, it commanded the cluster of cabins from some neighboring eminence.

The people of these French-Canadian river-side hamlets took life easily. Among them *Life among* were many engaged in the fur-trade at *the Creoles* certain seasons of the year — bourgeois, or masters, for the most part, serving as

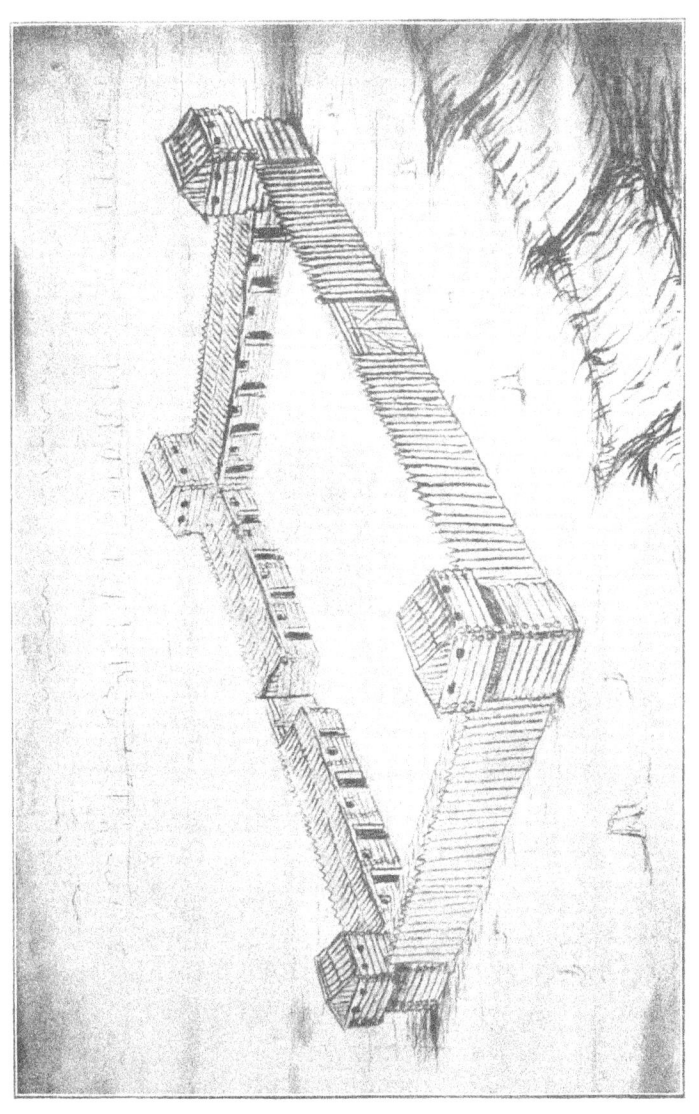

A KENTUCKY FORT

Ideal sketch, from contemporary descriptions and plans, by James R. Stuart

the agents or clerks of Montreal merchants; voyageurs, or boatmen, men-of-all-work who propelled the canoes when afloat, carried them and their cargoes over portages, transported packs of goods and furs through the forest inlands, cared for the camps, and acted as guards for the persons and property of their employers; coureurs de bois, or wood-rangers, men devoted to a life in the woods through the very love of adventure, sometimes conducting a far-reaching fur-trade on their own account, — the widest travellers and most daring spirits in all the great Northwest.

The habitants, or permanent villagers, were for the most part farmers in a small way. Down by the river stood their little log cabins, with well-sweeps and orchards, back of which stretched narrow, ribbon-like fields, remnants of which one may see to-day at Quebec and Montreal, or indeed at any of our old French towns in the West — for instance, Green Bay and Prairie du Chien. The French habitant was a social animal. He loved the little village wineshop, where, undisturbed by his sharp-eyed, sharp-visaged, prim and gossipy, white-aproned spouse, he could enjoy his pipe, his bowl, and his " fiddlers three." For they were famous fiddlers, these French-Canadians. On social occasions the fiddle was indispensable. No American wilderness was so far away that the little French fiddle had not been there. The Indians recognized it as a part of the furniture of every fur-trader's camp. At night, as the wanderers lounged around the blazing heap of logs, the sepulchral arches of the forest resounded with the piercing strains of the violin, accompanying the gayly sashed and turbaned voyageurs, as in metallic tones they chanted melodies of the river, the chase, love, and the wassail. In the village, no christening or wedding was complete without the fiddler; at the almost nightly social gatherings, in each other's puncheon-floored cabins, this cross-legged king of the feast was enthroned on a plank table.

The river was their highway. From earliest youth, they understood the handling of a canoe. Just as in the Far West the cowboy mounts his horse to cross the street, and refuses work that cannot be done on the back of a broncho, the French-Canadian went in his boat to visit his next-door neighbor.

It made small difference to these people who were in political control. All they sought was socially to be left alone, to enjoy life in their own simple fashion. On general principles, the attitude of King George, who wished the

Western hunting-grounds left unimpaired, was more to their liking than the aggressive, land-winning temper of the American settlers. Then again, over half of these French-Canadians had Indian wives, and in the veins of many flowed Indian blood. They were drawn to the savage tribes through relationship and sympathy. The men of New France were always cheek by jowl with the tribesmen, an amalgamation surprising to men of Anglo-Saxon parentage, who seem never to be able to sympathize with barbarians. Yet despite these ties, the French of the Illinois posts, having already found it easy to change masters, were willing enough to fraternize with the American backwoodsmen when once brought into communication with them.

Clark was well aware of this condition of affairs north of the Ohio. The French villages *Centres of* were centres of British influence, where *British in-* the natural hostility of the savages to *fluence* the American frontier settlements was being persistently excited by bribes and by appeals to their passions. Clark realized that so long as the Northwest was suffered to remain a safe rallying-point for war-parties, Kentucky would continue to suffer from forays and very likely the settlers be wholly exterminated or at best driven from the field. He resolved, therefore, to " carry the war into Africa," to establish a military frontier in the enemy's country. Spies were accordingly sent to Kaskaskia and Vincennes. They soon returned, reporting that the British were keeping but loose guard, and that while the French had conceived the notion, from British reports, that the Kentucky backwoodsmen were barbarians more cruel than the Indians about them, they were not more than lukewarm in their attachment to the king.

In August, 1777, Clark started overland to Virginia, where he consulted with Patrick *Clark's* Henry, then governor of that colony, *project* as well as with other prominent men, regarding his plan for capturing the British posts north of the Ohio. These gentlemen at once fell in with the audacious project; but as the success of the undertaking depended on secrecy, the aid given him by the governor was obtained from the legislature on the general plea that it was designed for the protection of Kentucky.[1]   Clark was made lieutenant-

[1] The public and private instructions given to Clark by Governor Henry are in the Appendix to Clark's letter to George Mason, of Virginia (dated Louisville, November 19, 1779), as edited by Pirtle, in *Ohio Valley Historical Series*, No. 3 (Cincinnati, 1869).

colonel (January 2, 1778), was given the equivalent of six thousand dollars in sadly depreciated currency, and was authorized to enlist in his cause three hundred and fifty Virginians wherever he might find them.

The jealousy between Virginia and Pennsylvania, and the impossibility of revealing his *Raising* purpose, made it difficult for Clark *volunteers* to raise volunteers; indeed, he met with considerable opposition from those who apparently suspected this Western movement, on political grounds, or were jealous of an attempt to sequester men whose services were needed in the defence of the mountain valleys. It was May (1778) before he could collect about a hundred and fifty borderers from the clearings and hunters' camps of the Alleghany foot-hills, both east and west of the range.[1]

---

[1] Clark says in his letter to Mason : " Many leading Men in the fronteers, . . . had like to have put an end to the enterprise, not knowing my Destination, and through a spirit of obstinacy they combined and did every thing that lay in their power to stop the Men that had Enlisted, and set the whole Fronteers in an uproar, even condescended to harbour and protect those that Deserted; I found my case desperate, the longer I remained the worse it was. . . . I plainly saw that my Principal Design [an attack on Detroit] was baffled. . . . I was resolved to push to Kentucky with what men I

They were a rough, and for the most part unlettered folk, these Virginia backwoodsmen *The back-* who formed Clark's little army of con-
woodsmen quest. There was of course no attempt among them at military uniform, officers in no wise being distinguished from men. The conventional dress of eighteenth-century borderers was an adaptation to local conditions, being in part borrowed from the Indians. Their feet were encased in moccasins. Perhaps the majority of the corps had loose, thin trousers of homespun or buckskin, with a fringe of leather thongs down each outer seam of the legs; but many wore only leggings of leather, and were as bare of knee and thigh as a Highland clansman; indeed, many of the pioneers were Scotch-Irish, some of whom had been accustomed to this airy costume in the mother-land. Common to all were fringed hunting shirts or smocks, generally of buckskin — a picturesque, flowing garment reaching from neck to knees, and girded about the waist by a leathern belt, from which dangled the

could gather in West Augusta; being Joined by Capt[s] Bowman and Helms who had raised a Comp[y] for the Expedition, but two thirds of them was stopt by the undesign'd Enemies to the Country that I have before mentioned: In the whole I had about one hundred & fifty Men Collected and set sail for the Falls [of the Ohio, now Louisville]."

tomahawk and scalping-knife. On one hip
hung the carefully scraped powder-horn; on
the other, a leather sack, serving both as game-
bag and provision-pouch, although often the
folds of the shirt, full and ample above the
belt, were the depository for food and ammunition. A broad-brimmed felt hat, or a cap of
fox-skin or squirrel-skin, with the tail dangling
behind, crowned the often tall and always
sinewy frontiersman. His constant companion
was his home-made flint-lock rifle — a clumsy,
heavy weapon, so long that it reached to the
chin of the tallest man, but unerring in the
hands of an expert marksman, such as was
each of these backwoodsmen.

They were rough in manners and in speech.
Among them, we must confess, were men who
had fled from the coast settlements because no
longer to be tolerated in a law-abiding community. There were not lacking mean, brutal
fellows, whose innate badness had on the un-
trammelled frontier developed into wickedness.
Many joined Clark for mere adventure, for
plunder, and deviltry. The majority, however,
were men of good parts, who sought to protect their homes at whatever peril — sincere
men, as large of heart as they were of frame,
many of them in later years developing into

citizens of a high type of effectiveness in a
frontier commonwealth. As a matter of history, most of them proved upon this expedition
to be heroes worthy of the fame they won and
the leader whom they followed.

On the border, military discipline was as
slight as in an Indian war-party. The officers,
elected by open vote, exercised little authority
over the wild, daring spirits whom they nominally led. The only enduring tie between them
was that of personal regard ; the only cohesion
in the force, reliance on the prowess and judgment of the commander. Clark had the full
confidence of his men, holding them by a personal influence which was as strong as it was
remarkable. Probably no other man on the
border could have done what he was about
to do.

" I set out from Redstone [Brownsville, Pa.]
the `12th of May," writes Clark in his famous
The letter to Mason, " leaving the Country
flotilla in great confusion, much distressed
by Indians." His little fleet consisted of the
usual flatboats then used by immigrants and
traders to the West. Stopping at Pittsburg
and Wheeling to take on the simple supplies
for which Governor Henry had given him requi-
sitions upon the military officers of the upper

Ohio country,[1] he cautiously floated down the Ohio. Indian attacks were imminent, for the river was frequently being crossed by war-parties; but fortunately the flotilla met with no opposition from this source. An exploring party bound for the Ozark joined them at the mouth of the Great Kanawha, and together the two expeditions " had a very pleasant voyage to the falls of the Ohio."

Early in June they arrived at the " Falls of the Ohio." Here, at the present Louisville, *At the Falls of the Ohio* the river is broken by falls, which both in ascending and descending necessitated the unloading of boats and the use of the portage path around the obstruction. In primitive days, a portage was of great importance strategically, for it controlled the waterway. For this reason, Clark tactfully chose as his base of operations the island in the centre of the falls, which commanded the portage path, and upon it

[1] " For the Transportation of the Troops, provisions, &c., d)wn the Ohio, you are to apply to the Commanding Officer at Fort Pitt for Boats, &c. . . . You are to apply to General Hand for powder & Lead necessary for this Expedition. If he can't supply it the person who has that which Capt Lynn bro^t from Orleans can. Lead was sent to Hampshire by my orders & that may be delivered you." — Henry's private instructions to Clark.

built a blockhouse fort and planted a crop of Indian corn.[1]

Another reason for the island camp was, that dissatisfaction had by this time become mani-

Desertion   fest among his men. Few knew of his purpose, and the mystery which necessarily hung around the expedition was doubtless preying on the minds of the weak-hearted. The commander found it essential to keep a strict guard on the boats and to institute a discipline which was irksome to all. One lieutenant, heading a small party, con-trived to escape, but the following day some of his men were captured, and the proper subordination was soon secured.

On the twenty-sixth of June, having been joined by a few volunteers from Kentucky and

A picked   the Holston valley, Clark's flotilla was
company   again on the move, the goal being Kaskaskia, the principal post in the Illinois country. It was a picked company, the weak-lings having been left at the island to guard the blockhouse and cultivate the cornfield.[2] Some of the bravest men on the frontier were

[1] Hence the present name, Corn Island.

[2] "About twenty families that had followed me much against my Inclination, I found now to be of service to me in guarding a Block-house that I had erected on the Island to secure my Provisions." — Clark's letter to Mason.

the captains of the four companies, and the equipment was as light as that carried by Indians on a foray.

The falls were " shot " during a total solar eclipse, an omen variously interpreted by the superstitious backwoodsmen. Henceforth the Ohio was followed to the now abandoned French stronghold, Fort Massac, some ten miles below the mouth of the Tennessee.[1] Just before leaving the island, Clark had received news of the alliance between the United States and France [2] in the prosecution of the Revolutionary War, and hoped that this would make it easier for him to win over the French in the Illinois and Wabash country.

The American commander feared to descend the Ohio to its mouth and then ascend the *The march* Mississippi, the ordinary route to *to Kaskas-* Kaskaskia, for his spies had brought *kia* word that that path was being patrolled by French and Indian scouts. He

[1] Built by the French in 1758, on their retreat from Fort Duquesne. The site is now a public park in the environs of Metropolis, Ill.

[2] See John Campbell's letter to Clark, dated Pittsburg, June 8, 1778, in *American Historical Review*, viii., p. 497. The original of this and most other manuscript material extant, relative to Clark, is in the Draper MSS., Wisconsin Historical Society.

therefore struck across country some hundred and twenty miles, being guided by an American hunter who had recently been in the French settlements. The poor fellow lost his way when not far out upon the path. This incident, Clark relates, " put the whole Troops in the greatest Confusion," and caused the leader, suspecting treachery, to threaten " to put the guide to Death if he did not find his way that Evening." Fortunately for all concerned, the sadly frightened pilot " in two hours got within his knowledge."

With great caution, Clark toilsomely pushed through the forest and over " those level Plains that is frequent throughout this extensive Country . . . much afraid of being discovered in these Meadows as we might be seen in many places for several miles." On the evening of the fourth of July his " little Army " of less than two hundred riflemen reached the east bank of the Kaskaskia River, on the opposite side from and above the town, which was about three miles away.[1]

[1] In a letter by Clark, apparently to Governor Henry, and doubtless written in the summer or autumn of 1777, the former describes Kaskaskia from reports made to him by spies : " It is situated 30 leagues above the mouth of the Ohio, on a river of its own name, five miles from its mouth and two miles east of the Mississippi. . . . The town of Kus-

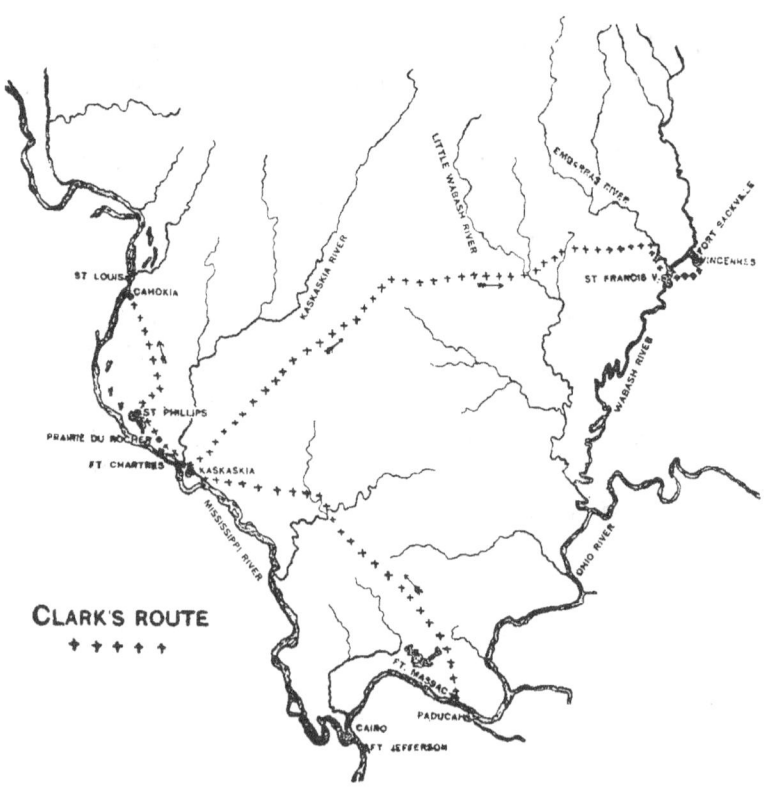

CLARK'S ROUTE
✛ ✛ ✛ ✛ ✛

Remaining under cover of the woods until dusk, the Americans moved forward along the bank, downstream, to a farmhouse a mile from the village. They took the family prisoners, and learned from them that Philippe de Rocheblave, the French commandant of the English fort, had " had some suspicean of being attacted and had some preparations, keeping out Spies, but they making no discoveries, had got off their guard." Rocheblave had frequently appealed to Detroit for assistance, but without avail. The captured habitants reported that the French militia were fairly well organized, and greatly feared

kuskies contains about one hundred families of French and English, and carry on an extensive trade with the Indians ; and they have a considerable number of negroes that bear arms and are chiefly employed in managing their farms that lay around the town, and send a considerable quantity of flour and other commodities to New Orleans. . . . The fort, which stands a small distance below the town is built of stockading about ten feet high, with blockhouses at each corner, with several pieces of cannon mounted, powder, ball, and all other necessary stores without guard or a single soldier. . . . The principal inhabitants are entirely against the American cause, and look on us as notorious rebels that ought to be subdued at any rate, but I don't doubt but after being acquainted with the cause they would become good friends to it." There is only a transcript of this letter in existence, and this is in the Draper MSS. ; it is published in full, edited by Professor F. J. Turner, in *Amer. Hist. Rev.*, April, 1903, pp. 491–494.

the Americans, while the Indians of the district bitterly hated the " Big Knives," [1] as they called the frontiersmen. There were four or five hundred men in the place, and it could only be taken by surprise. A few days before there had been an alarm in the fort, but a sense of security was now felt.

Clark was as quick in action as in thought. Having at the farm " found plenty of Boats to Cross in," his men were in two hours' time silently ferried across the Kaskaskia River. They were divided into two parties, one surrounding the town, which was above, although adjoining the fort, the other accompanying their leader and a French guide from the farmhouse under the brow of the river-bank to the postern gate, near the water's edge.

The myth-maker is of every age and every land. He has not spared American frontier history. We see his handiwork in

A pictu-resque Hero Tale

the Pocahontas story ; in popular tales concerning Jesuit mission-sites in the Old Northwest; in the apocryphal incidents of the siege of Wheeling; in the hero-tales of Boone in Kentucky, of the scouts Brady and

---

[1] The Indians thus styled the borderers, probably because whites first introduced among North American savages the use of knives.

Wetzel, of Brant, the Iroquois chieftain — to mention but a few. He has also befooled some of the chroniclers of the doings of George Rogers Clark.

We have been told that, as Clark and his men lay there by the postern gate, they could hear the sounds of French fiddles squeaking a quadrille, and now and then gay shouts and laughter. The officers of the post were, it is related, giving a ball to the habitants, in the large assembly room with its puncheon floor. The outlying houses were deserted. Men and women, villagers and garrison, Indians and coureurs de bois, were without regard to rank or race crowded into the hall, heeding nothing save the dance. Even the sentinels had deserted their posts to join in the festivities, and Kaskaskia, a victim to the irrepressible gayety of the French, was wholly unguarded.

Leaving his men at the gate, says the story-teller, Clark, alone with his guide, strode across the parade and, leaning against the door-post, with folded arms watched the gay scene — a patch of light and color in the heart of the gloomy wilderness. As he calmly stood there, an unbidden guest, an Indian lying curled in his blanket on the entry floor, started and gazed intently upon him. Another moment, the savage sprang to his feet and sounded the war-whoop.

In the midst of the general consternation, Rocheblave and his brother officers hurried to the door; but Clark, unmoved, bade them go on with the dance, but be pleased to remember that they were now holding revelry under the banner of Virginia and not that of Great Britain. Instantly Clark's detail, left at the gate, warned by the war-whoop rushed in and secured the garrison. It is a picturesque hero tale. One fastidious might say it smacked overmuch of melodrama; but I almost wish it were true, for our often sombre Western history seems now and then to need a lurid touch like this.[1]

While Clark's letter to Mason gives but the principal incidents in outline, we have the *The* credible statement of one of his men [2] *capture of* that Clark's party of about a dozen, *Kaskaskia* as they lay under the river-bank, were " saluted merrily " by keen-scented dogs,

[1] The tale appears to have first been published in Denny's " Memoir of Major Ebenezer Denny," Penn. Histor. Soc. *Publications* (1860), vii., pp. 217, 218. The scene has been represented by an artist in Lodge's *Story of the Revolution* (N. Y., 1898), ii., p. 20.

[2] Statement of Daniel Henry to L. C. Draper, in 1844, in the Draper MSS.

but this did not disturb the little garrison. Finding the fort gate open, they pushed on in the dark to Rocheblave's house, pointed out by the guide, found and captured the unsuspecting governor in an upper room, brought him below, and then gave " a loud huzza, answered by the other" party, which had now divided into squads of four or five men each. Yelling like mad, the now united Virginians easily overawed the puny garrison of Creoles, and, to resume our quotations from Clark, " in 15 minutes" were masters of the place without the firing of a gun.

Every street was guarded, and runners were sent out, "ordering the People on pane of Death to keep close to their Houses, which they observ'd." At daylight, the soldiers and the people were disarmed. By this stern promptness Clark had succeeded in thoroughly cowing the villagers — " nothing could excell the Confusion these People seemed to be in, being taught to expect nothing but Savage treatment from the Americans. Giving all for lost their Lives were all they could dare beg for, which they did with the greatest fervancy, they were willing to be Slaves to save their families. I told them it did not suit me to give them an answer at that time, they repared to their houses, trembling as if they were led to Execution; my principal would not suffer me to distress such a number of People, except, through policy it was necessary."

Their mercurial spirits soon rose, however, when they learned during the day that instead of being made the slaves of the bloodthirsty Virginians, they were, upon taking the oath of allegiance to the Republic, to be allowed to come and go at their pleasure, and meet in their little Catholic church as of old. Clark explained to a deputation of the people the American view of the war, and added that the Republic meant to free, not enslave, the people of the Illinois country, and would be a better friend to them than the British king.

"No sooner had they [a deputation of villagers who waited on him] heard this," pictur- *"An excess* esquely writes Clark, "than joy *of joy"* sparkled in their Eyes and [they] fell into Transports of Joy that really surprised me. . . . They returned to their families, and in a few minutes the scean of mourning and distress, was turned into an excess of Joy, nothing else seen nor heard. Addorning the streets with flowers Pavilians of different colours, compleating their happiness by singing, &c."

To a man, the Creoles took the oath of loyalty to the United States. Commander Rocheblave, however, had been violent and insulting in temper, and Clark, to teach the people a lesson, sent him on to Virginia as a prisoner and appropriated his black slaves, which were soon after sold for the equivalent of $2,500. This prize-money was divided among the riflemen, who were well pleased at the financial outcome of the expedition.

As for Father Pierre Gibault,[1] the Kaskaskia priest, he was a zealous Clark man from *Father* the time the generous conqueror gave *Gibault* him to understand that an American officer had " nothing to do with Churches more than to defend them from Insult. That by the laws of the State [Virginia] his Religion had as great Previledges as any other: This seem'd to compleat their happiness." The good father assured his new friend that although as a priest he had " nothing to do with temporal business, that he would give them such hints in the Spiritual way, that would be very conducive to the business."

[1] Whom Clark, singularly perverse in the spelling of foreign proper names, calls " Mr. Jeboth."

3

A small party of Americans, with some French volunteers now eager to serve the *Cahokia and* cause of Virginia, went rapidly on *Vincennes* horseback to Cahokia, "about sixty miles up the Country," where the people promptly fraternized with the invaders, and accepted Captain Joseph Bowman as local superintendent. At the same time, Gibault, on his own motion, in company with Dr. Le Font, principal of the Jesuit seminary at Kaskaskia, and a few others, went overland to Vincennes, "a Town about the size of Williamsburg." On the first of August they returned with the news that through the father's influence the American flag had been hoisted on the walls of the fort, from which the half-dozen British soldiers had deemed it wise to withdraw. Clark at once sent Captain Leonard Helm to take command of the French militia at Vincennes, while he remained at Kaskaskia.

Successful in his immediate designs, Clark's position was nevertheless perilous. "The numerous Tribes of Indians attached to the French was yet to enfluence, for I was too weak to treat them in any other way . . . every Nation of Indians could raise three, or four times our Number. . . . Savages, whose minds had long been poisoned by the English." Far to the north lay the British base in the Northwest. These southern towns were but the outposts of a formidable and resourceful enemy, concerning whose movements he could learn but little.

His chief desire was to strike at Detroit, as the centre of English operations; but for *A new* this he needed a far larger corps *difficulty* — indeed, he lacked sufficient men for his present plans, which involved several side expeditions among both French and Indians, in order to secure his foothold. A new difficulty now beset him, and increased the hazard. The greater part of his followers, their time of service having expired, were hot for returning home. " It was," he tells us, " with Difficulty that I could support that Dignity that was necessary to give my orders that force that was necessary, but by great preasants and promises I got about one hundred of my Detachment Enlisted for eight months, and to colour my staying with so few Troops I made a faint of returning to the Falls, as though I had sufficient confidence in the People, hoping that the Inhabitants would remonstrate against my leaving, which they did in the warmest terms. . . . Then seemingly by their request I agreed to stay with two Companies of Troops, and that I

hardly thought. as they alledged that so many
was necessary; but if more was wanted I could
get them from the Falls, where they were made
to believe there was a Considerable Garrison."

Those volunteers who persisted in returning
home having been sent off to the Falls, — with
Rocheblave in their custody, and bearing letters from Clark to Henry, "letting him know
my situation and the necessity of Troops in
the Country," — the commander settled down
for a winter at Kaskaskia. To fill the great
gap in his ranks, he enlisted young French
volunteers who, being "fond of the service,
the different Companies soon got Compleat."

The difficulties which surrounded him, and
his work of drilling the recruits, are best told
Drilling   in his own words: "My situation
recruits   and weekness convinced me that
more depended on my own Behaviour and
Conduct, than all the Troops that I had far
removed from the Body of my Country: situated among French, Spanyards, and Numerous
Bands of Savages on every quarter: Watching
my actions, ready to receive impressions favour-
able or not so of us, which might be hard to
remove, and would perhaps produce lasting
good, or ill effects. . . . Strict subordination
among the Troops was my first object, and

[I] soon effected it . . . Our Troops being all Raw and undissiplined You must [be] sensible of the pleasure I felt when harangueing them on Perade, Telling them my Resolutions, and the necessity of strict duty for our own preservation &c. For them to return me for Answer, that it was their Zeal for their Country that induced them to engage in the Service, that they were sencible of their situation and Danger; that nothing could conduce more to their safety and happiness, than good order, which they would try to adhere to, and hoped that no favour would be shewn those that would neglect it. In a short time perhaps no Garrison could boast of better order, or a more Valuable set of Men."

Another important duty consisted in obtaining a good understanding with the Spaniards who, from their northern capital, the *"Our friends the Span-yards"* neighbor hamlet of St. Louis, controlled Upper Louisiana. His advances were well taken by Don Francisco de Leyba, the lieutenant-governor. "Our friends the Spanyards," Clark writes, are "doing every thing in their power to convince me of their friendship." De Leyba, who met him at Cahokia, appears at once to have formed an attachment for the gallant Virginian, who on his part testifies that as he "was never before in comp^y with any Spanish Gent I was much surprised in my expectations; for instead of finding that reserve thought peculiar to that Nation, I here saw not the least symptoms of it, freedom almost to excess gave the greatest pleasure."

"Domestick affairs being partly well settled," Clark playfully continues, "the Indian Department came next the object of my attention and of the greatest importance." The sudden arrival in the country of the Big Knives had thrown the tribesmen in the "greatest consternation." For a time they knew not which cause to espouse. "They were generally at War against us, but the French and the Spainyards appearing so fond of us confused them, they counciled with the French Traders, to know what was best to be done, and of course was advised to come and selicit for peace, and did not doubt but we might be good Friends." By dint of a combination of threats, cajolery, and braggart talk, well suited to impress them, Clark skilfully brought the Indians to terms. His vigorous speeches, sent to Bowman at Cahokia ("Cohos" of Clark's manuscript) and Helm at Vincennes, were read by those commanders to the as-

The tribe-men con-fused

sembled tribes, and "did more service than a
Regiment of Men cou'd have done;" while
French and half-breed messengers carried
similar overtures through a wide belt of
country, going as far north as the Fox River
in Wisconsin.

Proceeding to Cahokia himself to meet
the Indians at a great council, "it was with
Savage astonishment," he writes, that he
friends "viewed the Amazeing number of Savages that soon flocked into the town of Cohos
to treat for peace, and to hear what the Big
knives had to say, many of them 500 miles
distant, Chipoways, Ottoways, Petawatomies,
Puans, Sacks, Foxes, Sayges, Tauways, Maw-
mies [1] and a number of other Nations, all living
east of the Messicippa, and many of them at
War against us." Indeed, the number of his
new-found savage friends that assembled at
Cahokia was so great that during the five
weeks of his stay there, "such a number of
Devils" gave him great anxiety and required
a stern hand to repress; for they were fond,
after the manner of wild animals, of testing
the strength of the stranger, who, however,
stoutly held his own among them.

[1] Chippewas, Ottowas, Potawatomis, Winnebagoes, Sauks,
Foxes, Osages, Iowas, Miamis.

Godefroy Linctot, the French trader at Prairie du Chien, openly espoused the American cause and did valuable service as Clark's agent north and west of the Illinois River, purchasing horses among the Sauks, and raiding the country. Clark's management of the Indians was superb, and they came to have a wholesome and lasting fear of the Big Knife chief; while those of the French who fell under his influence entertained for him a loving regard.

Meanwhile, General Hamilton at Detroit was greatly annoyed by the news from Vin-
Hamilton's cennes. With characteristic energy
war-party he sent agents out through the tribes of Michigan and Wisconsin, and made preparations for a formidable war-party for the retaking of that important post. The entire month of September was spent in fitting out the expedition. The seventh of October, headed by Hamilton himself, it left for the south, numbering a hundred and seventy-seven whites, chiefly Creole volunteers, and about three hundred Indians.

The heavily laden flotilla of batteaux proceeded up the Maumee, over the portage of
Vincennes nine miles, and down a tributary of
taken by the Wabash. The water was shallow;
Hamilton an early winter set in, forming ice on

the streams; and before the contingent reached Vincennes it was the seventeenth of December, seventy-one days after starting. Captain Helm and his one American soldier made a show of resistance, but on the French militia deserting to the enemy, it became necessary to surrender.[1] Some of Clark's spies from Kaskaskia, who were hanging on Hamilton's flanks, were also captured. If Hamilton had at once pushed forward and attacked Clark at Kaskaskia, there is no doubt that the Americans must either have succumbed or retired beyond the Mississippi into Spanish territory. But in midwinter the way was filled with great difficulties for the advance of an army column, hampered with baggage. Hamilton therefore remained at Vincennes, allowed all but some eighty or

---

[1] "When Governor Hamilton entered Vincennes, there were but two Americans there, Captain Helm, the commandant, and one Henry. The [latter] had a cannon well charged, and placed in the open fort gate, while Helm stood by it with a lighted match in his hand. When Hamilton and his troops got within good hailing distance, the American officer, in a loud voice, cried out, ' Halt ! ' This stopped the movement of Hamilton, who, in reply, demanded a surrender of the garrison. Helm exclaimed with an oath, ' No man shall enter until I know the terms.' Hamilton answered, ' You shall have the honors of war ; ' and then the fort was surrendered, with its garrison of one officer, and one man." — Butler's *Kentucky* (Louisville, 1834), p. 80, *note*.

ninety whites and a hundred Indians to return home, and spent the time planning for a great spring campaign against the Illinois, in which he proposed to batter down the forts with cannon, and then turning southward make a clean sweep of the Kentucky stations. Had he succeeded in this bold project, all American settlement west of the Alleghanies would have been destroyed, and the United States might have lost the West forever.

The news of the recapture of Vincennes was over a month in reaching Clark. Know-*A scare at* ing that the British expedition had *Kaskaskia* at least reached the old Indian village on the site of the present city of Fort Wayne, Indiana, but as yet uninformed of the result. Clark started early in January (1779) for Cahokia, in order to hold a conference there with the principal inhabitants of the Illinois country. On his way he and his "Guard of about six or seven Men and a few Gentlemen in Chairs" narrowly escaped being ambushed, three miles out of Kaskaskia, by a party of "40 Savages headed by white Men" whom Hamilton had sent out from Vincennes to take Clark prisoner, having given them "such Instructions for my treatment as did him no dishonour." Delayed by an accident, the travellers had by evening only reached the old French village of La Prairie du Rocher, fourteen miles northwest of Kaskaskia. Here they prepared to pass the night. While being entertained at a ball, an express rider arrived with the appalling news that Hamilton was within three miles of Kaskaskia, with eight hundred men. " I never saw greater confusion among a small Assembly than was at that time, every Person having their eyes on me, as if my word was to determine their good or Evil fate." As usual, Clark coolly ordered his horses saddled for the return, and told the frightened company " That I hoped that they would not let the news Spoil our Divirsion sooner than was necessary, that we would divirt ourselves until our horses was ready, forced them to dance, and endeavoured to appear as unconcerned as if no such thing was in Adjutation."

On reaching Kaskaskia, the inhabitants, as yet unattacked, were found confident that the enemy was but biding his time; and during the next few days Clark was obliged to exercise tact and firmness in a remarkable degree. The Creoles, confident that the Americans would lose, and that the English would treat them badly for having succored the enemy, at first affected neutrality. But after Clark had

made a feint of burning the town and of
hanging a villager who had circulated dis-
comforting rumors of a British advance, the
Kaskaskians again profusely expressed their
devotion to Virginia. Whereupon the astute
commander "altered my conduct towards them
and treated them with the greatest kindness,
granting them every request, my influence
among them in a few hours was greater than
ever." The incident closed happily with the
discovery that "the great Army that gave the
alarm consisted only of about forty Whites
and Indians making their Retreat as fast as
possible to St. Vincent, sent for no other purpose, as we found after than to take me."

This adventure convinced Clark — although
he had as yet received no news, for his spies
Clark   on the Wabash had been taken by
uneasy   the enemy— that Hamilton was now
at Vincennes. The French in the Illinois
elsewhere than at Kaskaskia where they now
stoutly professed confidence in the Americans,
were panic-stricken, and the neighboring tribes
grew insolent in their demands. Confidently
expecting an attack, the commander made
careful preparations, even to the extent of
planning to burn the outlying dwellings, so as
to afford no cover to the enemy. He felt sure

of his meagre garrison, but had the gravest doubts of coöperation from the Creoles outside. His requested reinforcements could hardly be expected at this season from Virginia and Kentucky. He philosophically declares that he " suffered more uneasiness than when I was certain of an immediate attact, as I had more time to reflect." The end of American rule seemed near.

The gloom lifted on the evening of the twenty-ninth of January, when Col. Francis *Vigo's in-* Vigo arrived from St. Louis with defi-*formation* nite information concerning the smallness of Hamilton's winter garrison at Vincennes, and his intended inaction until spring. Vigo, a Spanish merchant who had business connections with the governor of Upper Louisiana, had visited Clark upon the latter's capture of Kaskaskia, and not only promised his influence in behalf of the Virginians, but made them a substantial loan. Upon Clark's request he went to Vincennes, accompanied only by a servant, to ascertain the situation of affairs. Hamilton, suspicious of his intent, for a time held him on parole at the fort, but finally allowed him to depart on signing an agreement "not to do anything injurious to the British interests on his way to St. Louis." As promised,

Vigo proceeded to St. Louis in his piroque, but thereupon promptly re-embarked and crossed to Kaskaskia, bringing, as Clark writes, "every intilligence I could wish to have."

Clark was eminently a man of action. Recognizing that if Hamilton proceeded against him *Forestall-* all would be lost, he at once deter- *ing the* mined to forestall the enemy by mak- *enemy* ing the attack himself. "It was at this moment," he declares, "I would have bound myself seven years a Slave, to have had five hundred Troops."

"I had a Large Boat prepared and Rigged," — a rowing galley or batteau, called the "Willing," — "mounting two four pounders 4 large swivels Manned with a fine Comp [of forty men] commanded by Lieut. Rogers. . . . This Vessel when compleat was much admired by the Inhabitants as no such thing had been seen in the Country before. I had great Expectations from her." The galley was despatched in the evening of the fourth of February, with orders to patrol the Ohio and if possible to approach within ten leagues of Vincennes, on the Wabash, the purpose being to prevent ~~English~~ boats from descending upon the Kentucky settlements.

"I conducted myself as though I was sure of taking Mr. Hamilton, instructed my officers to observe the same Rule. In a day or two the Country seemed to believe it, many anctious to Retrieve their Characters turned out, the Ladies, began also to be spirited and interest themselves in the Expedition, which had a great effect on the Young Men." Persuaded by the Creole girls, both at Cahokia and Vincennes, " the Principal Young Men of the Illinois" flocked to the call of the tall Virginian. Upon the day following the departure of the " Willing," he was able to march out of Kaskaskia at the head of a hundred and seventy[1] bold fellows, American and French. "I cannot

"Inward assurance of success" account for it," declares our hero, " but I still had inward assurance of success, and never could when weighing every Circumstance doubt it: But I had some secret check."

In order to surprise Vincennes, it was of course necessary to avoid the usual river route by the Ohio and the Wabash. The expedition started off across the country, a distance of some two hundred and thirty miles. In summer it was a delightful region of alternating

[1] Clark says, "a little upwards of two hundred"; but Bowman's Journal (Pirtle's *Clark's Campaign in the Illinois*, p. 100), from which we obtain many details of the march, specifically gives the number as "170 men . . . [including] artillery, pack-horses," &c.

lakes, rivers, groves, and prairies — " I suppose one of the most beautiful Country in the world." In the dead of winter, it afforded fair travelling *A difficult* over the frozen plains and ice-bridged *march* streams. But now, in February, the weather had moderated and great freshets had flooded the broad area of lowland. The ground was boggy, progress was slow and difficult, there were no tents, the floods had driven away much of the game, — although " numbers of buffaloes" were killed early in the march, — and Clark and his officers were often at their wits' ends to devise methods for keeping their hard-worked men in good spirits. The several companies vied in hunting and cooking for each other; and at night held feasts in the Indian fashion around great camp-fires, at which there were singing and dancing, to the accompaniment of the inevitable French fiddle.

And thus the first week sped. Then came (February 13) the so-called " drowned lands" of *The* the Wabash, a wide stretch of sub- *"drowned* merged country extending the most of *lands"* the way from the Little Wabash into Vincennes. The two branches of the Little Wabash, with channels a league apart, were now so high that they made a single river five miles wide, with the water in no place less than three feet deep. "This would have been enough to have stoped any set of men that was not in the same temper we was in."

It was the following afternoon before a large canoe could be constructed, and on the third day this was employed in transporting the men and baggage across the deep channels, the horses swimming behind. In the shallow places, men and beasts plunged through the bush-strewn water and mud — the former "Building scaffolds at each [shallow] to lodge our Baggage on until the Horses Crossed to take them; it Rained nearly a third of our march, but we never halted for it."

There was no longer any game to be had, and it was now dangerous to discharge guns, be-*Fatigue* cause of the proximity to Vincennes. *and* Almost worn out by fatigue and *hunger* hunger, the expedition reached the Embarrass River on the seventeenth, twelve days out from Kaskaskia; but it was found impracticable to cross the Embarrass, now a raging flood. The best they could do was to find a swampy little hillock on which — amid "drizzly and dark weather" — they crowded together for the night, of course wet to the skin, shivering with cold, and with neither food nor fire.

Next morning, the sound of the sunrise gun at Vincennes, but nine miles away, came *Wallowing* booming over the waste of waters. *through* They were, however, still far from *the bog* having reached their goal. Wallowing through the bog, down the west bank of the Embarrass, they came at last to the Wabash, and here two days were spent in building canoes. " From the spot we now lay on [it] was about ten miles to Town, and every foot of the way put together that was not three feet and upwards under water would not have made the length of two miles and a half, and not a mouthful of Provision. . . . If I was sensible that you [George Mason] would let no Person see this relation, I would give You a detail of our suffering for four days in crossing those waters, and the manner it was done, as I am sure that You wou'd Credit it, but it is too incredible for any Person to believe except those that are well acquainted with me as You are, or had experienced something similar to it. I hope you will excuse me until I have the pleasure of seeing you personally." Clark's energies were taxed to the utmost to keep his Frenchmen from deserting, they being greatly depressed by the miseries of the situation, but the Americans were undaunted.

Details sent on a raft and in a canoe to steal boats in the neighborhood of the town re-
"Hard turned after two days without success,
fortune!" "for there was," says Bowman, "not one foot of dry land to be found. . . . Col. Clark sent two men in the canoe, down to meet the batteau [the "Willing"], with orders to come on day and night; that being our last hope, and [we] starving. . . . No provisions of any sort, now two days. Hard fortune!" At noon of the twentieth, a boat was brought in with five Frenchmen from Vincennes. The villagers reported that among Hamilton and his men there was no suspicion of an attack, while "the inhabitants were well disposed towards us." This news and the killing of a deer raised the spirits of the party.

On the twenty-first it rained all day. At daybreak the invaders were ferried to the east side of the Wabash, that on which lay Vincennes. Through the vast swamp, — "no dry land on any side for many leagues," — the water often up to their chins, the strongest waded, the canoes carrying the weak and famished. With infinite toil, but three miles had been covered when at dusk they sank exhausted upon another boggy island knoll, and for the seventh night — within sound of

" the evening and morning guns from the fort " — slept hungry and in clothes sopping wet.

Next day it was the same story, the brave fellows plunging on through the freezing flood, *The man* Indian file, the man of iron at the *of iron* head now and then leading off in a favorite song, which was caught up along the column and helped lighten the weary feet of the adventurers. That night was passed on a maple-grown hillock six miles out from Vincennes. It was bitter cold; in the morning (the 23d) there was ice half an inch thick on the smooth water, and the men were encased in arctic armor. The sun rose bright. Clark assured his stiffened, half-frozen, well-nigh famished crew that the next night would see them in Vincennes; then, dashing into the water at the head of the file, ordered his officers to close the rear and shoot any man who refused to march.[1]

[1] Law's *Colonial History of Vincennes* (Louisville, 1858), p. 32, gives this story, which apparently has been somewhat heightened in color : " In one of the companies was a small boy who acted as drummer. In the same company was a seargeant, standing six feet two inches in his stockings, stout, athletic, and devoted to Clark. Finding that his eloquence had no effect upon the men, in persuading them to continue their line of march, Clark mounted the little drummer on the shoulders of the stalwart sergeant, and gave orders to him

Now came the worst experience of all. The Horseshoe Plain before them had been trans-*A frightful* formed by the floods into a shallow *crossing* lake four miles wide. No clump of land stood above the water; it was one smooth unbroken expanse, on the farther side of which were heavy woods shielding them from the town. About the centre, the prolonged hardships of the march began at last to tell on all save the strongest. All along the line brave fellows dropped in the ranks, and the canoemen frantically plied between them and the land beyond, saving the helpless from drowning. The strong supported those who could still keep their feet, while Clark, with alternating gibe and stern command, exerted himself to animate his followers. The water was often to the shoulders of the tallest; and when at last the edge of the island grove was reached, there were few who did not sink to the ground exhausted, to be rallied only through great exertion. Fortunately some food was obtained

to plunge into the half-frozen water. He did so, the little drummer beating the *charge* from his lofty perch, while Clark, sword in hand, followed them, giving the command as he threw aside the floating ice — ' Forward ! ' Elated and amused with the scene, the men promptly obeyed, holding their rifles above their heads, and in spite of all obstacles, reached the high land beyond them, safely."

from a party of Indian women who chanced to pass in a canoe, fires were lighted, the weakest were treated to broth, and soon all were inspired to fresh courage.

Two miles away, through the woods and across another lake, they could see the town, and despair was followed by rejoicing.

Hamilton still unconscious

" Laying in this Grove some time to dry our Clothes by the Sun we took another Prisoner," a Creole out shooting ducks, and from him learned that Hamilton was still unconscious of his danger. Two hundred Indians had, however, just arrived in town. This last information was discouraging, for that made the force in Vincennes — British, French, and Indian — four times his own. " A thousand Ideas," he says, " flushed in my Head at this moment." He now thought it impolitic to surprise the place, for in the fight some of the French and Indians might be killed and this would embitter the rest; whereas his informant told him the French were lukewarm and would only fight if forced to it.

" I resolved to appear as Daring as possible, that the Enemy might conceive by our be-

Clark's letter to the villagers

haviour that we were very numerous and probably discourage them." Accordingly he sent by this man the following letter[1] to the villagers, who lived apart from the fort, which was on a rising ground overlooking the town :

To the Inhabitants of Post St. Vincents :

Gentlemen, — Being now within two miles of your village with my army, determined to take your Fort this night, and not being willing to surprize you, I take this method to request such of you as are true citizens, and willing to enjoy the liberty I bring you, to remain still in your houses. And those, if any there be, that are friends to the King, will instantly repair to the fort, and join the *Hair-buyer General,* and fight like men. And if any such, as do not go to the Fort shall be discovered afterwards, they may depend on severe punishment. On the contrary, those that are true friends to liberty, may depend on being well treated. And I once more request them to keep out of the streets ; for every one I find in arms on my arrival, I shall treat as an enemy.

G. R. Clark.

As they gathered in the public square of Vincennes to hear the letter read, Clark's name

[1] Given in Bowman's Journal, in Pirtle, p. 104. But while Pirtle gives Clark's letter to Mason *verbatim et literatim,* Bowman's Journal is taken by him from the Louisville *Literary News-Letter* (November 21, 1840), for which publication it was obviously "improved" in diction, orthography, punctuation, and capitalization ; we thus have only a paraphrase of Clark's letter, not the actual document.

inspired the Creoles with awe. His sudden appearance out of the swamps appalled them, and they were so frightened by his tone of confident menace that none dared show enough favor to the British to go up and warn the garrison, who had seen the sudden commotion in the village, but were not aware of the cause.

Clark's camp could be seen from the town, although not from the fort. An open plain *A ruse* lay between Vincennes and the grove wherein the invaders were drying themselves in the sun. Realizing that he must make some show of force while his letter was being considered, he marched his men back and forth just within the edge of the wood; "but taking advantage of the Land, disposed the lines in such a manner that nothing but the Pavilions [flags of different commands] could be seen, having as many of them as would be sufficient for a thousand Men, which was observed by the Inhabitants who had Just Receiv'd my letter, counted the different Colours and Judged of our numbers accordingly. But I was careful to give them no oppertunity of seeing our Troops before dark, which it would be before we could Arrive. The Houses obstructed the Forts observing us and were not Allarmed as I expected." As for the Indians, they quickly withdrew out of range, to await the issue of the coming fight between the Big Knives and the red-coats.

At sundown, Clark divided his party into two sections; he commanded one, and Bowman *The attack on Vincennes* the other. There was now order and regularity, for the drill which the men had taken at Kaskaskia was beginning to tell. At seven o'clock, Bowman's men surrounded the town, while Clark's pushed through to the fort. The Creoles greeted them with cheers as with swinging gait they marched up through the village street, and freely gave them assistance and much-needed ammunition. Even the Indians, in their admiration of the bold, leather-clad Virginians, offered to take a hand. "A considerable number of British Indians made their escape out of Town. The Kickepous and Peankeshaws to the amount of about one hundred, that was in Town immediately Armed themselves in our favour and Marched to attact the Fort. I thanked the Chief for his intended service, told him the Ill consequence of our People being mingled in the dark . . . he approved of it and sent off his Troops . . . and staid with me giving all the Information he could."

The garrison were still unprepared. Not a

word of this transformation scene had come up
from the village. Hamilton thought that the
first shots were fired by drunken Indians, but
to his consternation he soon saw in the brilliant
moonlight that the stockade was surrounded
by American borderers, and that there was
serious business at hand. At the angles of
the palisaded fort were strong blockhouses,
the second floors of which were eleven feet
above the ground, and in each of these were
cannons and swivels. Clark had no cannon,
for his artillery, taken from the Kaskaskia fort,
had soon been forced to abandon the march;
but his riflemen — each of whom was an expert
shot and well sheltered " behind Houses, Pal-
ings, and Ditches, &c., &c.," and " a considerable intrenchment before the gate where I
Intended to plant my Artillery when Arrived "
— finally silenced the guns by pouring such
a constant fire through the loopholes that it
was impossible for the gunners to withstand it.
The Americans themselves were unharmed.
" Fine sport for the sons of Liberty," exultantly
wrote Bowman in his diary for that day.

In the matter of marksmanship, the British
and the French-Canadian militia were no match
for the backwoodsmen, and by sunrise it was
evident that the long night's siege had sadly

crippled the garrison, although "As soon as daylight, the Fort began to play her small arms very briskly."

At nine o'clock, Clark's men paused to take "a breakfast, it being the only [regular] meal *Clark's* of victuals since the 18th inst." — six *warning* days. Meanwhile Clark sent a white flag to Hamilton with a letter inviting him to save himself from "the impending storm that now threatens," and surrender his garrison and stores. But that officer tartly declined "to be awed into an action unworthy of British subjects," and thereupon the firing was hotly resumed.

In the course of the morning a party of French and Indian scouts, in the employ of the *Terroriz-* British, came noisily into town with *ing the* scalps and prisoners from a recent *enemy* foray against American settlers. Before they discovered the changed situation, Clark's men set upon them, killing and scalping two and partly wounding most of the others. Six were captured, and then, in the sight of the garrison, deliberately tomahawked and thrown into the river. This served the double purpose of inspiring terror among the other Indians, by showing them how powerless the English were to aid them, and of creating a panic among the French volunteers within the fort. The English themselves remained stubborn, but they were few in number.

After two hours of fighting, during which several men in the fort were wounded from *Clark* shots coming through the portholes, *demands* Hamilton sent out a flag and re-*uncondi-* *tional sur-* quested a truce of three days. Clark *render* responded with the following note, demanding unconditional surrender: [1]

> Colonel Clarks Compliments to Mʳ Hamilton and begs leave to inform him that Coḷ Clark will not agree to any Other Terms than that of Mʳ Hamilton's Surendering himself and Garrison, Prisoners at Discretion.
>
> If Mʳ Hamilton is Desirous of a Conferance with Coḷ Clark he will meet him at the Church with Captⁿ Helms.
>
> Feby 24ᵗʰ 1779.   G. R. Clark

Hamilton agreed to the conference, which was held in the little French church. The English commander sought to soften the terms, but Clark was unyielding. " Towards the close of the Evening," articles were signed, by which

[1] The original is in the Draper MSS., and is reproduced in the present volume in facsimile.

Hamilton agreed to deliver to Clark at ten o'clock the following morning, Fort Sackville — the English name of Vincennes post — " as it is at present with all the Stores, &c . . . The Garrisson are to deliver themselves up as Prisoners of War and March out with their Arms and Acoutriments, &c., &c . . . Three days time be allowed the Garrison to settle their Accompts with the Traders and Inhabitants of this Place . . . The Officers of the Garrisson to be allowed their necessary Baggage, &c., &c." To these articles, Hamilton attached a memorandum stating that they were " Agreed to for the following reasons: The remoteness from succors; the state and quantity of provisions, &c.; unanimity of officers and men in its expediency; the honourable terms allowed; and, lastly, the confidence in a generous enemy."

At the appointed hour on the morning of the twenty-fifth, we learn from Bowman's *The surrender* diary that " Lieutenant Governor Hamilton and his garrison of about eighty men marched out [past Bowman and Mc Carty's companies], whilst Col. Clark, Captains Williams' and Worthington's companies marched into the Fort, relieved the centries, hoisted the American colours, secured all the arms." Thirteen guns were fired, as a national salute; but in the midst of the jubilation a premature explosion of cartridges occurred in one of the batteries, by which Bowman, Worthington, and four privates were severely burned. The fort was rechristened " Patrick Henry," in honor of the Governor of Virginia, in whose service the little band of conquerors were enlisted.

The capture of Vincennes was one of the most notable and heroic achievements in American history. Clark had conducted a forced march of about two hundred and thirty miles through almost unheard-of difficulties. With a small party of ragged and half-famished militiamen, nearly half of whom were Creoles,[1] he had captured, in the heart of a strange and hostile country, without the aid of his artillery, a heavy stockade mounted by cannons and swivels and manned by a trained garrison. It was a bold scheme, of his own planning, and skilfully

An heroic achievement

---

[1] In the Draper MSS. is a letter from John Rogers to Major Jonathan Clark, written May 6, 1779, while en route to Virginia with the detachment guarding Hamilton and the other prisoners. He says, " We made 101 prisoners and had only 130 men 60 of which were French there was seven men wounded in the Fort and Seven Indians killed that were Comeing in with two prisoners."

carried out. At his back were some of the best fighting men on the border, but with him rests the principal credit.

Hamilton, after being sharply reprimanded by Clark for sending scalping parties against the frontier settlements, was early in March sent in irons to Virginia,[1] with twenty-six of his fellows; the others were paroled, for Clark had no means of subsisting them.

Captain Helm, now released from captivity, ascended the Wabash with fifty men, and two days before the departure of the prisoners to Virginia intercepted a flotilla of seven batteaux coming to Vincennes from Detroit, with " Provisions, Indian goods, &c." —$50,000 worth, guarded by forty French volunteers headed by two of Hamilton's officers. The booty was divided among the Virginians, who considered themselves richly recompensed for their task.

[1] Hamilton was kept in close confinement at Williamsburg, and despite the protests of the British the State of Virginia "refused to exchange him on any terms" until towards the close of the Revolution. Washington wrote that he "had issued proclamations and approved of practises, which were marked with cruelty towards the people that fell into his hands, such as inciting the Indians to bring in scalps, putting prisoners in irons, and giving them up to be the victims of savage barbarity." He was Lieutenant-Governor of Quebec in 1785, and died as Governor of Dominica in 1796.

And now came welcome news from Governor Patrick Henry, thanking the troops for *Illinois a* their capture of Kaskaskia, the news *Virginian* of which had been some months in *county* reaching Virginia, and promising them a good reward.[1] As a direct consequence of their victory, and the taking of the oath of fealty by the inhabitants, Illinois had been constituted by the legislature (November, 1778) as a county of Virginia, and John Todd, an old Kentucky friend of Clark, was commissioned as county lieutenant. This appointment was especially welcomed by Clark, for he did not enjoy the details of civil administration which had thus far fallen to his lot. "The Civil Departm⁴· In the Illinois," he wrote to Mason, " had heretofore rob'd me of too much of my time that ought to be spent in Military reflection, I was now likely to be relieved by Col? Jn˙ Todd appointed by the Government for that purpose; I was anctious for his Arrival & happy in his appointment."

A few days later, some of the long-expected reinforcements arrived from Virginia and Ken- *Belated* tucky; but not more than half of the *reinforce-* number expected by Clark, who felt *ments*

[1] In after years, they received 150,000 acres of land in Indiana, opposite Louisiana.

compelled by this fact and a fresh outbreak of the Indians of Ohio, to postpone his cherished expedition against Detroit. After establishing small garrisons at Vincennes, Cahokia, and Kaskaskia, and making several important treaties with the Illinois and Wisconsin Indians, he introduced Todd to the people at Kaskaskia, the county seat, on the twelfth of May, and then retired to his principal headquarters at the Falls of the Ohio, "where I Arrived safe on the 20th day of August."

We have dwelt in such detail upon Clark's romantic expedition for the conquest of the *Results* Northwest, that we must close with *achieved* but a brief summary of the results achieved. During the remainder of the Revolutionary struggle, the Indian tribes between the Wabash and the Mississippi were in large part friendly to the Americans. The red men feared Clark, the border men fairly adored him, and the French were awed by and respected him — although the Creoles were at all times restive under his stern discipline and his cavalier method of forcing from them military supplies, and sighed for the time when France might once more control the Mississippi Valley. He was admittedly the one man on the frontier who by the exercise of his personal influence could keep the country in order, and counteract threatened British attempts to regain their lost hold. His fame spread through the Southern tribes, and the British colony at Natchez feared lest he should direct a movement against them. He established Fort Jefferson on the Mississippi, on the border line between Kentucky and Tennessee. In 1780, he marshalled the men of Kentucky in one last assault against the hostile tribes east of the Wabash, quelling them at Chillicothe and Piqua, thus insuring peace for another twelvemonth. The following year, now brigadier-general of the Virginia militia west of the mountains, he was in the mother colony, and at the head of a hastily-organized force of two hundred and forty riflemen ambuscaded a party of English troops on the James River. A year later, he led forth a thousand tall Kentucky riflemen to ravage the Indian villages on the Big Miami, in retaliation for the disastrous raid made that summer by Brant, McKee, Girty, and other British-Indian leaders.

All this while, Clark held to his designs *The Detroit project* upon Detroit. He made a trip to Virginia to interest public men in his scheme, and greatly alarmed the English by his preparations for the proposed expedition; but the coast colonies were to the last too busy with their own affairs to grant him the necessary assistance, and, much to his disappointment, what he wished to make the crowning achievement of his career was never carried out.

Although Clark was of great service to Kentucky and Virginia, in keeping in order Indians and French along the Ohio frontier during the remainder of the Revolutionary War, his repu-

Clark's power wanes tation, and consequently his power, had reached its climax with the capture of Vincennes. After a few years, overcome by the drink habit and nettled by what he considered the ingratitude of the Republic in not properly rewarding his services, he became morose, and while always honored, was able to exercise comparatively small influence among the younger generation.

Not long after the definitive treaty of peace with Great Britain, when Clark was still in touch with the principal men of the East, Thomas Jefferson made to him a proposition

Jefferson's interesting proposition which is especially interesting at the present time — no less than that of heading an expedition to explore a route to the Pacific. In a letter from Annapolis

(December 4, 1783),[1] Jefferson writes to Clark, thanking him for sending certain specimens of "shells & seeds," and for promising "as many of the different species of bones, teeth & tucks of the Mammoth as can now be found" — for the great statesman, then in retirement, was assiduously collecting for his private scientific museum at Monticello.   He then adds: "I find they have subscribed a very large sum of money in England for exploring the country from the Mississippi to California.   they pretend it is only to promote knolege.   I am afraid they have thoughts of colonising into that quarter some of us have been talking here in a feeble way of making the attempt to search that country.   but I doubt wether we have enough of that kind of spirit to raise the money.   how would you like to lead such a party?   tho I am afraid our prospect is not worth asking the question."   Nothing came of this offer; but just twenty years later Clark's younger brother, William, together with Meriwether Lewis, started under Jefferson's auspices upon a similar expedition, which won for them imperishable renown.

In 1793, Clark imprudently accepted a commission as major-general from Genet, the

[1] The original is in the Draper MSS.

French diplomatic agent at Washington, and sought to raise a filibustering legion in the West, to overcome, in behalf of the French, the *Clark and* Spanish settlements on the Missis-*Genet* sippi,[1] in coöperation with a similar expedition from Georgia against the Floridas. At this time the Kentuckians were much concerned because Spain, which held the mouth and the west bank of the Mississippi, would not allow them the free navigation of that river, so essential to the marketing of their crops; they were incensed at the United States government, which appeared to neglect these and other Western interests. Genet, taking advantage of this widespread dissatisfaction among the borderers, sought their aid in ousting Spain from the mouth of the river and along the Gulf, and replacing her by France. The intrigue was ill managed by the blustering Genet, who also had insufficient financial resources, and the French fleet was so occupied with affairs in San Domingo that it could not coöperate. Nevertheless Clark, despite his failing powers, was making quite effective headway in Ken-

[1] See the admirably full treatment of this episode, by Prof. F. J. Turner, in his "Correspondence of Clark and Genet," first report of the Historical MSS. Commission, Amer. Histor. Ass'n *Report* for 1896, pp. 930–1107.

tucky, where he had two hundred men under arms, when President Washington, in the interests of neutrality, suddenly put a stop to the conspiracy, and at the same time Genet was recalled by his government. Had Genet and Clark successfully carried out their plans, France would have regained a substantial foothold in the Mississippi Valley, and the course of Western history been materially altered. Washington thus rendered to the West, indeed to the Republic at large, a service of inestimable importance.

Clark's later years were spent in comparative neglect at his simple home in the then small village of Clarksville, in view of Corn Island, which had been his military base during the time when he won the Northwest for *Clark's later years* the American cause. The story is told, although not well established, that when commissioners sought him in his old age, bearing a richly ornamented sword voted him by the State of Virginia, he received the compliments of his visitors in sullen silence. Then bursting forth in rage, he is said to have broken the weapon with his crutch, crying: "When Virginia needed a sword, I gave her one. She sends me now a toy. I want bread!" Dying in 1818 at his sister's home near Louisville, his ashes lie at Cave Hill cemetery, in that city, where he is accounted the most honored of Kentucky's dead.

It is difficult to overestimate the importance of Clark's conquest. Lord Dunmore's War *Importance of the conquest* was one step ; it extended Virginia's "sphere of influence" westward to the Muskingum. But Clark. of his own motion and largely at the expense of his private fortune, chiefly supporting his soldiers on the country and paying them from its plunder, in a series of brilliant achievements captured the Southern key-points of the great Northwest, and held them with military force and his strong personal influence until the treaty of peace with England in 1783.

The English peace commissioners at first claimed the Northwest as a part of Canada; *Effect on the treaty of peace* but throughout the protracted nego- tiations Jay and Franklin persisted in demanding the country which Clark had so gallantly won and was still holding. What appears to have had more effect upon the English treaty commissioners than the fact of military occupancy, was Frank- lin's argument that unless room for growth were given the United States, a permanent peace could not be expected between the two

countries — that the tide of emigration westward over the Alleghanies could not be
stemmed; that the rough, masterful borderers
could not be restrained from intrenching on
the English wilderness, and a never-ending
frontier fight, disastrous to all concerned,
would be inevitable. The situation was admitted. Later, Lord Shelburne, who was
chiefly responsible for yielding this point,
reinforced his position by maintaining in Parlia-
ment that after all the fur-trade of the Northwest was not worth fighting for, and the fur-trade
was all that Englishmen wished of that vast
area. Nevertheless, Jay and Franklin could
have found no footing for their contention, had
Clark not been in actual possession of the
country. It certainly was a prime factor in the
situation.

Aside from this, we are indebted to George
Rogers Clark for a series of military achievements nowhere, all conditions considered,
excelled in the proud annals of American
heroism; and for a glowing inspiration to
patriotic endeavor, that will never die so long
as our youth are instructed in the history of
the land.

II

THE DIVISION OF THE NORTHWEST INTO STATES

II

THE DIVISION OF THE NORTHWEST
INTO STATES

WASHINGTON, "first in war, first in peace, and first in the hearts of his countrymen," was first also in making suggestions as to the boundary lines of Northwestern *Washing-* States. September 7, 1783, we find *ton's sug-* him writing to James Duane, then a *gestion* member of Congress from New York, regarding the future of the country beyond the Ohio.[1] After giving some wise suggestions as to the management of both Indians and whites in that vast region, he declares that the time is ripe for the blocking out of a State there. The veteran surveyor says: "From the mouth of the Great Miami River, wch empties into the Ohio, to its confluence with the Mad River, thence by a Line to the Miami fort and Village on the other Miami River, wch empties into

---

[1] Ford's *Writings of Washington*, x., pp. 310, 311.

Lake Erie, and Thence by a Line to include the
Settlement of Detroit, would, with Lake Erie
to the noward, Pensa. to the eastwd., and the
Ohio to the soward, form a governm^t sufficiently
extensive to fulfil all the public engagements,
and to receive moreover a large population
by emigrants." He continues: " Were it not
for the purpose of comprehending the Settlement of Detroit within the Jurisd^n of the new
Governm^t, a more compact and better shaped
district for a State would be, for the line to
proceed from the Miami Fort and Village
along the River of that name to Lake Erie;
leaving in that case the settlement of Detroit,
and all the Territory no. of the Rivers Miami
and St. Joseph's between the Lakes Erie, St.
Clair, Huron, and Michigan, to form hereafter
another State equally large, compact, and
water-bounded."

Thus did Washington, with that clear-head-
edness and far-sightedness which caused him
in practical matters like this to outrank most
Americans of his day, roughly map out the
present States of Ohio and Michigan. Five
weeks later (October 15), Congress adopted
this second suggestion almost literally, in establishing a region for colonization north of the
Ohio, into which no red man was thereafter to

be allowed a foothold — if the law could stop
him.[1]

Early the following March, Congress instructed a committee of which Thomas Jeffer-

I.   JEFFERSON'S PLAN, 1784.

Jefferson's son was chairman, to fashion a plan
plan   of government for the entire North
west, — or, as it was then called, the Western

---

[1] *Secret Journals of Congress*, i., p. 258. Duane was chairman of the committee reporting these resolutions.

Territory, — which had now become public domain through the surrender of the land claims of those States which had hitherto stoutly held that they owned everything west of their coast lines, as far as the Pacific Ocean. To Jefferson is to be given the credit for drafting the report of this committee, which was first taken up by Congress on the nineteenth of April, and after some amendment adopted on the twenty-third. The original draft[1] has come down to us in history, famous, among other features, for Jefferson's proposition to divide the Northwest, on parallels of latitude, into ten States, most of them to bear fantastic names which smack of the classical revival then deeply affecting American thought: Sylvania, Michigania, Assenisipia, Illinoia, Polypotamia, Chersonesus, Metropotamia, Saratoga, Pelisipia, and Washington. While Congress practically accepted his scheme of territorial division, each section was wisely left to choose its own title when it should enter the Union.[2]

These resolutions were in force until the

---

[1] In the handwriting of Jefferson, and now preserved at Washington, in the archives of the Department of State.

[2] See Randall's *Life of Jefferson*, i., pp. 397, 398, for full text of the resolutions as adopted. They are also given in *Wis. Hist. Colls.*, xi., p. 61.

Congress of the Confederation, in session at
Ordinance Philadelphia, adopted July 13, 1787,
of 1787   "An ordinance for the government
of the Territory of the United States north-

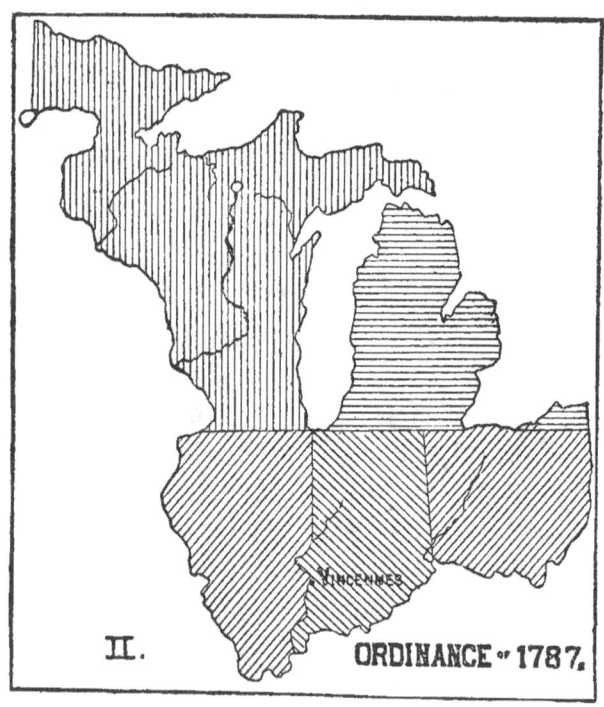

II.   ORDINANCE *of* 1787.

west of the river Ohio." What thereafter
was familiarly known as the Northwest Territory lay west of Pennsylvania and north and
west of the Ohio River. Its western limit was
the Mississippi River, which had been estab-

lished by the treaty of Paris (February 10, 1763) as the boundary between the British possessions and the French province of Louisiana, and confirmed as the western boundary of the United States by our first treaty with Great Britain (September 3, 1783); the northern limit was the line between British America and the United States. The land embraced in this vast tract was, in great part, the Virginia cession, made in 1784; to the north of that lay the strip ceded by Connecticut in 1786 and 1800; farther north, the Massachusetts cession of 1785; while the territory north of latitude 43° 43' 12" had been acquired from Great Britain in 1783.[1]

The fifth article of the Ordinance was as follows: "There shall be formed in the said *The famous* territory not less than three nor *boundary* more than five States; and the *article* boundaries of the States, as soon as Virginia shall alter her act of cession and consent to the same,[2] shall become fixed and established as follows, to wit: The Western State, in the said territory, shall be bounded by the Mississippi, the Ohio, and the Wabash rivers; a direct line drawn from the Wabash

[1] See map in McMaster's *Hist. People U. S.*, ii.
[2] Which she did in 1788.

and Post Vincents [Vincennes, Indiana], due north, to the territorial line between the United States and Canada; and by the said territorial line to the Lake of the Woods and Mississippi. The middle State shall be bounded by the said direct line, the Wabash from Post Vincents to the Ohio, by the Ohio, by a direct line drawn due north from the mouth of the Great Miami to the said territorial line, and by the said territorial line. The Eastern State shall be bounded by the last-mentioned direct line, the Ohio, Pennsylvania, and the said territorial line: *Provided, however,* And it is further understood and declared, that the boundaries of these three States shall be subject so far to be altered, that, if congress shall hereafter find it expedient, they shall have authority to form one or two States in that part of the said territory which lies *north of an east and west line drawn through the southerly bend or extreme of Lake Michigan.* And whenever any of the said States shall have sixty thousand free inhabitants therein, such State shall be admitted, by its delegates, into the Congress of the United States, on an equal footing with the original States, in all respects whatever."

In order to give the Ordinance an assurance

6

of stability, it was solemnly provided, in section
14 of the preamble, that: "The following
articles shall be considered as articles of compact, between the original States and the
people and States in the said Territory, and
*forever remain unalterable, unless by common
consent.*" It will be interesting to see how
Congress finally divided the Old Northwest
into States; and why it was that while five
commonwealths were formed therefrom as provided by the Ordinance, in the end none of
them was bounded exactly as stipulated in
the famous fifth article.

Twelve years later,[1] the Congress of the
United States, which had succeeded the Con-
Erection of gress of the Confederation, made its
Indiana first division of the Northwest Terri-
Territory tory.[2] The act provided: "That
from and after the fourth day of July next, all
that part of the Territory of the United States
northwest of the Ohio River which lies to the
westward of a line beginning at the Ohio, opposite to the mouth of the Kentucky River, and
running thence to Fort Recovery [near the

[1] Act approved May 7, 1800. The Ordinance itself had
been confirmed by act of Congress approved August 7, 1789.

[2] See St. Clair's letter to Harrison, on the division of the
Northwest Territory, *St. Clair Papers*, ii., pp. 489, 490.

present Greenville, Ohio], and thence north until it shall intersect the territorial line between the United States and Canada, shall, for the purposes of temporary government, constitute a

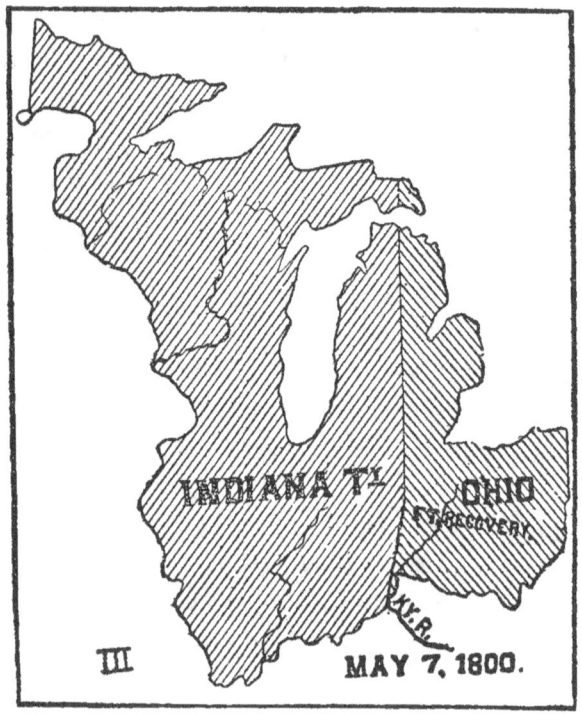

separate Territory, and be called the Indiana Territory." The country east of this line was still to be called the Northwest Territory, with its seat of government at Chillicothe; while Vincennes was to be the seat of government

for Indiana Territory. That portion of the
line running from the point on the Ohio, opposite the mouth of the Kentucky, northeastward
to Fort Recovery, was designed to be but a
temporary boundary, it being one of the lines
established between the white settlements and
the Indians, by the treaty of Greenville, July
30, 1795.

The act of Congress approved April 30, 1802,
enabling " the people of the eastern division "
Admission of the Northwest Territory (Ohio) to
of Ohio   draft a State constitution, obliged
them to accept as their northern boundary " an
east and west line drawn through the southerly
extreme of Lake Michigan," in accordance
with the limits prescribed by the original ordinance.   In the State constitutional convention,
held at Chillicothe in November that year, this
line had, without a murmur, been acceded to in
committee, when suddenly it came to the ears
of the members that an experienced trapper,
then in the village, claimed for Lake Michigan
a more southerly head than had been given to
it by the majority of the map-makers.

It appears that the committee of Congress
which drafted the Ordinance of 1787 obtained
from the Department of State a copy of
Mitchell's map, which had been published in

1755 by the British Lords Commissioners for Trade and Plantations in America. This placed the southern bend of Lake Michigan at 42° 20'. A pencilled line thereon, evidently made by a member of the committee, passes due east from the bend and intersects the international line at a point between River Raisin and Detroit. It was this chart which the trapper claimed to be incorrect.[1] The Chillicothe convention became alarmed at the report, and made haste to attach a proviso to the boundary article, as follows: " *Provided always, and it is hereby fully understood and declared by this convention,* That if the southerly bend or extreme of Lake Michigan should extend so far south, that a line drawn due east from it should not intersect Lake Erie, or if it should intersect the said Lake Erie east of the mouth of the Miami River of the lake, then, and in that case, with the assent of the Congress of the United States, the northern boundary of this State shall be

[1] Burnet's *Notes on Northwest Territory* (1847), p. 360. Mitchell's error was perpetuated in later maps by other cartographers, notably in Pownall's chart (1779). Had the library been reasonably well equipped, the committee might have had access to one published by Thomas Hutchins in 1778, nine years before the passage of the Ordinance. Hutchins placed the southern bend about where it was afterwards proved to be by Talcott's survey — 41° 37' 07.9".

established by, and extending to, a direct line, running from the southern extremity of Lake Michigan to the most northerly cape of the Miami bay," etc.

" The eastern division" of the Northwest Territory, now organized under the name of the State of Ohio. was formally admitted as such to the Union, by act approved February 19, 1803. Nothing was said in the recognition act relative to the boundary; it was taken for granted by the Ohio people that the proviso was accepted.

On the eleventh of January, 1805, an act of Congress was approved, erecting the Terri-
Erection of tory of Michigan out of " all that
Michigan part of the Indiana Territory which
Territory lies north of a line drawn east from the southerly bend or extreme, of Lake Michigan, until it shall intersect Lake Erie, and east of a line drawn from the said southerly bend through the middle of said lake to its northern extremity, and thence due north to the northern boundary of the United States." This was, in short, the present Southern Peninsula of Michigan, with a southern boundary as established by the Ordinance of 1787, together with that portion of the upper peninsula lying east of the meridian of Mackinac.

Congress had admitted Ohio to the Union with a tacit recognition of the northern boundary laid down in her constitutional proviso; yet so little thought had been given to the

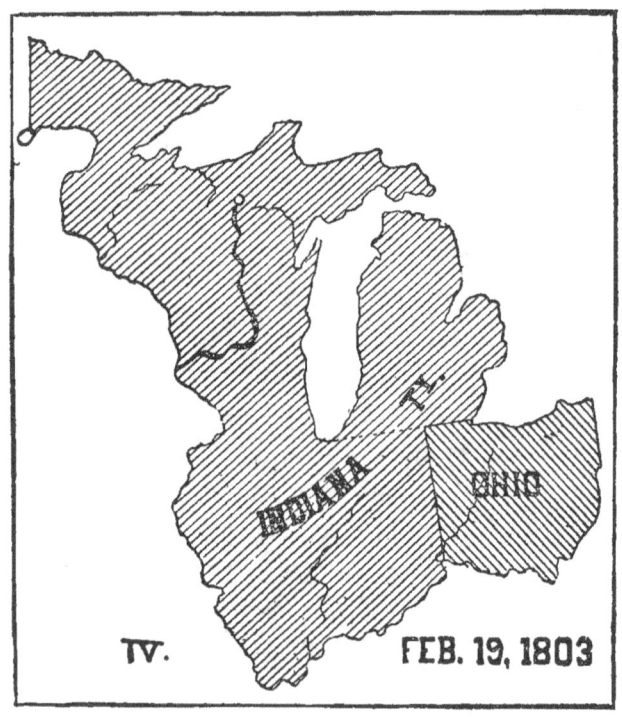

matter, and geographical knowledge of the West was still so vague, that this circumstance had been overlooked, and Michigan Territory was allowed a southern limit which, while in strict accordance with the Ordinance, seriously overlapped the territory assigned to Ohio. Thus, when, in later years, the location of the southerly bend of Lake Michigan was determined, a serious boundary dispute arose, Michigan claim-

ing the Ordinance as a compact which could not be broken by Congress without common consent; while Ohio tenaciously clung to the strip of country which the constitution-makers at Chillicothe had in the eleventh hour secured for her. The wedge-shaped strip in dispute averaged six miles in width, across Ohio, embraced some four hundred and sixty-eight square miles, and included the lake-port of Toledo and the mouth of the Maumee River, the possession of which was deemed well worth quarrelling over. Congress passed an act for determining the boundary (May 20, 1812), but owing to trouble with Great Britain the lines were not run until 1818, and then not satisfactorily. July 14, 1832, another act of Congress for the settlement of the northern limit of Ohio was passed; and as a result of extensive observations by Captain A. Talcott of the United States Engineer Corps, that officer was able to report in detail, in January, 1834, and again in November, 1835,[1] to the effect that the southern bend of Lake Michigan is in latitude 41° 37′ 07.9″, while the north cape of Maumee Bay is in 41° 44′ 02.4″.

Michigan had in 1834 begun to urge her claims to statehood, insisting on the southern boundary prescribed for the fourth and *Michigan-* fifth States by the ordinance. Vir-*Ohio* ginia, whose consent as the chief *boundary* land-giver had been necessary to the legalizing of that document, was importuned

[1] *Senate Docs.*, No. 1, 24th Cong., 1st sess., vol. i, p. 203.

by Governor Mason to intercede in behalf of
the peninsula Territory. The officials of the
Old Dominion were in accord with the movement, but this fact failed to produce any effect
on Congress, for the political sympathy of the
actual State of Ohio was just then more important to the dominant party than the possible
good-will of the projected State of Michigan.

Without waiting for an enabling act, a convention held at Detroit in May and June, 1835,
adopted a State constitution for submission to
Congress, demanding entry into the Union
"in conformity to the fifth article of the ordinance" of 1787 — of course the boundaries
sought being those established by that article.
During the summer there were popular disturbances in the disputed territory, and some
gunpowder harmlessly wasted. In December,
President Jackson in a special message laid
the matter before Congress. Congress quietly
determined to "arbitrate" the quarrel by giving to Ohio the disputed tract, and offering
Michigan, by way of partial recompense, the
whole of what is to-day her Upper Peninsula.[1]
Michigan, however, did not want the sup-
posedly barren and worthless country to her
northwest, protested long and loud against

[1] Act approved June 15, 1836.

what she deemed to be an outrage, and declared that she had no community of interest with the northern peninsula, being for half of the year separated from it by insurmountable natural barriers. Moreover, she asserted, it rightfully belonged to the fifth State to be formed out of the Northwest Territory. But Congress persisted in making this settlement of the quarrel one of the conditions precedent to the admission of Michigan into the Union. In September, 1836, a State convention, called for the sole purpose of deciding the question, rejected the proposition on the ground that Congress had no right, according to the terms of the Ordinance, to annex such a condition. A second convention, however, approved of it (December 15), and Congress promptly accepted this decision as final.[1] Thus Michigan came into the sisterhood of States, January 26, 1837, with the territorial limits which she to-day possesses.[2]

In following the fortunes of Michigan, we have necessarily run somewhat ahead of our story. When Michigan Territory was erected

---

[1] Hough's *Amer. Const.*, i., p. 663.

[2] The arguments on the Ohio-Michigan claims will be found at length in *Senate Docs.*, No. 211, vol. iii., 1835–36, and *Reports of Coms.*, No. 380, vol. ii., 1835–36.

in 1805, Indiana Territory had been left with
the Mississippi River as its western border, the
Ohio as its southern, the international boundary and the south line of Michigan as its

northern, while its eastern limits were the west
line of Ohio, the middle of Lake Michigan, and
the meridian of Mackinac.   This included the
present States of Indiana, Illinois, Wisconsin,
and the greater part of Michigan's Upper
Peninsula.

The next division was ordained by act of Congress approved February 3, 1809, when *Erection of Illinois Territory* that portion of Indiana Territory lying west of the lower Wabash River and the meridian of Vincennes was erected into the Territory of Illinois. Indiana was thus left with her present boundaries, except that on the south side she owned a funnel-shaped strip of water and of land just west of the middle of Lake Michigan, between the Vincennes meridian and the then western boundary of Michigan Territory — what is now, roughly speaking, the County of Door, in Wisconsin, together with the Counties of Delta, Alger, and Schoolcraft, and the greater part of Chippewa and Mackinac, in Michigan.

When Indiana was admitted to the Union (act approved April 19, 1816), her northern boundary was established by Congress on a line running due east of a point in the middle of Lake Michigan ten miles north of the southern extreme of the lake. This was recognized as a distinct violation of the great Ordinance; but the excuse was offered that Indiana must be given a share of the lake coast, and as there were then no important harbors or towns involved, Michigan made no serious objection to this particular encroachment on her territory.

The contraction of the northern bounds of Indiana, however, left unclaimed the before-

No Man's mentioned strip of water in Lake
Land Michigan and the generous belt of

peninsula country to the north. Literally it was "No Man's Land." States and Territories had been formed around it, but these semi-insulated sections of ore and pine lands were claimed by none, such was the prevalent ignorance concerning the public domain in the then far Northwest.

The act of April 18, 1818, enabling Illinois to become a State, abridged her territory to its present limits, and gave to Michigan " all that part of the territory of the United States lying north of the State of Indiana, and which was included in the former Indiana Territory, together with that part of the Illinois Territory which is situated north of and not included within the boundaries prescribed by this act." By this statute, what we may call No Man's Land, and all of the Northwest Territory west of it, were " for temporary purposes only " assigned to Michigan Territory, which now embraced all the country between the Mississippi River and Lakes Erie, St. Clair, and Huron, and lying north of Ohio, Indiana, and Illinois.

Illinois's northern boundary The northern boundary of Illinois was fixed at 42° 30', which is over sixty-one miles north of the southern bend of Lake Michigan, the southern boundary prescribed by the Ordinance for the fourth and fifth States to be formed out of the old Northwest Territory. Thus were the express terms of the Ordinance, which had been declared to be " forever unalterable except by common consent," again violated, without so much as

saying " by your leave " to the settlers west
of Lake Michigan who lived north of 42° 30'.
What was afterwards Wisconsin was thereby
deprived, through the shrewd manipulation of
Nathaniel Pope, Illinois's delegate in Congress
at that time, of eight thousand five hundred
square miles of rich agricultural and mining
country and numerous lake-ports. Pope spe-
ciously argued that Illinois must become intimately connected with the growing commerce
of the Northern lakes, or else she would be led,
from her commercial relations upon the great
rivers trending to the South, to join a Southern
confederacy in case the Union were disrupted.[1]

An act of Congress approved June 28, 1834,
added to the Territory of Michigan, " for tem-
Michigan   porary purposes," the lands lying
spreads   north of the State of Missouri and
westward   between the Mississippi River on the
east and the Missouri and White Earth [2] rivers
on the west, which had been acquired from
France in 1803 as a part of the Louisiana

[1] *Annals of Congress*, 1818, vol. ii., p. 1677 ; Ford's *Hist.
of Ill.*, p. 22 ; Davidson and Struve's *Hist. of Ill.*, p. 295.

[2] A small northern tributary of the Missouri having its
source some thirty miles south of the international boundary ; it empties into the Missouri near the western boundary
of Mountraille County, Dakota, about eighty-five miles west
of the meridian of Bismarck.

Purchase.[1] Michigan Territory now extended, therefore, from Detroit westward to a point eighty-five miles northwest of the site of the present city of Bismarck, Dakota.

The people west of Lake Michigan had long been desirous of having a territorial govern-
Dissatisfac- ment of their own. The seat of gov-
tion west of ernment of Michigan Territory was at
Lake Michi- Detroit, six hundred miles from the
gan
centre of settlement west of the lake, and during half of the year nearly inaccessible therefrom; the laws of Michigan were practically dead-letters among them; civil machinery west of the lake was chiefly conspicuous for its absence, and there were commercial as well as sectional and political jealousies between the people on either side of the great inland sea.

As early as 1824, James Duane Doty, a federal judge living at Green Bay, had inter-

---

[1] The clause of this act relating to area is as follows : " All that part of the territory of the United States bounded on the east by the Mississippi river, on the south by the state of Missouri and a line drawn due west from the northwest corner of said state [then on the meridian of Kansas City] to the Missouri river ; on the southwest and west by the Missouri river and the White Earth river, falling into the same ; and on the north by the northern boundary of the United States, shall be, and hereby is, for the purpose of temporary government, attached to and made part of the Territory of Michigan."

7

ested Senator Thomas H. Benton in a projected "Territory of Chippewau." The bill[1]
was drawn by Doty and forwarded to Benton
in November of that year, together with a petition for its passage signed by the inhabitants
of the proposed Territory. It is interesting to

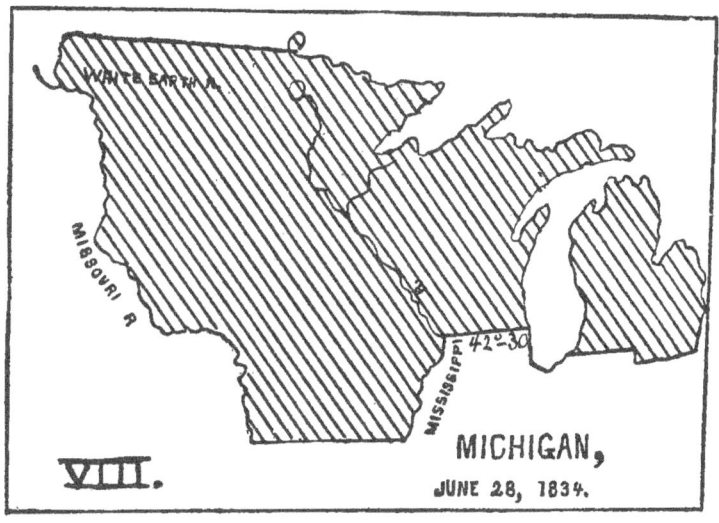

MICHIGAN,
JUNE 28, 1834.

VIII.

note the ideas prevalent among them at that
time concerning the proper limits of what is
now Wisconsin. The boundaries sought by
the Doty bill were: "All that part of the
Michigan Territory included within the following boundaries, that is to say: On the south by

[1] Doty MSS., in the possession of the Wisconsin Historical Society.

the northern boundary line of the State of Illinois, crossing the Mississippi River at the head of Rock Island, and by the northern boundary line of the State of Missouri; on the west by the Missouri River; on the north by the boundary line of the United States to the southern extremity of Drummond's Island at the mouth of the River St. Mary, and thence by a line running from said island to the southern extremity of Bois Blanc Island in Lake Huron, thence by a line equally distant from the island and main land to the centre of the straits between Lakes Michigan and Huron, and thence up the middle of the said straits and Lake Michigan to the northeastern corner of the State of Illinois."

Throughout the protracted agitation incident to this project, Judge Doty wrote numerous *Protracted* letters to influential congressmen, ex-*agitation* planatory of the situation. In 1827, we find him willing to call the proposed new Territory " Wiskonsin" in honor of its principal river. In February, 1828, the house committee on territories was committed to its favor, but it soon received a serious set-back from a memorial sent in by the people of Detroit, who strenuously objected to surrendering to the proposed new territory that portion of their

Upper Peninsula which lay to the east of the Mackinac meridian.[1] The memorialists showed that they were holding active commercial relations with the settlers around the straits of Mackinac, to whom they were also closely allied, socially and politically.

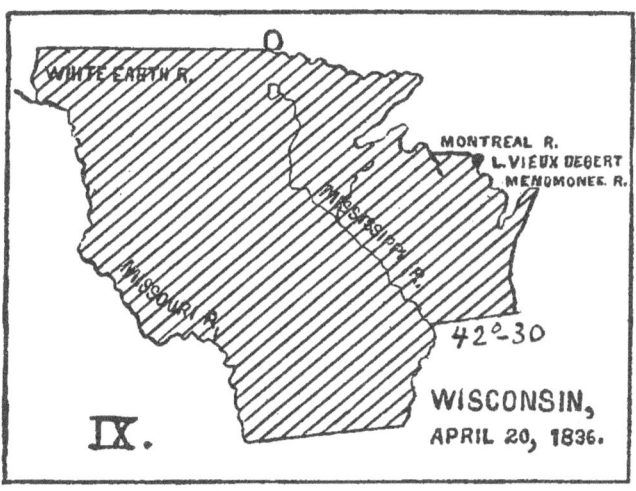

In 1830, the effort was renewed by Doty in a bill to establish the Territory of Huron, with the same boundaries as those prescribed for Chippewau.[2] Four years later, after several

[1] *Michigan Herald*, Detroit, February, 1828.

[2] In Washburne's *Edwards Papers* (pp. 439, 440) there is a letter from Hooper Warren, editor of the Galena *Gazette*, to Gov. Ninian Edwards, of Illinois, dated Galena, October 6, 1829, in which he thus refers to letters on the boundary

sessions of lobbying, a substitute was offered, entitled " A bill establishing the territorial government of Wisconsin," with boundaries

question written by Doty to that paper : " I hope you have read the numbers of our Green Bay correspondent. He is Judge Doty. You are among others to whom he requested us to send the papers containing his essays. *I want you to answer them.* You will see that the whole of his arguments respecting Ohio and Indiana do not apply to Illinois, as our boundary has the assent of Congress, while that of the former states has not. I will further suggest to you that the Ordinance does not say that the east and west line from the southerly bend of Lake Michigan *shall be the boundary ;* but that congress *may* form one or more states *north* of that line — and would not the southern boundary of the state of Wisconsin at 42° 30′ be in accordance with that *injunction* or *permission ?* Further, Illinois has a *natural* right to a port on Lake Michigan, which the old line would cut her off from. This subject is of more importance than you may think it is. A large portion, perhaps a majority, of the people here, are of Judge Doty's opinion, and are wishing and expecting the old line to be established. I have been informed that Judge D. has said that should a case of jurisdiction come before him, he would decide against us. The contention in Michigan proper is for *ten* miles only, which Ohio and Indiana have got *north* of the ' east and west line.' "

See *Wis. Hist. Colls.*, x., pp. 236, 237, for instance of confusion existing, at this time, as to the location of the Wisconsin–Illinois boundary — the election commissioners of Jo Daviess County, Illinois, opening a poll at Platteville, Wisconsin. E. B. Washburne says, in connection with this fact : " The boundary line between Illinois and Michigan Territory was not officially defined until 1830." — ED.

the same as before, except that the country to
the east of the Mackinac meridian was not now
claimed, a House committee having reported
in 1832 that "the due line north from Mac-
kinau should be retained as more in conso-
nance with the Ordinance of 1787." [1]   The bill
hung fire on account of the Ohio-Michigan
dispute, with the result that, as already stated,
Wisconsin, the fifth and last division in the
Northwest Territory, was stripped of the entire
Upper Peninsula.   The selected land line between Wisconsin and Michigan — connecting
the Montreal and Menominee rivers — appears
to have been the suggestion, in 1834, of Senator Preston of South Carolina.[2]   An old map of
Wisconsin, then in vogue, erroneously showed
a continuous water-course between those two
points, thus making an island of the peninsula.

The bill establishing the new Territory
was approved April 20, 1836, Wisconsin
Erection of being therein assigned these limits:
Wisconsin " Bounded on the east by a line drawn
Territory from the northeast corner of the State
of Illinois, through the middle of Lake Michigan, to a point in the middle of said lake and
opposite the main channel of Green Bay, and

[1] Governor Doty's Message, December 4, 1843.
[2] *Wis. Hist. Colls.*, iv., p. 352.

through said channel and Green Bay to the mouth of the Menomonee River; thence through the middle of the main channel of said river to that head of said river nearest to the Lake of the Desert; thence in a direct line

to the middle of said lake; thence through the middle of the main channel of the Montreal River to its mouth; thence with a direct line across Lake Superior to where the territorial line of the United States last touches said lake northwest; thence on the north with the said

territorial line to the White Earth River; on
the west by a line from the said boundary line
following down the middle of the main channel
of White Earth River to the Missouri River,
and down the middle of the main channel of
the Missouri River to a point due west from
the northwest corner of the State of Missouri;
and on the south, from said point, due east to
the northeast corner of the State of Missouri;
and thence with the boundaries of the States
of Missouri and Illinois, as already fixed by
acts of Congress."

It was Hobson's choice, with both Wisconsin
and Michigan. Congress assumed the right
to govern and divide the Northwest Territory
to suit itself, regardless of the solemn compact
of 1787, and there seemed nothing to do but
submit. The future proved that Michigan had
in the great northern peninsula been awarded
more than an equivalent for the narrow belt of
country lost to Ohio, and had no reason to
grumble; while Wisconsin lost in the trans-
action a wide tract of territory which belongs
to her geographically, and which had been
assigned to her in the preliminary delibera-
tions concerning the political division of the
Northwest. But while the consent of Michigan
had been formally asked and reluctantly given

to this violation of the great Ordinance, that of Wisconsin was not sought, either as to her northeastern or her southern boundary.

The matter of her southern boundary was the occasion of much uneasiness in Wisconsin *Wisconsin's* between 1838 and 1846. We have *southern* seen that the act erecting that Terri-*boundary* tory (1836) recognized the northern boundary of Illinois as established in 1818. But in December, 1838, the Wisconsin Legislature memorialized Congress, declaring that the determination of Illinois's northern boundary twenty years before was "directly in collision with, and repugnant to, the compact entered into by the original States, with people and states within the Northwestern Territory"; and praying that, as a measure of justice, "the southern boundary of [Wisconsin] Territory may be so far altered as to include all the Country lying north of a line drawn due west from the southern extreme of Lake Michigan." The strip asked for was over sixty-one miles in width, embraced eight thousand, five hundred square miles of unusually fertile soil, many excellent water-powers, and the sites of Chicago, Rockford, Freeport, Galena, Oregon, Dixon, and several other prosperous towns.

The memorial was pigeon-holed by the Senate judiciary committee. But the Wisconsin Legislature, urged on by Governor Dodge, returned to the charge a year later, with resolutions declaring that Congress had violated the Ordinance of 1787, and that "a large and valuable tract of country is now held by the State of Illinois, contrary to the manifest right and consent of the people of the Territory." The people living in the disputed tract in Illinois were invited to express their opinion of the matter at the ballot-box. Public meetings were held at several affected Illinois towns; and a convention representing the Illinois counties of Jo Daviess, Stephenson, Winnebago, Boone, McHenry, Ogle, Carroll, Whitesides, and Rock Island was held at Rockford (July 6, 1840), which declared that Wisconsin had a sound claim to the fourteen northern counties of Illinois. A popular election was held in Stephenson County, February 19, 1842, whereat of the five hundred and seventy votes cast, all but one were in favor of uniting with Wisconsin; and in August, Boone County's vote was similarly demonstrative.

Outside of the Legislature, the people of Wisconsin themselves exhibited small interest

in the discussion. But at Madison, the territorial lawmakers continued their agitation, occasionally spicing their pugnacious memorials
to Congress with thinly veiled threats of seces-
sion, and such verbal boasts as, " The moral
and physical force of Illinois, of the whole
Union, cannot make us retrace our steps!"
In Congress, Illinois tactics prevented action
on Wisconsin's claims; and gradually the Wisconsin Legislature tired of the one-sided contest. In the first constitutional convention at
Madison (1846), an attempt was made by some
of the members to refer the boundary dispute to
the Federal Supreme Court; but this proposition failed — largely owing, it was claimed, to
the dislike of some of the Wisconsin politicians
to coming into competition with those in Northern Illinois. The constitution-makers therefore peaceably accepted the southern boundary
which Congress had established; and thus the
question was laid at rest forever.

By act of June 12, 1838, Congress contracted
the limits of Wisconsin by creating from its
trans-Mississippi tract[1] the Territory of Iowa.

[1] The language of the clause is as follows : " All that part
of the present Territory of Wisconsin which lies west of the
Mississippi River and west of the line drawn due north from
the headwaters or sources of the Mississippi to the territorial

This, however, was in accordance with the original design when the country beyond the *Iowa de-* Mississippi was attached to Michigan *tached from* Territory for purposes of temporary *Wisconsin* government; hence no objection to this arrangement was entertained by Wisconsin. The establishment of Iowa had reduced Wisconsin to her present limits, except that she still held, as her western boundary, the Mississippi River to its source, and a line drawn due north therefrom to the international boundary.

In this condition Wisconsin remained until the act of Congress approved August 6, 1846, *Wisconsin's* enabling her people to form a State *northwest* constitution. Settlements had now *boundary* been established along the Upper Mississippi and in the St. Croix valley, far

line" [international boundary]. By a memorial to Congress of the Wisconsin Territorial Legislature, approved January 14, 1841 (*Senate Docs.*, No. 171, 26th Cong., 2d sess., vol. iv.), it will be seen that under this act of June 12, 1838, there was some ambiguity as to the western boundary description ; the Wisconsin memorialists held that "the effect of the act confined the western boundary-line of Wiskonsin to the edge of the waters of the Mississippi river, and took away the jurisdiction of Wiskonsin over any part or portion of the Mississippi, either concurrent or otherwise." Congress finally changed the phraseology, so that Wisconsin's western boundary became "the center of the main channel of that river."

removed from, and having neither social nor commercial interests in common with, the bulk of settlement in Southern and Eastern Wisconsin. The northwestern settlers did not wish to be permanently connected with Wisconsin, but

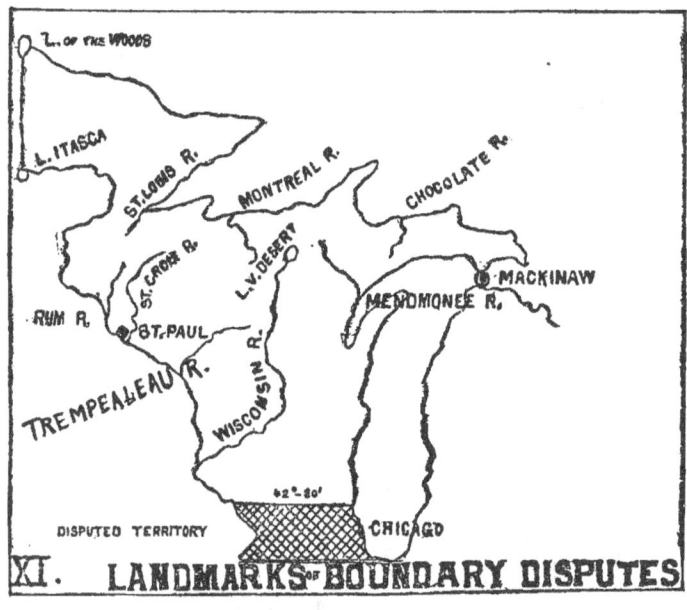

XI. LANDMARKS—BOUNDARY DISPUTES

did desire to cast their fortunes with a new Territory, to be called Minnesota, which was to be formed west of the Mississippi. They therefore brought strong influences to bear in Congress, and the enabling act in question gave to Wisconsin practically the same northwestern line that she has to-day — from the first rapids

of the St. Louis River due south to the St.
Croix River and thence to the Mississippi.
This set off from Wisconsin and assigned to
Minnesota an area of twenty-six thousand
square miles, with the city of St. Paul included.
There was a sharp contest over the matter,
both in Congress and in the Wisconsin constitutional conventions of 1846 and 1847–48,
with the result that the St. Croix people won,
and Wisconsin, the fifth and last State of the
Northwest Territory, became a member of the
Union (act approved May 29, 1848), with her
present limits: shorn on the south by Illinois,
on the northeast by Michigan, and on the
northwest by Minnesota.

In 1837, Wisconsin Territory had a diplomatic flurry with Missouri regarding the southern bounds of her trans-Mississippi tract, but
as that country was merely attached to Wisconsin for temporary purposes and was afterwards absorbed by Iowa, the particulars of the
dispute are not now pertinent.   Neither is
An inter-   the animated disturbance created by
national   the Wisconsin Legislature in 1843–44
dispute   over the terms of the international
boundary treaty of 1842, of importance at this
day; for when Wisconsin became a State, the
strip of country northwest of Lake Superior,

which she claimed had been wrongfully encroached upon by Great Britain, to the extent
of ten thousand square miles, became the
property of Minnesota, which fell heir to the
international dispute.[1]

[1] For detailed treatment, see Thwaites's " Boundaries of
Wisconsin," *Wis. Hist. Colls.*, xi.

III

THE BLACK HAWK WAR

III

THE BLACK HAWK WAR

A LTHOUGH many of its incidents were paltry enough, few events in the early history of the West were as picturesque, as tragical, or as fraught with weighty conse-

Partisan misrepre- sentations quence, as the Black Hawk War, which occurred in 1832. Certainly none have been so persistently mis-

represented for partisan purposes. Immediately after the close of the war, numerous persons who had served with the army hastened to record their impressions in the frontier newspapers and in book form. These publications seem chiefly to have been designed as electioneering documents to glorify the war records of certain officials engaged in the service, and correspondingly to belittle the deeds of others. This gave rise, through a score or more of years, to acrimonious controversies, conducted through the media of published documentary collections, speeches, newspapers, and unpublished letters. As the result of these prejudiced accounts, there have developed in the public mind vague and in large measure incorrect notions of the war, its causes, its incidents, and the relative merits of its chief participants. It is the attempt of this paper to dispel, it may be, some of these errors by presenting a sketch of the famous uprising of the Sauks, in the preparation of which partisan sympathy has not entered, the truth alone being sought from original sources.

On the third of November, 1804, the United States government concluded a treaty with the allied Sauk and Fox Indians, by which, mainly *Treaty of* for the paltry annuity of a thousand 1804 dollars, the confederacy ceded to the whites fifty million acres of land, comprising in general terms the eastern third of the present State of Missouri, and the territory lying between the Wisconsin River on the north, the Fox River of the Illinois on the east, the Illinois on the southeast, and the Mississippi on the west. There was an unfortunate clause in this compact (article seven), which became one of the chief causes of the Black Hawk War. Instead of obliging the Indians at once to vacate the ceded territory, it was stipulated that, " as long as the lands which are now

ceded to the United States remain their property " — that is to say, public land — " the In-

dians belonging to the said tribes shall enjoy
the privilege of living or hunting upon them."[1]

[1] *Treaties between the United States of America and the
several Indian Tribes* (Washington, 1837), p. 109.

Within the limits of the cession was the chief seat of Sauk power [1] — a village lying on the north side of Rock River, three miles above *The old* its mouth and the same distance south *Sauk village* of Rock Island, in the Mississippi. It was picturesquely situated, contained the principal cemetery of the nation, and was populated by about five hundred families, being one of the largest Indian towns on the continent. The soil was alluvial in its composition, producing large crops of corn and pumpkins, and the aboriginal villagers took great pride in a rudely cultivated tract some three thousand acres in extent, lying north of the town and parallel with the Mississippi.

From the beginning of the nineteenth century the principal character in this village was Makataimeshekiakiak, or Black Sparrow Hawk — commonly styled ~~Black Hawk~~. Born at the

---

[1] The allied Sauks and Foxes had, from the middle of the eighteenth century, occupied the banks of the Mississippi, between the mouths of the Missouri and the Wisconsin. The confederation, in times of peace, was more nominal than real. There was much jealous bickering between the tribes. In general, the Foxes, who occupied the west bank, and were the smallest tribe numerically, were more conciliatory toward the whites than were the Sauks, who dwelt chiefly along the east bank.

Sauk village in 1767, he was neither an heredi-
tary nor an elected chief, but by common
Black consent became the leader of that
Hawk community. Although not possessed
of superior physical, moral, or intellectual en-
dowments, the force of circumstances caused
him to become a national celebrity in his day
and a conspicuous figure in Western history for
all time. He was a restless, ambitious savage,
possessed of some of the qualities of successful
leadership, but without the capacity to attain
the highest honors in the Sauk and Fox confederacy. He early became a malcontent,
jealous of Keokuk, Wapello, Morgan, and the
other recognized chiefs, continually sought
excuses for openly differing with them on
questions of policy, and in council arrayed
his followers against them. He was much of
a demagogue, and aroused the passions of
his people by appeals to their prejudices and
superstitions.

It is probable that he was never, in the exercise of this policy, dishonest in his motives.
Doubtless he was sincere in the opinions he
championed. But he was easily influenced by
the British military and commercial agents, —
who were continually engaged, previous to the
War of 1812–15, in cultivating a spirit of hos-

tility between the Northwestern tribes and the Americans, — and was led by them always to consider himself under the special protection of the " British father " (general military agent) at Malden.[1]   A too-confiding disposition was ever leading his judgment astray.   He was readily duped by those who, white or red, were interested in deceiving him.   The effect of his daily communication with the Americans was often rudely to shock his high sense of honor, while the uniform courtesy of the treatment accorded him upon his annual begging visit to Malden contrasted strangely with the attitude of the inhabitants on the Illinois border.

Black Hawk was about five feet, four or five inches in height, and rather spare as to flesh; his somewhat pinched features exaggerated the

[1] In his *Autobiography* (Boston, 1834), — probably authentic for the most part, but written in a stilted style which we doubtless owe to the editor, Patterson, — Black Hawk calls the president at Washington his " great father," and the agent at Malden his " British father."   Ford's *History of Illinois* (Chicago, 1854), p. 110, *note*, questions the accuracy of the autobiography; he says that " Black Hawk knew little, if anything, about it "; that it " was written by a printer, and was never intended for anything but a catchpenny publication," and that it is a " gross perversion of facts."   Later historians, not as strong Indian-haters as Ford, have taken a more favorable view of the book.

BLACK HAWK

m the painting by R. M. Sully, in possession of the Wisconsin Historical Society

prominence of the cheek-bones of his race;
he had a full mouth, inclined to be somewhat
open when at rest; a pronounced Roman nose;
fine "piercing" eyes, often beaming with a
kindly and always with a thoughtful expres-
sion; practically no eyebrows; a high, full
forehead; a head well thrown back, with a
pose of quiet dignity, and his hair plucked out,
with the exception of the scalp-lock, in which,
on ceremonial occasions, was fastened a bunch
of eagle feathers.[1]   The conservative braves of
the confederacy, who were friendly to the
Americans, appear in the main to have regarded the Hawk with kindly compassion.
He was thought by them to be misguided, to
be the credulous catspaw for others, but his
sincerity was not often doubted.   His own followers, who, from the closeness of their intercourse with the Canadian authorities were
known as the "British Band," as a rule held
him in the highest regard.[2]

[1] An admirable original portrait of Black Hawk, by R. M.
Sully, painted in 1833 while the subject was a prisoner at
Fortress Monroe, hangs in the portrait gallery of the Wisconsin Historical Society; a photographic engraving of this
is herewith published.

[2] See Reynolds's *My Own Times* (2d. ed., Chicago, 1879),
p. 204, for his estimate of Black Hawk.   Ford, who himself
served in the Black Hawk War, says, in his *History of Illinois*

At the outbreak of hostilities between Great
Britain and the United States, in 1812, Black
Hawk naturally sided with Tecumseh and the
British.   Accompanied by a band of two hun-
Aids   dred Sauk braves, he served under the
Tecumseh great Shawnee chief until the death
of the latter at the battle of the Thames, October 5, 1813.[1]   Black Hawk — who had, in
company with the Potawatomi chiefs, Shaubena and Billy Caldwell, been near to Tecumseh when he fell — at once hurried home.
He would, he tells us in his Autobiography,
have remained quiet thereafter, until the close
of the war, but for a fatal injury which had
during his absence been inflicted by a party
of white ruffians upon an aged friend whom he
had left behind at the village.   In consequence
of this outrage, it was the thirteenth of May,
1816, — nearly eighteen months after the signing of the treaty of Ghent, — before the British
Band of the Sauks could be induced to

(Chicago, 1854), p. 109: " Black Hawk was distinguished for
courage, and for clemency to the vanquished.   He was an
Indian patriot, a kind husband and father, and was noted
for his integrity in all his dealings with his tribe and with the
Indian traders.   He was firmly attached to the British, and
cordially hated the Americans."

   [1] See Cruikshank, on Black Hawk's record in the War of
1812–15, *Wis. Hist. Colls.*, xii., pp. 141, 142.

cease their retaliatory border forays along the Upper Mississippi and sign a treaty of peace with the United States.

After burying the hatchet, Black Hawk settled into the customary routine of savage life — *Bitterness* hunting in winter, loafing about his *against* village in summer, improvidently ex- *Americans* isting from hand to mouth though surrounded by abundance, and occasionally varying the monotony by visits to Malden, from whence he would return laden with provisions, arms, ammunition, and trinkets; his stock of vanity increased by wily flattery, and his bitterness against the Americans correspondingly intensified. It is not surprising that he should have hated the Americans. They brought him naught but evil. He was continually being disturbed by them, and a cruel and causeless beating which he received from a party of white settlers in the winter of 1822–23 was an insult treasured up against the American people as a whole.

In the summer of 1823, squatters, covetous of the rich fields cultivated by the British Band, be- *Encroach-* gan rudely to take possession of them. *ment of* The treaty of 1804 had guaranteed to *squatters* the Indians the use of the ceded territory so long as the lands remained the property of the United States and were not sold to individuals. The frontier line of homestead settlement was still fifty or sixty miles to the east; the country between had not yet been surveyed, and much of it not explored; the squatters had no rights in this territory, and it was clearly the duty of the federal government to protect the Indians within it until sales were made. The Sauks would not have complained had the squatters settled in other portions of the tract, and not sought to steal the village which was their birthplace and contained the cemetery of their tribe.[1] There were physical outrages of the most flagrant nature. Indian cornfields were unblushingly included within the areas appropriated and fenced by the intruders, squaws and children were whipped for venturing beyond the bounds thus set, lodges were burned over the heads of the occupants. A reign of terror ensued, in which Black Hawk's frequent remonstrances to the white authori-

---

[1] "I had an interview with Keokuk [head chief of the confederacy], to see if this difficulty could not be settled with our Great Father, and told him to propose to give any other land that our Great Father might choose, even our lead mines, to be peaceably permitted to keep the small point of land on which our village was situated. . . . Keokuk promises to make an exchange if possible." — *Autobiography*, pp. 85, 86.

ties were in vain. The situation year by year became more unbearable. When the Indians returned each spring from their winter's hunt they found their village more of a wreck than when they had left it in the preceding autumn. It is surprising that they acted so peacefully while the victims of such harsh treatment.

Keokuk and the United States Indian agent at Fort Armstrong — which had been built on *Black Hawk stubborn* Rock Island about 1816 — continually advised peaceful retreat across the Mississippi. But Black Hawk was stubborn as well as romantic, and his people stood by him when he appealed to their love of home and veneration for the graves of their kindred. He now set up the claim that the Sauk and Fox representatives in the council which negotiated the treaty of 1804 did not consent that the land on which stood Black Hawk's village should be the property of the United States.[1] This was the weak point in

[1] "After questioning Quashquame [one of the signers of the treaty of 1804] about the sale of the lands, he assured me that he never had consented to the sale of our village." — *Autobiography*, p. 85. Yet Quashquame had signed the treaties of Portage des Sioux (September 13, 1815) and St. Louis (September 3, 1822), wherein the treaty of 1804 was explicitly reaffirmed.

his position.　At each treaty to which he had
" touched the quill " since that date he had,
with the rest of his nation, solemnly reaffirmed
the integrity of the compact of 1804.　That he
understood the nature of its provision, there
is no reason to doubt.　But this fact he now
conveniently ignored.[1]　His present views
were indorsed by the mischief-making British
agent at Malden, by the Winnebago Prophet,
and by others of his advisers.　All of these
told him that were it true the government had
not yet bought the site of his village, he should
hold fast to it, and the United States would not
venture to remove him by force.[2]

---

[1] Black Hawk signed the treaties of St. Louis (May 13,
1819), St. Louis (September 3, 1822), and Prairie du Chien
(August 19, 1825), each of which reaffirmed the treaty of
1804.

[2] He was easily satisfied with delphic advice : " I heard
that there was a great chief on the Wabash, and sent a
party to get his advice.　They informed him that we had not
sold our village.　He assured them, then, that if we had not
sold the land on which our village stood, our Great Father
would not take it from us.　I started early to Malden to see
the chief of my British Father, and told him my story.　He
gave the same reply that the chief on the Wabash had
given. . . . I next called on the great chief at Detroit, and
made the same statement to him that I had to the chief of
our British Father.　He gave me the same reply. . . . This
assured me that I was right, and determined me to hold out,
as I had promised our people." — *Autobiography*, pp. 94, 95.

White Cloud, the Prophet, was Black Hawk's evil genius. He was a shrewd, crafty Indian, *White Cloud, the Prophet* half Winnebago and half Sauk, possessing much influence over both nations from his assumption of sacred talents, and was at the head of a Winnebago village some thirty-five miles up the Rock River. He possessed some traits of character similar to those of Tecumseh's brother, but in a less degree. His hatred of the whites was inveterate; he appears to have been devoid of humane sentiments; he had a reckless disposition, and sowed the seeds of native revolt apparently to gratify his passion for war. White Cloud was about forty years of age when his sinister agitation bore fruit; nearly six feet in height, stout and athletic; he had a large, broad face; a short, blunt nose; full eyes, large mouth, thick lips, a full head of shaggy hair. His general appearance indicated deliberate, self-contented savagery. In council, the Prophet displayed much zeal and persuasive oratory. In the matter of dress he must at times have been picturesque. An eye-witness, who was in attendance on a Potawatomi council wherein the wizard was urging the cause of Black Hawk, describes him as dressed in a faultless white buckskin suit, fringed at the seams; wearing a towering head-dress of the same material, capped with a bunch of fine eagle feathers; each ankle girt with a wreath of small sleigh-bells which jingled at every step, while in his nose and ears were ponderous gold rings gently tinkling one against the other as he shook his ponderous head in the warmth of harangue.[1]

In the spring of 1830 Black Hawk and his band returned from an unsuccessful hunt to find their town almost completely shattered, many of the graves ploughed over, and the whites more abusive than ever. During the winter the squatters, who now had been seven years illegally upon the ground, formally preempted a few quarter-sections of lands at the mouth of the Rock, so selected as to cover the village site and the Sauk cornfields. This was clearly a trick to accord with the letter but to violate the spirit of the treaty of 1804. There was still a belt, fifty miles wide, of practically unoccupied territory to the east of the village,

---

[1] The name of the Prophet, in the Winnebago tongue, was Waubakeeshik, meaning "white eye," having reference to the fact that one of his pupils was without color. Pioneers recently living, who remembered the Prophet, differed in opinion as to whether he was totally blind in that organ. He died among the Winnebagoes in 1840 or 1841.

and no necessity, for several years to come, for disturbing the Sauks in the natural progress of settlement.

The indignant Black Hawk at once proceeded to Malden, to pour his sorrows into the ears of his " British father." Here he received additional assurance of the justice of his cause, and upon his return visited the Prophet, at whose village he met some of the Potawatomis and Winnebagoes, who also gave him words of encouragement.

Returning to his village in the spring of 1831, after another gloomy and profitless winter's *The whites* hunt, he was fiercely warned away *threatened* by the whites. In a firm and dignified manner he notified the settlers that, if they did not themselves remove, he should use force. He informs us in his Autobiography that he did not mean bloodshed, but simply muscular eviction.[1] His announcement was construed

---

[1] " The white people brought whiskey into our village, made our people drunk, and cheated them out of their homes, guns, and traps. This fraudulent system was carried to such an extent that I apprehended serious difficulties might take place unless a stop was put to it. Consequently I visited all the whites and begged them not to sell whiskey to my people. One of them continued the practice openly. I took a party of my young men, went to his home, and took his barrel and broke in the head and turned out the whiskey. I did

by the whites, however, as a threat against their lives ; and petitions and messages were showered in by them upon Governor John Reynolds, of Illinois, setting forth the situation in terms that would be amusing in their exaggeration were it not that they proved the prelude to one of the darkest tragedies in the history of the Western border.   The governor fell in with the popular spirit, and at once issued a flaming proclamation calling out a mounted volunteer force to "repel the invasion of the British *The Hawk* Band."   These volunteers, sixteen *coerced* hundred strong, coöperated on the twenty-fifth of June with ten companies of regulars under General Edmund P. Gaines, the commander of the Western division of the army, in a demonstration before Black Hawk's village.[1]

this for fear some of the whites might be killed by my people when drunk." — *Autobiography,* p. 89.

"I now determined to put a stop to it, by clearing our country of the intruders. I went to the principal men and told them that they must and should leave our country, and gave them until the middle of the next day to remove in. The worst left within the time appointed — but the one who remained represented that his family (which was large) would be in a starving condition if he went and left his crop, and promised to behave well if I would consent to let him remain until fall in order to secure his crop. He spoke reasonably, and I consented." — *Ibid.*, p. 101.

[1] "It is astonishing, the war-spirit the Western people

During that night the Indians, in the face of this superior force, quietly withdrew to the west bank of the Mississippi, whither they had previously been ordered. On the thirtieth they signed with General Gaines and Governor Reynolds a treaty of capitulation and peace, solemnly agreeing never to return to the east side of the river without express permission of the United States government.[1] The rest of the summer was spent by the evicted savages in a state of misery. It being now too late to raise another crop of corn and beans, they suffered much for the actual necessaries of life.

Another difficulty soon arose. The previous year (1830), a party of Menominees and Sioux *The Me-* had murdered some member of the *nominee* British Band. A few weeks after the *massacre* removal, Black Hawk and a large war-party of the Sauks ascended the Mississippi, and, in retaliation, massacred, scalped,

possess. As soon as I decided to march against the Indians at Rock Island, the whole country, throughout the northwest of the state, resounded with the war clamor. Everything was in a bustle and uproar. It was then eighteen or twenty years since the war with Great Britain and these same Indians, and the old citizens inflamed the young men to appear in the tented field against the old enemy." — Reynolds, p. 209.

[1] See text of treaty. — *Autobiography*, pp. 218, 219.

and fearfully mutilated all but one of a party
of twenty-eight Menominees who were encamped on an island nearly opposite Fort
Crawford, at Prairie du Chien. On the complaint of the Menominees, General Joseph
Street, the Indian agent at that post, demanded that the Sauk murderers be delivered
to him for trial, under existing treaty provisions. As none of the Menominee murderers
had been given up, his foray was, according
to the ethics of savage warfare, one of just
reprisal. Black Hawk therefore declined to
accede; but although this was the custom
of his race, he was therein clearly rebelling
against the United States government through
its Indian Department.

Neapope, second in command of the British
Band, had, prior to the eviction, gone upon
Bad   a visit to Malden. He returned to
advice   his chief in the autumn, by way of
the Prophet's town, with glowing reports of
proffered aid from the British and the Winnebagoes, Ottawas, Chippewas, and Potawatomis, in the regaining of the village.[1]

---

[1] "He (Neapope) informed me, privately, that the
Prophet was anxious to see me, as he had much good
news to tell me, and that I would hear good news in the
spring from our British father. 'The Prophet requested me

Neapope, possessed of considerable military genius, was an ardent disciple of the Prophet, as well as a reckless mischief-maker on his own account.[1]

The advice of White Cloud was, that Black Hawk should proceed to the Prophet's town the following spring and raise a crop of corn, assurances being given him that by autumn the several allies, armed and equipped by the British, would be ready to join the Sauk leader in a general movement against the whites in the valley of the Rock.

to inform you of all the particulars. I would much rather, however, you should see him, and learn all from himself. But I will tell you, that he has received expresses from our British father, who says that he is going to send us guns, ammunition, provisions, and clothing, early in the spring. The vessels that bring them will come by way of Mil-wa-ke [Milwaukee]. The Prophet has likewise received wampum and tobacco from the different nations on the lakes — Ottawas, Chippewas, Potawatomis; and as for the Winnebagoes, he has them all at his command. We are going to be happy once more.' "— *Autobiography*, p. 109.

[1] Neapope (pronounced *Nah-pope*) means "soup." He was regarded as something of a curiosity among his fellows, because he used neither whiskey nor tobacco. Being a "medicine man," he was in demand at feasts and councils as an agency through which "talks" could be had direct with the Great Spirit. He had the reputation of being better versed in the Sauk traditions than any other member of the tribe. His history after the close of the Black Hawk War is unknown.

Relying upon these rose-colored representations, Black Hawk spent the winter on the
British   then deserted site of old Fort Mad-
Band re-   ison, on the west bank of the Mis-
cruited
sissippi, near the mouth of the Des
Moines, engaged in quietly recruiting his
band. The urgent protests of Keokuk, who
feared that the entire Sauk and Fox confederacy
would become implicated in the war for which
the Hawk was evidently preparing, but spurred
the jealous and obstinate partisan to renewed
endeavors.[1]

At this period the territory embraced in
the Sauk and Fox cession of 1804 was an al-
Early   most unbroken wilderness of alternat-
trails   ing prairies, oak groves, rivers, and
marshes. The United States government had
not surveyed any portion of it, nor had it been
much explored by white hunters or pioneers;
while the Indians themselves were acquainted
with but narrow belts of country along their
accustomed trails. In the lead regions about
Galena and Mineral Point, there were a few
trading posts and small mining settlements.

[1] " Keokuk, who has a smooth tongue and is a great
speaker, was busy in persuading my band that I was wrong,
and thereby making many of them dissatisfied with me. I
had one consolation, for all the women were on my side, on
account of their cornfields." — *Autobiography*, p. 98.

An Indian trail along the east bank of the Mississippi connected Galena and Fort Armstrong, on Rock Island. A coach road known as "Kellogg's Trail," opened in 1827, connected Galena with Peoria and the settlements in southern and eastern Illinois. A daily mail coach travelled this, the only wagon road north of the Illinois River, and it was often crowded with people going to and from the mines, which were the chief source of wealth for the northern pioneers. Here and there along this road lived a few people engaged in entertaining travellers and baiting stage horses — "Old Man" Kellogg at Kellogg's Grove; one Winter, on Apple River; John Dixon at Dixon's Ferry, on Rock River; "Dad Joe," at Dad Joe's Grove; Henry Thomas, on West Bureau Creek; Charles S. Boyd, at Boyd's Grove, and two or three others of less note. Indian trails crossed the country in many directions, between the villages of the several bands and their hunting and fishing grounds, and these were used as public thoroughfares by whites and reds alike.[1] One of these connected Galena and Chicago, by the way of Big

[1] See *Wis. Hist. Colls.*, xi., p. 230, on the evolution of highways from Indian trails; also the several volumes in Hulbert's *Historic Highways of America* (Cleveland, 1902–03).

Foot's Potawatomi village, at the head of the body of water now known as Lake Geneva. There was another, but seldom used, between Dixon's and Chicago. The mining settlements were also connected by old and new trails, and two well-travelled ways led respectively to Fort Winnebago, at the portage of the Fox and Wisconsin rivers, and to Fort Howard, on the lower Fox. In Illinois, the most important aboriginal highway was the great Sauk trail, extending in almost an air line across the State from Black Hawk's village to the south shore of Lake Michigan, and thence to Malden; over this deep-beaten path the British Band made their frequent pilgrimages to Canada.

Between Galena and the Illinois River, the largest settlement was on Bureau Creek, where *Frontier settlements* some thirty families were gathered. There were small aggregations of cabins at Peru, La Salle, South Ottawa, Newark, Holderman's Grove, and a little cluster of eight or ten on Indian Creek. The lead-mining colonies in the portion of Michigan Territory afterwards set aside as Wisconsin were chiefly clustered about Mineral Point and Dodgeville.[1] At the mouth of Milwaukee

[1] See map of lead mines in 1829, *Wis. Hist. Colls.*, xi., p. 400.

River, on Lake Michigan, the fur-trader, Solomon Juneau, was still monarch of all he surveyed; while at Chicago there was a population of but two or three hundred, housed in primitive abodes nestled under the shelter of Fort Dearborn. Scattered between these settlements were a few widely separated farms, managed in a crude, haphazard fashion; squatters were more numerous than homesteaders, and at best little attention was paid to metes and bounds.

The settlers were chiefly hardy backwoodsmen who had graduated from the Pennsylvania, *Character* Ohio, Kentucky, and Indiana clear-*of settlers* ings, and " come West " to better their fortunes, or because neighbors were becoming too numerous in the older regions. Generally they were poor, owning but little more than their cabins, their scanty clothing, a few rough tools, teams of " scrub " horses or yokes of cattle, and some barnyard stock. They were, for the most part, in the prime of life, enterprising, bold, daring, skilled marksmen, and accustomed to exposure, privations, and danger. There were no schools, and the only religious instruction received by these rude pioneers was that given by adventurous missionaries who penetrated the wilderness with the self-sacrificing energies of the fathers of the church, compensating with zeal for what they lacked in culture.

But upon the heels of these worthies had come thieves, counterfeiters, cut-throats, social outlaws from the East. Reckless and aggressive, they too often gave to the community a character of lawless adventure. Such men haunt the frontiers of civilization; and aborigines, from being more frequently brought into collision with these than with the more conservative majority, are apt naturally to form an opinion of our race that is far from flattering.[1]

Conditions in Illinois were ripe for an Indian war. Many elements in the white population foresaw benefits to be derived from it. Occupation would be given to the small but noisy class of pioneer loafers, and government money would circulate freely; to the numerous and respectable body of Indian-haters — persons who had at some time suffered in person or property from the red savages, and had come to regard them as

Ready for an Indian war

---

[1] Nicolay and Hay's *Abraham Lincoln — A History*, i., chaps. ii. and iii., gives a graphic picture of pioneer life in Illinois in 1830; but their account of the Black Hawk War, chap. v., unfortunately contains numerous errors.

little better than wild beasts — it offered a chance for reprisal; to the political aspirant, a brilliant foray presented opportunities for the achievement of personal popularity, and indeed the Black Hawk War was long the chief stock in trade of many a subsequent statesman; while to persons fond of mere adventure, always a large element on the border, the fighting of Indians presented superior attractions.

On the sixth of April, 1832, Black Hawk and Neapope, with about five hundred warriors *Illinois in-* (chiefly Sauks), their squaws and chil-*vaded* dren, and all their possessions, crossed the Mississippi at the Yellow Banks, below the mouth of the Rock, and invaded the State of Illinois. During the winter, the results of the Hawk's negotiations with the Winnebagoes and Potawatomis had not been of an encouraging nature. He now suspected that the representations of the Prophet and Neapope were exaggerated, and his advance from Fort Madison up the west bank of the Mississippi was accordingly made with some forebodings; but the Prophet met him at the Yellow Banks, and gave him such positive reassurances of ultimate success, that the misguided Sauk confidently and leisurely continued his jour-

ney.[1]   He proceeded up the east bank of the
Rock as far as the Prophet's town — some four
hundred and fifty of his braves being well
mounted, while the others, with the women,
children, and equipage, occupied the canoes.
The intention of the invaders was, as before
stated, to raise a crop with the Rock River
Winnebagoes at or immediately above the
Prophet's town, and prepare for the war-path
in the fall, when there would be a supply of
provisions.   Progress was so beset by difficulties, heavy rains having made the stream turbulent and the wide river bottoms swampy,
that the band was twenty days in travelling the
intervening forty miles.

Immediately upon crossing the Mississippi,
Black Hawk had despatched messengers to
Shaubena's the Potawatomis, asking them to
services   meet him in council of war on Sycamore Creek (now Stillman's Run), opposite
the present site of Byron.   The Potawatomis

---

[1] " The Prophet then addressed my braves and warriors.
He told them to follow us, and act like braves, and we had
nothing to fear, but much to gain.   That the American war
chief might come, but would not, nor dare not, interfere with
us so long as we acted peaceably.   That we were not yet
ready to act otherwise.   We must wait until we ascend Rock
River and receive our reinforcements, and we will then be
able to withstand any army ! " — *Autobiography*, p. 113.

were much divided in opinion as to the proper course to pursue. Shaubena, a chief of much ability, who since the War of 1812–15 had formed a sincere respect and attachment for the whites, succeeded in inducing the majority of the braves at least to remain neutral; but the hot-heads, under Big Foot and a despicable half-breed British agent, Mike Girty, were fierce for taking the war-path. Shaubena, after quieting the passions of his followers, set out at once to make a rapid tour of the settlements in the Illinois and Rock valleys, carrying the first tidings of approaching war to the pioneers, even extending his mission as far east as Chicago.[1]

General Henry Atkinson[2] had arrived at Fort Armstrong early in the spring, in charge *Troops* of a company of regulars, for the pur-*called out* pose of enforcing the demand of the Indian department for the Sauk murderers of the Menominees. He did not learn of the invasion until the thirteenth of April, seven days after the crossing, and at once notified Governor Reynolds that his own force was too small for the emergency and that a large detachment of militia was essential. The gov-

---

[1] See Matson's *Memories of Shaubena* (Chicago, 1880).
[2] The Indians called him " White Beaver."

ernor immediately issued another fiery proclamation (April 16), calling for a special levy
of mounted volunteers to assemble at Beardstown, on the lower reaches of Illinois River,
upon the twenty-second of the month.

The news spread like wild-fire. Some of the
settlers flew from the country in hot haste,
Stockade   never to return; but the majority of
forts   those who did not join the State troops
hastened into the larger settlements or to other
points convenient for assembly, where rude
stockade forts were built on Kentucky models,
the inhabitants forming themselves into little
garrisons, with officers and some degree of
military discipline.[1]

---

[1] The following named forts figured more or less conspicuously in the ensuing troubles:

In Illinois — Galena, Apple River, Kellogg's Grove, Buffalo Grove, Dixon's, South Ottawa, Wilburn (nearly opposite
the present city of Peru), West Bureau, Hennepin, and Clark
(at Peoria).

In Michigan Territory (now Southwestern Wisconsin) —
Union (Dodge's smelting works, near Dodgeville), Defiance
(Parkinson's farm, five miles southeast of Mineral Point),
Hamilton (William S. Hamilton's smelting works, now
Wiota), Jackson (at Mineral Point), Blue Mounds (one and
a half miles south of East Blue Mound), Parish's (at Thomas
J. Parish's smelting works, now Wingville), Cassville, Platte-
ville, Gratiot's Grove, Diamond Grove, White Oak Springs,
Old Shullsburg, and Elk Grove.

Fort Armstrong was soon a busy scene of preparation. St. Louis was at the time the

Atkinson organizes the army only government supply dépôt on the Upper Mississippi; and limited transportation facilities, and the bad weather incident to a backward spring, greatly hampered the work of collecting troops, stores, boats, and camp equipage. General Atkinson, energetic and possessed of much executive ability, overcame these difficulties as rapidly as possible. He had military skill, courage, perseverance, and knowledge of Indian character, and during his preparations for the campaign took pains personally to assure himself of the peaceful attitude of those Sauks and Foxes not members of the British Band. He also sent two sets of messengers to Black Hawk, ordering him to withdraw at once to the west bank of the river, on the peril of being driven there by force of arms. To both messages the Sauk leader, now blindly trusting in the Prophet, sent defiant answers.[1]

[1] " Another express came from the White Beaver [Atkinson], threatening to pursue us and drive us back, if we did not return peaceably. This message roused the spirit of my band, and all were determined to remain with me and contest the ground with the war chief, should he come and attempt to drive us. We therefore directed the express to say to the war chief, ' If he wished to fight us, he might come on ! ' We

Meanwhile the volunteers, easily recruited amid the general excitement, rendezvoused at *Volunteers* Beardstown. They were organized *mobilized* into four regiments, under the commands of Colonel John Thomas, Jacob Fry, Abraham B. Dewitt, and Samuel M. Thompson; there were also a spy (or scout) battalion under Major James D. Henry, and two " odd battalions " under Majors Thomas James and Thomas Long.[1] The entire force, some six-

were determined never to be driven, and equally so, not to make the first attack, our object being to act only on the defensive." — *Autobiography*, p. 114.

Wakefield's *History of the War* (Jacksonville, Ill., 1834), pp. 10–12, gives an interesting report of a visit to Black Hawk's camp at the Prophet's town, made April 25–27, by Henry Gratiot, Indian agent for the Rock River band of Winnebagoes. Gratiot bore one of the messages from Atkinson, which Black Hawk declined to receive. See *Wis. Hist. Colls.*, ii., p. 336; x., pp. 235, 493, for details of this mission, and sketch of Gratiot.

[1] See roster in Armstrong's *The Sauks and the Black Hawk War* (Springfield, Ill., 1887), appendix. Abraham Lincoln, afterwards President of the United States, was captain of a company in the Fourth (Thompson's) regiment. Wakefield, the historian, served in Henry's spy battalion. Jefferson Davis, later president of the Confederacy, was a lieutenant of Co. B., First United States infantry, which was stationed at Fort Crawford (Prairie du Chien) during January and February, 1832, but Davis himself is on the rolls as " absent on detached service at the Dubuque mines by order of Colonel Morgan." He was absent from his company on furlough, from March 26 to August 18, 1832; hence, it would

teen hundred strong — all horsemen except three hundred who had by mistake been enlisted as infantry — was placed under the charge of Brigadier-General Samuel Whiteside who had previously been in command of frontier rangers and enjoyed the reputation of being a good Indian fighter. Accompanied by Governor Reynolds, the brigade proceeded to Fort Armstrong, which was reached on the seventh of May, and General Atkinson swore the volunteers into United States service. The governor, who remained with his troops, was recognized and paid as a major-general; while Lieutenant Robert Anderson (later of Fort Sumter fame) was detailed from the regulars to be inspector-general of the Illinois militia.

On the ninth, the start was made, Black *The army* Hawk's trail up the east bank of the *sets out* Rock being pursued by Whiteside and the mounted volunteers. Atkinson fol-

appear from the records that he took no part in the Black Hawk War further than to escort the chief to Jefferson Barracks. Nevertheless, an anonymous campaign biography of Davis, published at Jackson, Miss., 1851, in the interest of his candidacy for the governorship, and presumably inspired by the candidate himself, says that he "earned his full share of the glories, by partaking of the dangers and hardships of the campaign. Here he remained in the active discharge of his duties, and participating in most of the skirmishes and battles, until shortly after the battle of Bad Axe."

lowed in boats with cannon, provisions, and the bulk of the baggage; with him were the three hundred volunteer footmen and four hundred regular infantry, the latter gathered from Forts Crawford (Prairie du Chien) and Leavenworth, and under the command of Colonel Zachary Taylor, afterwards President of the United States.[1] The rest of the baggage was taken by Whiteside's land force in wagons. The travelling was bad for both divisions. The heavy rains had swollen the stream; the men frequently waded breast deep for hours together, pushing the keel and Mackinac boats against the rapid current and lifting them over the rapids; while upon the swampy trails the baggage wagons were often mired, and the horsemen obliged to do rough service in pushing and hauling freight through the black muck and over tangled roots. For many days the troops had not a dry thread upon them; the tents were found to be of poor quality, and but meagre protection from the driving storms on the Illinois prairies.[2]

[1] Major William S. Harney, the hero of Cerro Gordo, also served with the regulars in this campaign.

[2] "A great portion of the volunteers had been raised in the backwoods, and rafting and swimming streams were familiar to them." — Reynolds, p. 226.

Whiteside was thus enabled to out-distance Atkinson. Arriving at the Prophet's town, he found it deserted and the trail up the river fresh, so he pushed on as rapidly as possible to Dixon's, where he arrived on the twelfth. Here he found two independent battalions, three hundred and forty-one men all told, under Majors Isaiah Stillman and David Bailey.[1] They had been at the ferry for some days, with abundance of ammunition and supplies, in which latter Whiteside was now deficient. These commands were not of the regular levy, and objected to joining the main army except on detached service as rangers. Imbued with reckless enthusiasm, they were impatient at the slow advance of the expedition, and anxious at once to do something brilliant, feeling confident that all that was necessary to end the war was for them to be given a chance to meet the enemy in open battle.

Stillman's scouts Obtaining Whiteside's permission to go forward in the capacity of a scouting party, the independents set out bravely on the morning of the thirteenth, under

---

[1] This made the total volunteer force 1,935 men. The Stillman and Bailey battalions were afterwards organized as the Fifth Regiment, under Colonel James Johnson.

Stillman.   Late in the afternoon of the fourteenth they pitched camp in a small clump of
open timber, three miles southwest of the
mouth of Sycamore Creek.   It was a peculiarly
strong position for defence.   The troop completely filled the grove, which was surrounded
by a broad, undulating prairie.   With an
Indian enemy averse to fighting in the open,
the troopers might readily have repulsed ten
times their own number.

Black Hawk had tarried a week at the
Prophet's town, holding fruitless councils with
Tribemen   the wily and vacillating Winnebagoes.
in council   He now for the first time learned
positively that he had been deceived.   But
to keep his engagement at Sycamore Creek,
he pushed on, faint at heart, though vaguely
hoping better things of the Potawatomis.
Going into camp with his principal men, in a
large grove near the mouth of the creek, he
met the chiefs of that tribe, and soon found
that Shaubena's counsels had rendered it impossible to gain over to his cause more than
about a hundred of the hot-head element.
Black Hawk asserted in after years that he had
at this juncture fully resolved to return at once
to the west of the Mississippi should he again
be summoned to do so by General Atkinson,

never more to disturb the peace of the white settlements. As a parting courtesy to his guests, however, he was on the evening of the fourteenth making arrangements to give them a dog feast, when the summons came in a manner little anticipated.

The white-hating faction of the Potawatomis was encamped on the Kishwaukee River some seven miles north of Black Hawk, and with them the majority of his own party. The Hawk says that not more than forty of his braves were with him upon the council ground. Towards sunset, in the midst of his preparations, he was informed that a party of white horsemen were going into camp three miles down the Rock. It was Stillman's corps, but the Sauk — then unaware of the size of the force which had been placed in the field against him — thought it a small party headed by Atkinson, and sent three of his young men with a white flag. to parley with the new arrivals and convey his offer to meet the White Beaver in council.[1]

The rangers, who had regarded the expedition as a big frolic, were engaged in preparing their camp, in irregular picnic fashion, when

[1] *Autobiography*, pp. 117, 118.

the truce-bearers appeared upon a prairie
knoll, nearly a mile away.   A mob of the
troopers, in helter-skelter form, some with
saddles on their horses and some without,
rushed out upon the astonished envoys, and
hurried them into camp amid a hubbub of
yells and imprecations.   Black Hawk had sent
five other braves to follow the flagmen at a
safe distance, and watch developments.   This
second party was sighted by about twenty of
the horsemen, who had been scouring the
plain for more Indians.   They were said to
have been, like others of Stillman's men at the
time, much excited by the too free use of
intoxicants.   Hot chase was given to the spies,
and two of them were killed.   The other three
galloped back to the council grove and reported to their chief that not only two of their
own number, but the three flag-bearers as well,
had been cruelly slain.   This flagrant disregard
of the rules of war caused the blood of the old
Sauk to boil with righteous indignation.   Tear-
ing to shreds the flag of truce which, when the
spies broke in upon him, he himself had been
preparing to carry to the white camp, he
fiercely harangued his thirty-five braves and
bade them, at any risk, to avenge the blood
of their tribesmen.

The neutral Potawatomi visitors at once withdrew from the grove and hastily sped to *Stillman's defeat* their villages, while Black Hawk and his party of forty Sauks, [1] sallied forth on their ponies to meet the enemy. The entire white force, over three hundred strong, was soon seen rushing towards them in a confused mass. The Sauks withdrew behind a fringe of bushes, their leader hurriedly bidding them to stand firm. On catching a glimpse of the grim array awaiting them, the whites paused; but before they had a chance to turn, the Hawk sounded the war-whoop, and the savages dashed forward and fired. The Sauk chief tells us that when he ordered it, he thought the charge suicidal, but, enraged at the treachery of the troopers, he and all with him were willing to die in securing reprisal.

On the first fire of the Indians, the whites, without returning the volley, fled in great consternation, pursued by about twenty-five savages, until nightfall ended the chase. But nightfall did not end the rout. The volunteers, beset by the genius of fear, dashed through

---

[1] " Black Hawk in his book says he had only forty in all, and judging from all I can discover in the premises, I believe the number of warriors were between fifty and sixty." — Reynolds, p. 234.

their own impregnable camp, left everything behind them, and plunged madly through swamps and creeks till they reached Dixon's, twenty-five miles away, where they straggled in for the next twenty hours. Many of them did not stop there, but kept on at a keen gallop till they reached their own firesides, fifty or more miles farther, carrying the report that Black Hawk and two thousand bloodthirsty warriors were sweeping all Northern Illinois with the besom of destruction. The white casualties in this ill-starred foray amounted to eleven killed, while the Indians lost the two spies and but one of the flag-bearers, who had been treacherously shot in Stillman's camp — his companions owing their lives to the fleetness of their ponies.

The flight of Stillman's corps was wholly inexcusable. It should, in any event, have stopped at the camp, which was easily defensible.[1] Stillman, no doubt, exerted himself to

---

[1] "I never was so surprised, in all the fighting I have seen — knowing, too, that the Americans, generally, shoot well — as I was to see this army of several hundreds, retreating without showing fight, and passing immediately through this encampment. I did think that they intended to hault here, as the situation would have forbidden attack by my party, if their number had not exceeded half mine, as we would have been compelled to take the open prairie, whilst

his utmost to rally his men, but they lacked discipline and that experience which gives soldiers confidence in their officers and each other. Their worst fault was their dishonorable treatment of bearers of a flag of truce, a symbol which few savage tribes disregard. But for this act of treachery, the Black Hawk War might have been a bloodless demonstration. Unfortunately for our own good name, this violation of the rules of war was more than once repeated by the Americans during the contest which followed.

From this easy and unexpected victory, Black Hawk formed a low opinion of the valor of the militiamen, and at the same time an *The Hawk* exaggerated estimate of the prowess *at Kosh-* of his own braves. Almost wholly *konong* destitute of provisions and ammunition, he was elated at the capture of Stillman's abundant stores. Recognizing that war had been forced upon him [1] and was hence-

they could have picked trees to shield themselves from our fire." — *Autobiography*, p. 122.

[1] "I had resolved upon giving up the war, and sent a flag of peace to the American war chief, expecting as a matter of right, reason, and justice, that our flag would be respected (I have always seen it so in war among the whites), and a council convened, that we might explain our grievances, having been driven from our village the year before, without per-

forth inevitable, he despatched scouts to watch the white army while he hurriedly removed his women and children, by way of the Kishwaukee, to the swampy fastnesses of Lake Koshkonong, near the headwaters of Rock River, in Michigan Territory (now Wisconsin). He was guided thither by friendly Winnebagoes, who deemed the position impregnable. From here, recruited by parties of Winnebagoes and Potawatomis, Black Hawk descended into Northern Illinois, prepared for active border warfare.

The story of Stillman's defeat inaugurated a *A reign of terror* reign of terror between the Illinois and Wisconsin rivers, and much consternation throughout the entire West. The name of Black Hawk, whose forces and the

mission to gather the corn and provisions, which our women had labored hard to cultivate, and ask permission to return, — thereby giving up all idea of going to war against the whites. Yet, instead of this honorable course which I have always practised in war, I was forced into war, with about five hundred warriors, to contend against three or four thousand.

"The supplies that Neapope and the Prophet told us about, and the reinforcements we were to have, were never more heard of, and it is but justice to our British father to say, were never promised — his chief having sent word in lieu of the lies that were brought to me, 'for us to remain at peace, as we could accomplish nothing but our own ruin, by going to war.'" — *Autobiography*, pp. 123, 124.

nature of whose expedition were grossly exaggerated, became associated the country over with tales of savage cunning and cruelty. The bloodthirsty Sauk long served as a household bugaboo. Shaubena and his friends again rode post-haste through the settlements, sounding the alarm. Many of the frontiersmen, lulled into a sense of security by the long calm following the invasion at Yellow Banks, had returned to their fields. But there was now a hurrying back into the forts; they flew like chickens to cover, on the warning of the Hawk's foray. The rustle in the underbrush of a prowling beast; the howl of a wolf on the prairie; the fall of a forest bough; the report of a hunter's gun, were sufficient in this time of panic to blanch the cheeks of the bravest men, and cause families to fly in the agony of fear for scores of miles, leaving all their possessions behind them.[1]

[1] Wakefield, pp. 56-60, relates some amusing and apparently truthful anecdotes of the scare. Here is one of them : " In the hurried rout that took place at this time, there was a family that lived near the [Iroquois] river [in northeastern Illinois] ; they had no horses, but a large family of small children ; the father and mother each took a child ; the rest were directed to follow on foot as fast as possible. The eldest daughter also carried one of the children that was not able to keep up. They fled to the river where they had to

On the day of the defeat, Whiteside, with a thousand four hundred men, proceeded to the *The army* field of battle and buried the dead. *disbanded* On the nineteenth, Atkinson and the entire army moved up the Rock, leaving Stillman's corps at Dixon to care for the wounded and guard the supplies. But the army was no sooner out of sight than Stillman's cowards added infamy to their record, by deserting their post and going home. Atkinson hastily returned to Dixon with the regulars, leaving Whiteside to follow Black Hawk's trail up the Kishwaukee.

Whiteside's men, however, now began to weary of soldiering. They declared that the

cross. The father had to carry over all the children, at different times, as the stream was high, and so rapid the mother and daughter could not stem the current with such a burden. When they all, as they thought, had got over, they started, when the cry of poor little Susan was heard on the opposite bank, asking if they were not going to take her with them. The frightened father again prepared to plunge into the strong current for his child, when the mother seeing it, cried out, 'Never mind Susan ; we have succeeded in getting ten over, which is more than we expected at first — and we can better spare Susan than you, my dear.' So poor Susan, who was only about four years old, was left to the mercy of the frightful savages. But poor little Susan came off unhurt; one of the neighbors, who was out hunting, came along and took charge of little Susan, the eleventh, who had been so miserably treated by her mother."

Indians had gone into the unexplored and impenetrable swamps of the north, and could never be captured; even were that possible, Illinois volunteers were not compelled to serve out of the State, in Michigan Territory; they also claimed to have enlisted for but one month. After two or three days' fruitless skirmishing, and before reaching the State line, the council of officers determined to abandon search. Turning about, they marched southward to Ottawa, where they were, on the twenty-seventh and twenty-eighth of May, at their own request, mustered out of the service by Governor Reynolds. En route from the Kishwaukee to Ottawa, the militiamen stopped at the Davis farm on Indian Creek, where a massacre of whites (p. 160) had occurred a few days before, and the mutilated corpses of fifteen men, women, and children were lying on the greensward, unsepulchred. This revolting spectacle, instead of nerving the troops to renewed action in defence of their homes, appears to have still further disheartened them.[1]

Thus did the first campaign of the war end, as it had begun, with an exhibition of

[1] See Reynolds's statement of the case, in *My Own Times*, pp. 238, 239.

rank cowardice on the part of the Illinois militia.

Governor Reynolds was active, and at once arranged for a fresh levy of " at least two thousand " men to serve through the war, to rendezvous at Beardstown, June 10; while the federal government ordered a thousand regulars under General Winfield Scott to proceed from the seaboard to the seat of war, Scott being directed to conduct all future operations against the enemy. Meanwhile, at Atkinson's earnest appeal, three hundred mounted volunteer rangers, under Henry Frye as colonel and James D. Henry as lieutenant-colonel, agreed to remain in the field to protect the northern line of Illinois settlements until the new levy could be mobilized.[1]

A fresh levy

---

[1] General Whiteside enlisted as a private in this battalion. Abraham Lincoln was also a member, being enlisted May 27 as a " private horseman," in Captain Elijah Iles's company. He was mustered out at Ottawa, June 16, when the regular levy had taken the field. June 20 he re-enlisted in Captain Jacob M. Early's company, an independent body of rangers not brigaded, and served throughout the war. Besides these three hundred volunteer rangers, divided into six companies, General Atkinson had some three hundred regulars on Rock River, the entire force available to check the enemy, until the new levy could assemble.

Black Hawk, upon descending Rock River from Lake Koshkonong, divided his people *Irregular* into war-parties, himself leading the *hostilities* largest, about two hundred strong. He was assisted by small scalping parties of Winnebagoes, who were always ready for guerilla butchery when the chance for detection was slight, and by about a hundred Potawatomis under Mike Girty.

During the irregular hostilities which now broke out in northern Illinois and just across the Michigan (now Wisconsin) border, pending the resumption of the formal campaign, some two hundred whites and nearly as many Indians lost their lives, great suffering was induced among the settlers, and panic among the latter was widespread. Many of the incidents of this partisan strife are rich in historic and romantic interest and have been productive of elaborate discussions in the press and in documentary collections; but in a paper of this scope only a few of the most striking events can be alluded to.[1]

---

[1] Nearly every volume of the *Wisconsin Historical Collections* contains articles and documents bearing on this war, which it would be burdensome to cite here in detail ; many of them are invaluable, while some, in the light of later developments, are worthless.

On the twenty-second of May a party of thirty Potawatomis and three Sauks, under *Notable* Girty, surprised and slaughtered *skirmishes* fifteen men, women, and children congregated at the Davis farm, on Indian Creek, twelve miles north of Ottawa, Illinois. Two daughters of William Hall — Sylvia, aged seventeen years, and Rachel, aged fifteen — were spared by their captors. Being taken to Black Hawk's stronghold above Lake Koshkonong, they were there sold for two thousand dollars in horses and trinkets to White Crow, a Winnebago chief who had been sent out by Henry Gratiot, sub-agent for the Winnebagoes, to conduct the negotiation. The girls were safely delivered into Gratiot's hands at Blue Mounds, on the third of June.

On the evening of the fourteenth of June, a party of eleven Sauks killed five white men at Spafford's farm, on the Peckatonica River, in what is now La Fayette County, Wisconsin. Colonel Henry Dodge, with twenty-nine men, followed, and the next day overtook the savages in a neighboring swamp. In a hot brush lasting but a few minutes, the eleven Indians were killed and scalped, while of Dodge's party three were killed and one wounded. The details of no event in the entire war have been so thoroughly discussed and quarrelled over as those of this brief but bloody skirmish.[1]

On the twenty-fourth of June, Black Hawk's own party made a desperate attack on Apple River Fort, fourteen miles east of Galena, Illinois. For upwards of an hour the little garrison sustained the heavy siege, displaying remarkable vigor, the women and girls moulding bullets, loading pieces, and in general proving themselves border heroines. The red men retired with small loss, after laying waste by fire the neighboring cabins and fields. The following day this same war party attacked, with singular ferocity, Major Dement's spy battalion of Posey's brigade, a hundred and fifty strong, at Kellogg's Grove, sixteen miles to the east. General Posey came up with a detachment of volunteers to relieve the force, and continued the skirmish. The Indians were routed, losing about fifteen killed, while the whites lost but five.[2]

[1] Notably in *Wis. Hist. Colls.*, ii., iv., v., vi., vii., viii., x.

[2] Kellogg's Grove, afterwards Waddams's, and now Timms's, is situated in the southwestern portion of Kent township, Stephenson County, Illinois, about nine miles south of Lena. The five men killed in the skirmish of June 25, 1832, had been buried at different points within the grove. During the summer of 1886 their remains were collected by order of the county board of supervisors, and

At Plum River Fort, Burr Oak Grove, Sinsiniwa Mound, and Blue Mounds, skirmishes
of less importance were fought.

The people of the lead-mining settlements in
what is now southwestern Wisconsin, deemed

The lead- themselves peculiarly liable to attack,
mine dis- fearing that the troops centred on
trict Rock River would drive the enemy
upon them across the Illinois border. The
news of the invasion at Yellow Banks was
received by the miners early in May, and active preparations for defence and offence were
at once undertaken. Colonel Henry Dodge,
one of the pioneers of the lead region, and
an energetic citizen largely interested in
smelting, held a commission as chief of the
Michigan militia west of Lake Michigan, and
assumed direction of military operations north
of the Illinois line. With a company of
twenty-seven hastily equipped mounted rangers he made an expedition to Dixon, with a
view both to reconnoitre the country and

decently interred upon a commanding knoll at the edge of
the copse. With these were placed those of five or six other
victims of the Black Hawk War, who had fallen in other
portions of the county. Over these remains, a monument
costing five hundred dollars was erected by the board, being
formally dedicated September 30, 1886, under the auspices
of W. R. Goddard post of the G. A. R.

solicit aid from Governor Reynolds's force. He failed in this latter mission, however, and returned to the mines carrying the news of Stillman's defeat.[1] After making preparations for recruiting three additional companies, Dodge proceeded with Indian Agent Gratiot and a troop of fifty volunteers to White Crow's Winnebago village at the head of Lake Mendota (Fourth Lake), on a point of land now known as Fox's Bluff, some four miles northwest of the present Madison. The Winnebagoes were always deemed a source of danger to the mining settlements, and it was desirable to keep them quiet during the present crisis. Colonel Dodge held council with them on the twenty-fifth of May, and received profuse assurances of their fidelity to the American cause; but the partisan leader appears to have justly placed small reliance upon their sincerity.[2]

[1] "General Dodge was camped in the vicinity [Dixon's], on the north side of Rock River, and I wrote him, at night [May 14–15], the facts of Stillman's disaster, and that his frontiers of Wisconsin would be in danger. He returned immediately to Wisconsin." — Reynolds, p. 235.

[2] Dodge's " talk " is given in Smith's *History of Wisconsin* (Madison, 1854), i., pp. 416, 417. See *Wis. Hist. Colls.*, ii., p. 339, for White Crow's taunt flung at Dodge, that the whites were " a soft-shelled breed," and could not fight. For sketch of this chief — whose Indian name was Kaukishkaka (The

Returning from this council, Dodge set out from his headquarters at Fort Union on an

Dodge's Rough Riders

active campaign with two hundred mounted rangers enlisted for the war. These men, gathered from the mines and fields, were a free-and-easy set of fellows, imbued with the spirit of adventure and an intense hatred of the Indian race. While disciplined to the extent of obeying orders whenever sent into the teeth of danger, these Rough Riders of seventy years ago swung through the country with small regard for the rules of the manual, and presented a striking contrast to the habits and appearance of the regulars.

On the third of June they arrived at Blue Mounds, just in time to receive the Hall girls brought in by White Crow. The Crow and his companions being now offensive in their manner, Dodge had them thrown into the guard-house, and held for a time as hostages for the good behavior of the rest of the Lake Mendota band. On the eleventh, he was joined by a small party of Illinois rangers from Galena, under Captain J. W. Stephenson, the united force proceeding to Atkinson's re-

Blind), he having lost an eye in a brawl — see *id.*, x., pp. 495, 496. Washburne's estimate of him, *ibid.*, p. 253, is unfavorable; others of his white contemporaries speak with enthusiasm of his strength as a native orator, and his manly bearing.

cruiting quarters, then at Ottawa, where Dodge conferred with the general as to the future conduct of the campaign. After remaining a few days, the rangers returned to the lead mines to complete the local defences.

In less than three weeks from the date of Stillman's defeat, Atkinson and Reynolds had *The new* together recruited and organized a *army* new mounted militia force, and on the fifteenth of June the troops rendezvoused at Fort Wilburn (near Peru). There were three brigades, respectively headed by Generals Alexander Posey, M. K. Alexander, and James D. Henry. Each brigade contained a spy battalion. The aggregate strength of this volunteer army was three thousand two hundred, which was in addition to Frye's rangers, half of whom continued their services to protect the settlements and stores west of the Rock River. With these, Dodge's rangers, and the regular infantry, the entire army now in the field numbered about four thousand effective men.

A party of Posey's brigade was sent in ad-*The ad-* vance from Fort Wilburn to scour *vance to* the country between Galena and the *Koshko-* *nong* Rock, and disperse Black Hawk's war-party. It was this force that had the brush with the Sauks at Kellogg's Grove on the twenty-fifth of June, already alluded to. Meanwhile, Alexander's and Henry's brigades had arrived overland at Dixon's. On arrival of news of the defeat of the Indians at Kellogg's, Alexander was despatched in haste to Plum River to intercept the fugitives should they attempt to cross the Mississippi at that point; while Atkinson, with Henry and the regulars, remained at Dixon's to await developments. On learning that Black Hawk's main camp was still near Lake Koshkonong, Atkinson at once marched up the east bank of the Rock, leaving Dixon's on the afternoon of June 27. The main army, now consisting of four hundred regulars and two thousand one hundred volunteer troops, was joined the following day by a party of seventy-five friendly Potawatomis, who seemed eager to join in the prospective scrimmage.

On the thirtieth, the army crossed the Illinois-Wisconsin boundary about one mile east of the site of Beloit, near the Turtle village of the Winnebagoes, whose inhabitants had flown at the approach of the column.[1] Sauk signs were

[1] In the Beloit *Weekly Free Press* for October 15, 1891, and January 21, 1892, Cornelius Buckley discusses in detail the place of crossing the boundary, and the site of Atkinson's

fresh, for after his defeat at Kellogg's at the hands of Posey and Dement, Black Hawk had, instead of crossing the Mississippi, fled directly to his stronghold, reaching the Rock above the mouth of the Kishwaukee three or four days in advance of the white army. It was this warm trail that Atkinson's men, with the vehemence of bloodhounds, were now following. When possible, at the close of each day, the troops selected a camp in the timber, were protected by breastworks, and at all times slept on their arms, for there was constant apprehension of a night attack; the rear guard of the savages, prowling about in the dark, were frequently fired on by the sentinels.

The outlet of Lake Koshkonong was reached on the second of July. Hastily deserted Indian *Fruitless* camps were found, with white scalps *scouting* hanging on the poles of the tepees. Scouts made a tour of the lake, but beyond a few stragglers nothing of importance was seen. A few Winnebagoes hanging upon the flanks of the column were captured, and after their

camp, which latter he places "near the northeast corner of the southwest quarter of section 25, town 1, and range 12, and 480 rods north of the State line . . . and directly north of the old fair grounds."

kind gave vague and contradictory testimony;
one of them was shot and scalped for his
impertinence.   Several succeeding days were
spent in fruitless scouting.   July 4, Alexander arrived with his brigade, reporting that
he had found no traces of red men on the
Mississippi.   On the sixth, Posey reported
with Dodge's squadron.

Dodge was at Fort Hamilton (Wiota) on
the twenty-eighth of June, reorganizing his
rangers, when Posey arrived from Kellogg's
Grove, bringing from Atkinson orders to bring
Dodge's command with him and join the main
army on the Koshkonong.   At Sugar River,
Dodge was joined by Stephenson's Galena
company and by a party of twenty friendly
Menominees and eight or ten white and half-
breed scouts under Colonel William S. Hamilton, a son of the famous Alexander, and then
a prominent lead miner.   This recruited his
Rough Rider squadron so that it now numbered
about three hundred.   Proceeding by the way
of the Four Lakes (neighborhood of Madison),
White Crow and thirty Winnebagoes offered
to conduct Posey and Dodge to Black Hawk's
camp, and unite with them for that purpose.
After advancing for several days through almost impassable swamps, the corps were within

short distance of the locality sought, when an express came from Atkinson ordering them to proceed without delay to his camp on Bark River, an eastern affluent of Lake Koshkonong, for he believed the main body of the enemy to be in that vicinity. This order much provoked Dodge, but it proved to be opportune. Black *Black* Hawk's camp occupied a position *Hawk's* advantageous for defence, at the sum- *camp* mit of a steep declivity on the east bank of the Rock, where the river was difficult of passage, being rapid and clogged with boulders.[1] White Crow's solicitude as a guide was undoubtedly caused by his desire to lead this small force, constituting the left wing of the army, into a trap where it might have been badly whipped if not annihilated.

The army was thus formed: Posey's brigade and Dodge's rangers comprised the left wing, on the west side of the Rock; the regulars under Taylor, and Henry's volunteers, were the right wing, commanded by Atkinson in person, and marched on the east bank; while Alexander's brigade, also on the west bank, was the centre. While marching across country, Dodge had conceived a poor opinion of Posey's men, and on the arrival of the left

[1] The site of the present village of Hustisford, Wisconsin.

wing at headquarters, solicited a change of companions. To secure harmony, Atkinson caused Posey and Alexander to exchange positions.

While the treacherous White Crow had been endeavoring to entrap the left wing, other Winnebagoes of the neighborhood informed Atkinson that Black Hawk was encamped on an island in the Whitewater River, a few miles east of the American camp on the Bark. In consequence, the commander was from the seventh to the ninth of July running a wild-goose chase through the broad morasses and treacherous sink-holes of that region. It was because of this false information that Atkinson had hastily summoned the left wing to his aid, and thus in the nick of time unwittingly saved it from grave danger. Through lack of concert in their lying, the wily Winnebagoes failed of their purpose, for in the meantime the Hawk, startled from his cover by the manœuvring in his neighborhood, fled westward to the Wisconsin River.

Governor Reynolds, and several other promi-
Illinois men discouraged
nent Illinois men who were with the army, had become discouraged. They therefore promptly left for home by way of Galena, impressed with the opinion

that the troops, now in wretched physical condition, almost destitute of food, and flound-
ering aimlessly through the Wisconsin bogs,
were pursuing an ignis-fatuus and the Black
Hawk could never be captured.[1]

On the same day (July 10), Henry's and
Alexander's brigades were despatched with
At Fort Dodge's squadron to Fort Winnebago,
Winnebago at the portage of the Fox and Wisconsin rivers, eighty miles to the northwest,
for much-needed provisions, it being the
nearest supply point. The Second Regiment
of Posey's brigade, under Colonel Ewing, was

---

[1] " On the 10th of July, in the midst of a considerable
wilderness, the provisions were exhausted, and the army forced
to abandon the pursuit of the enemy for a short time.
Seeing the difficulties to reach the enemy, and knowing the
extreme uncertainty of ever reaching Black Hawk by these
slow movements, caused most of the army to believe we
would never overtake the enemy. This condition of affairs
forced on all reflecting men much mortification, and regret
that this campaign also would do nothing. Under these circumstances, a great many worthy and respectable individuals,
who were not particularly operative in the service, returned
to their home. My staff and myself left the army at the
burnt village, on Rock River, above Lake Koshkonong, and
returned by Galena to the frontiers and home. When I
reached Galena, the Indian panic was still raging with the
people there, and I was compelled to order out more troops
to protect the citizens — although the militia of the whole
country was in service." — Reynolds, pp. 251, 252.

sent down the Rock to Dixon's, with an officer
accidentally wounded; while, with the rest of
his troops, Posey was ordered to Fort Hamilton to guard the mining country, which
Dodge's absence had left exposed to the
enemy.   Atkinson himself fell back to Lake
Koshkonong, and built a fort a few miles up
Bark River, on the eastern limit of the present
village of Fort Atkinson.

On arrival at Fort Winnebago, the troopers
found there a number of Winnebago Indians,
all of them free with advice to the white chiefs.
There was also at the fort a famous half-breed
scout and trader named Pierre Paquette, who
had long been a trusted servant of the American Fur Company.   He informed Henry and
Dodge of the location of Black Hawk's stronghold, confirming White Crow's story, but
with added information as to its character.
With twelve Winnebago companions, he was
promptly engaged as pilot thither.   While the
division was at the fort, there was, from some
unknown cause, a stampede of its horses, the
animals plunging madly for thirty miles
through the neighboring swamps, where upwards of fifty were lost.[1]

[1] Reynolds, pp. 254, 255; also *Wis. Hist. Colls.*, x., p.
314.

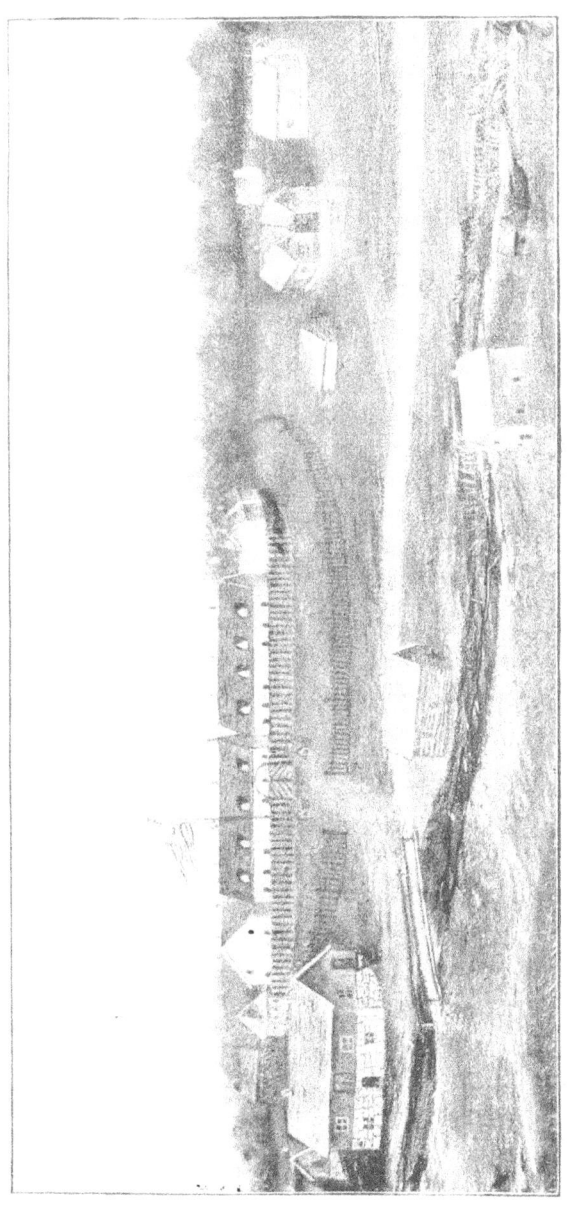

FORT WINNEBAGO IN 1834

From the painting by Ira A. Ridgeway, based on tradition and contemporary plans.

Henry and Dodge, resolute Indian fighters, decided to return to camp by way of the Hustisford rapids, and there engage Black Hawk if *Mutinous* possible. But Alexander's men re-*conduct* fused to enter upon this perilous expedition, and insisted on obeying Atkinson's orders to return to headquarters by the shortest available route. Alexander easily yielded to his troopers' demands, and this mutinous example would have corrupted Henry's brigade but for the firmness of that commander, who was a strict disciplinarian. Alexander returned direct to camp (July 15), with the men whose horses had been lost in the stampede, and twelve days' provisions for the main army. The same day, Henry and Dodge, the former in command, started out with twelve days' supplies for their own force, accompanied by Paquette and the Winnebago guides. The ranks had been depleted from many causes, so that roll-call on the sixteenth disclosed but six hundred effective men in Henry's brigade, and about a hundred and fifty in Dodge's squadron.

On the eighteenth, the troopers reached Rock River and found the Winnebago village at which Black Hawk and his band had been quartered, but the enemy had fled. The Winnebagoes insisted that their late visitors were now at Cranberry Lake,[1] a half day's march up the River, and the white commanders resolved to proceed thither the following day. They had arrived at the village at noon, and at two in the afternoon Adjutants Merriam of Henry's, and Woodbridge of Dodge's, bearing information of the supposed discovery, started south to Atkinson's camp, thirty-five miles down the river. Little Thunder, a Winnebago chief, accompanied them as guide. When nearly twenty miles out, and halfway between *A hot* the present sites of Watertown and *trail* Jefferson, the messengers suddenly struck a broad, fresh trail trending to the west. Little Thunder became greatly excited, and shouted and gestured vehemently, but the adjutants were unable to understand a word of the Winnebago tongue. When the chief suddenly turned his pony and dashed back to Henry's camp, they were obliged to hasten after him, as further progress through the tangled thickets and wide morasses without a pilot was inadvisable. Little Thunder had, it seemed, returned to inform his people that the trail of Black Hawk in his flight to the Missis-

[1] Afterwards Horicon Lake, in Dodge County — now drained.

sippi had been discovered, and to warn them that further dissembling was useless.[1]

In the camp of the volunteers, this news was received with great joy. Their sinking spirits at once revived, and the following morning pursuit on the fresh scent was undertaken with an enthusiasm that henceforth had no occasion *The* to lag. All possible encumbrances *pursuit* were left behind, so that progress should be unimpeded. The course lay slightly to the north of west, through the present towns of Lake Mills and Cottage Grove. The Chicago & Northwestern Railway between Jefferson Junction and Madison follows quite closely Black Hawk's trail from the Rock River to the Four Lakes. Deep swamps and sink-holes were met by the army, nearly the entire distance. The men had frequently to dismount and wade in water and mud to their armpits, while the first night out a violent thunderstorm with phenomenal rainfall, followed by an unseasonable drop in the temperature, increased the natural difficulties of the march. But the fickle Winnebago stragglers, who in this time of want and peril were deserting the band of Sauk fugitives, and fawning upon their white pursuers, reported the Hawk but two

[1] *Wis. Hist. Colls.*, ii., p. 407.

miles in advance, and the volunteers eagerly
hurried on with empty stomachs and wet clothes.
By sunset of the second day (July 20) they
reached the lakes, going into camp for the
night a quarter of a mile north of the northeast extremity of Lake Monona (Third Lake).[1]
That same night, Black Hawk was strongly

[1] Wakefield, who was with the army, gives this interesting
picture (p. 66) of the now famous Four-lake country, as it
appeared to him, July 20, 1832 : " Here it may not be unin-
teresting to the reader to give a small outline of those lakes.
From a description of the country, a person would very naturally suppose that those lakes were as little pleasing to the
eye of the traveller as the country is. But not so. I think
they are the most beautiful bodies of water I ever saw. The
first one that we came to [Monona] was about ten miles in
circumference, and the water as clear as chrystal. The earth
sloped back in a gradual rise ; the bottom of the lake appeared to be entirely covered with white pebbles, and no
appearance of its being the least bit swampy. The second
one that we came to [Mendota] appeared to be much larger.
It must have been twenty miles in circumference. The
ground rose very high all around ; — and the heaviest kind of
timber grew close to the water's edge. If those lakes were
anywhere else, except in the country they are, they would
be considered among the wonders of the world. But the
country they are situated in is not fit for any civilized nation
of people to inhabit. It appears that the Almighty intended
it for the children of the forest. The other two lakes
[Kegonsa (First) and Waubesa (Second)] we did not get
close enough for me to give a complete description of them ;
but those who saw them, stated that they were very much
like the others."

ambushed, seven or eight miles beyond, near the present village of Pheasant Branch, at the western extremity of Lake Mendota.

At daybreak of the twenty-first, the troops were awakened, and, after fording Catfish River where the Williamson Street bridge now crosses *At Madison* it, swept in regular line of battle across the isthmus between Monona and Mendota lakes, Ewing's spies to the front. Where to-day is built the park-like city of Madison, the capital of Wisconsin, was then a heavy forest with frequent dense thickets of underbrush. The line of march was along the shore of Monona to about the present site of the Fauerbach brewery, thence almost due west to Mendota, the hilly shores of which were closely skirted through the present campus of the University of Wisconsin, across intervening swamps and hills to Pheasant Branch, and thence due northwest to Wisconsin River, which here sweeps in majestic curves between corrugated, grass-grown bluffs, some two or three hundred feet in height. The advance was so rapid that, during the day, forty horses succumbed between the Catfish and the Wisconsin. When his animal gave out, the trooper would trudge on afoot, throwing away his camp-kettle and other encumbrances, thus following the example of the fugitives, whose trail was strewn with Indian mats, kettles, and miscellaneous equipage discarded in the hurry of flight. Some half-dozen inoffensive Sauk stragglers, chiefly old men who had become exhausted by the famine now prevailing in the Hawk's camp,[1] were at intervals shot and scalped by the whites — two of them within the present limits of Madison.

It was three o'clock in the afternoon before the enemy's rear guard of twenty braves under Neapope was overtaken. Several running skirmishes ensued. The timber was still thick, and it was impossible at first to know whether or not Neapope's party were the main body of the fugitives. The weakness of the tribesmen after a time became apparent, and thereafter when they made a feint the spies would charge and easily disperse them.

At about half-past four o'clock, when within

[1] "During our encampment at Four Lakes, we were hard put, to obtain enough to eat to support nature. Stuck in a swampy, marshy country (which had been selected in consequence of the great difficulty required to gain access thereto), there was but little game of any sort to be found — and fish were equally scarce. . . . We were forced to dig roots and bark trees, to obtain something to satisfy our hunger and keep us alive. Several of our old people became so much reduced, as actually to die with hunger." — *Autobiography,* p. 130.

a mile and a half of the river, and some twenty-five miles northwest of the site of Madison, *Battle of Wisconsin Heights* Neapope's band, reinforced by a score of braves under Black Hawk, made a bold stand to cover the flight of the main body of his people down the bluffs and across the broad island-studded stream. Every fourth man of the white column was detailed to hold the horses, while the rest of the troopers advanced on foot. The savages, yelling like madmen, made a heavy charge, and endeavored to flank the whites, but Colonel Frye on the right and Colonel Jones on the left repulsed them with loss. The Sauks now dropped into the grass, here nearly six feet high; but after a half-hour of hot firing on both sides, with a few casualties evenly distributed, Dodge, Ewing, and Jones charged the enemy with the bayonet, driving them up a rising piece of ground at the top of which a second rank was found, skilfully covering the retreat. After further firing, the Indians swiftly descended through the rank herbage of the bluffs to join their main body, now engaged in crossing the river. It had been raining softly during the greater part of the battle, and difficulty was experienced in keeping the muskets dry; nevertheless a sharp fire was kept up between the lines until dusk. At the base of the bluffs there was swampy ground some sixty yards in width, thick strewn with willows, and then a heavy fringe of timber on a strip of firm ground along the river-bank. As the Indians could reach this vantage-point before being overtaken, it was deemed best to abandon the pursuit for the night.

Black Hawk, skilful in military operations, personally conducted the battle, on the part of the Sauks, and from a neighboring knoll, where he was seated on a white pony, directed and encouraged his men with clear, loud voice.[1]

After dusk had set in, a considerable party of the fugitives, composed mainly of women, children, and old men, were placed on a large raft and in canoes begged from the Winnebagoes, and sent down the river in the hope that the soldiers at Fort Crawford, guarding the mouth of the Wisconsin, would allow these non-combatants to cross the Mississippi in peace. But too much reliance was placed on the humanity of the Americans. Lieutenant

[1] Black Hawk says that he lost six warriors in this engagement at Wisconsin Heights (opposite Prairie du Sac). Mrs. Kinzie's *Wau Bun* (New York, 1856) says, it was reported at Fort Winnebago that fifty Sauks were killed. Wakefield puts the number at sixty-eight killed outright, and twenty-five mortally wounded.

Joseph Ritner, with a small detachment of regulars, was sent out by Indian Agent Joseph M. Street[1] to intercept these forlorn, half-starved wretches, a messenger from the field of battle having apprised the agent of their approach. A short distance above Fort Crawford, Ritner fired on them, killing fifteen men and capturing thirty-two women and children, and four men. Nearly as many more were drowned during the onslaught; while of the rest, who escaped to the wooded shores, all but a half-score perished with hunger or were massacred by a belated party of three hundred Menominee allies from the Green Bay district, under Colonel Stambaugh and a small staff of white officers.[2]

During the night after the battle of Wisconsin Heights — as that affair has since been known in history — there were frequent alarms from prowling Indians, and the men, fearing an attack, were nearly always under arms. About an hour and a half before dawn of the twenty-second, a loud, shrill voice, speaking in an unknown tongue, was heard from the direction of the

An unsuccessful appeal

[1] Stationed at Prairie du Chien.

[2] See "Boyd Papers," *Wis. Hist. Colls.*, xii., for the documentary history of Stambaugh's expedition.

eminence known to have been occupied by
Black Hawk during the previous afternoon.
There was at once a panic in the camp, for it
was thought that the savage leader was giving
orders for an attack, and Henry thought it desirable to bolster the courage of his men by
making them a patriotic speech, during which
the interrupted harangue of the savage ceased.

It was afterwards learned that the orator
was Neapope, who had spoken in the Winnebago tongue, under the presumption that
Paquette and the Winnebago pilots were still
in camp.   But during the night they had left
for Fort Winnebago, and it chanced that no
one among the troops had understood a word
of the speech — an offer of conciliation, addressed to the victors.   Neapope had said that
with the Sauks were their squaws, children, and
old people ; they had unwillingly been forced
into war, they were literally starving, and if
allowed to cross the Mississippi in peace would
nevermore do harm.   But the plea fell on un-
witting ears, and thus failed the second earnest
attempt of the British Band to close the war.
As for Neapope, finding that his mission had
failed, — apparently through the hardness of
the American heart, — he fled to the Winnebagoes, leaving his half-dozen companions to

return with the discouraging news to Black Hawk, now secretly encamped with the remnant of his band in a neighboring ravine north of the Wisconsin.[1]

The twenty-second of July was spent by the white army on the battlefield, making preparations to march to the rude local fort at Blue Mounds for supplies. It was now known that during the night the enemy had escaped across or down the river; and the troops were insufficiently provisioned for a long chase through the unknown country beyond Wisconsin River.

On the twenty-third, Henry marched with his corps to Blue Mounds, and late that even-
Preparing for the pursuit ing was joined by Atkinson and Alexander, who, on being informed by express of the discovery of the trail and the rapid chase, had left the fort on the Koshkonong and hastened on to the Mounds to join the victors. Atkinson assumed command, distributed rations to the men, and ordered that the pursuit be resumed.

On the twenty-seventh and twenty-eighth, the Wisconsin was crossed on rafts at Helena,

---

[1] *Autobiography*, pp. 131–133. Black Hawk does not mention this incident of Neapope's night harangue. Reynolds reports it, p. 262; so also Ford, p. 146, and Wakefield, p. 86.

then a deserted log village, whose cabins had
furnished material for the floats.[1] Posey here
joined the army with his brigade, and thus all
of the generals were now reunited. The march
was commenced at noon of the twenty-eighth,
the four hundred and fifty regulars, now under
General Brady, — with Colonel Taylor still of
the party, — in advance ; while Dodge, Posey,
and Alexander followed in the order named,
Henry bringing up the rear in charge of the
baggage. It appears that much jealousy had
been displayed by Atkinson, at the fact that
the laurels of the campaign, such as they were,
had thus far been won by the volunteers.
Henry, as chief of the victors at Wisconsin
Heights, was especially unpopular at headquarters. But the brigadier and his men
trudged peacefully on behind, judiciously
pocketing what they felt to be an affront.[2]

[1] See *Wis. Hist. Colls.*, xi., p 403 ; and Libby's " Chronicle
of the Helena Shot Tower," *ibid.*, xiii., pp 335–374. The
town, built for the accommodation of the employees of a
shot-making company, had been deserted at the outbreak of
the war, most of the men being now members of Dodge's
rangers.

[2] Ford, pp. 146–155, publishes some interesting correspondence, showing that Dodge was disposed to claim more
than his share of the honors of this and some other engagements in the war, and to ignore Henry as his superior officer.
Those men under Dodge, who have written about the cam-

After marching four or five miles northeastward, the trail of the fugitives was discovered
A forbid- trending to the north of west, towards
ding path the Mississippi. The country between
the Wisconsin and the great river is rugged
and forbidding in character; it was then unknown to whites, and almost equally unfamiliar
to the Winnebago guides. The impediments
were many and serious, swamps and turbulent
rivers being freely interspersed between steep,
thickly wooded hills. However, the fact that
they were noticeably gaining on the enemy
constantly spurred the troopers to great endeavors. The pathway was strewn with the
bodies of dead Sauks, who had died of wounds
and starvation, and there were frequent evidences that to sustain life the fleeing wretches
were eating the bark of trees and the sparse
flesh of their fagged-out ponies.[1]

paign, extol the superior merits of their chief; but in Illinois
pioneer reminiscences, Henry is invariably the hero of the
occasion.

[1] "I started over a rugged country, to go to the Mississippi, intending to cross it, and return to my nation.
Many of our people were compelled to go on foot, for want
of horses, which, in consequence of their having had nothing
to eat for a long time, caused our march to be very slow. At
length we reached the Mississippi, having lost some of our
old men and little children, who perished on the way with
hunger." — *Autobiography*, p. 133.

On Wednesday, the first of August, Black Hawk and his now sadly depleted and almost

The   famished band reached the Missis-
Mississippi, sippi at a point two miles below the
at last   mouth of the Bad Axe, a small east-
ern tributary, and about forty north of the Wisconsin. In these upper reaches the broad river is diverted into several channels by long, narrow islands heavily wooded by swamp oaks and willows, and thick strewn with giant wind-rows of drift, lodged by spring freshets. Here Black Hawk undertook to cross; there were, however, but two or three canoes to be had, and the work was slow. One large raft, laden with women and children, was despatched to thread its way under cover of the islands along the east side of the river, towards Prairie du Chien; but on the way it capsized, probably impelled upon one of the sprawling snags which ofttimes rendered early river navigation a perilous undertaking, and nearly all of its occupants were drowned.

In the middle of the afternoon, the steamer " Warrior," of Prairie du Chien, used to trans-port army supplies, appeared on the scene with John Throckmorton as captain.[1]   On

[1] See Fonda's report of the " Warrior's " part in the battle, *Wis. Hist. Colls.,* v., pp. 261–264.

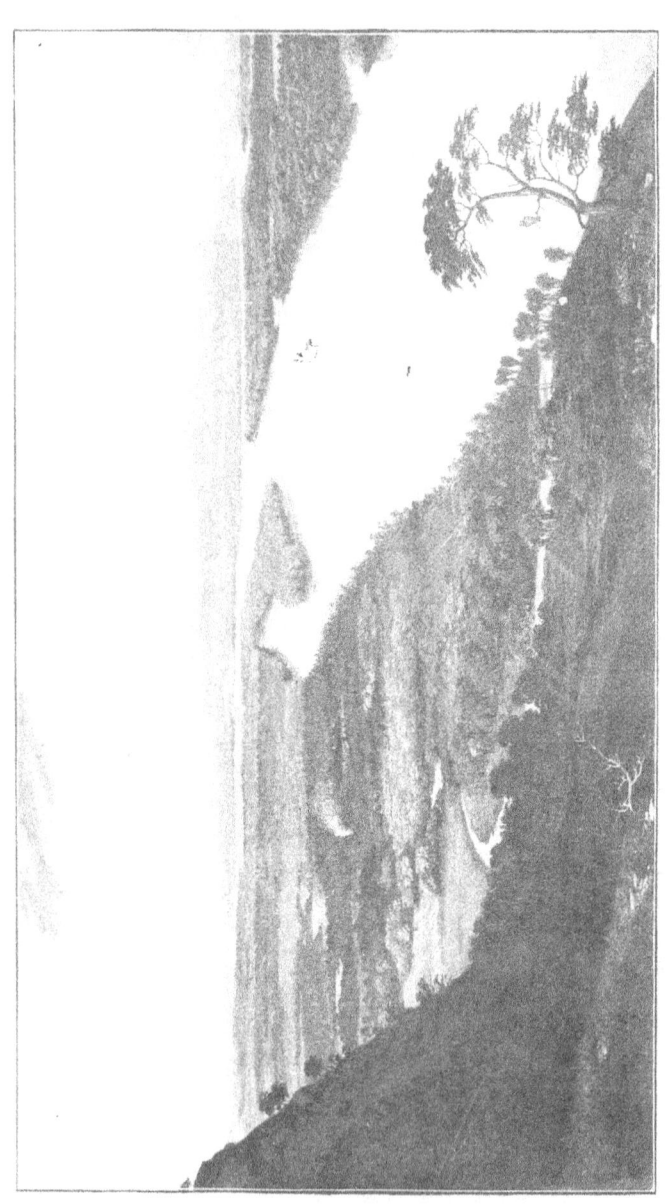

SCENE OF BATTLE OF THE BAD AXE

From the painting by Samuel M. Brookes, in possession of the Wisconsin Historical Society

board were Lieutenants Gaines P. Kingsbury and Reuben Holmes, with fifteen regulars and six volunteers. The party had been up the river to notify the friendly Sioux chief Wabasha, — whose village was on the site of Winona, Minnesota, — that the Sauks were headed in that direction. As the steamer *The Battle of the Bad Axe* neared the shore, Black Hawk appeared on the bank with a white flag, and in the Winnebago tongue called to the captain to send a boat ashore, as the fugitives wished to give themselves up. A Winnebago stationed in the bow interpreted the request, but the captain affected to believe that an ambush was intended, and ordered the Hawk to come aboard in his own craft. This the Sauk could not do, for the only canoes at his command were engaged in transporting his women and children across the river, and were not now within hail. His reply to this effect was quickly met by three successive rounds of canister-shot, which ploughed with deadly effect through the little group of Indians on shore. There followed a fierce fire of musketry on both sides, in which twenty-three Indians were killed, while the whites suffered the loss of but one wounded. The "Warrior," now being short of fuel, towards night returned to Prairie du Chien to " wood up," the soldiers much elated at their share in the campaign.

During the night a few more savages crossed the river into Minnesota; but Black Hawk, foreseeing that disaster was about to befall his people, gathered a party of ten warriors, among whom was the Prophet, and these, with about thirty-five squaws and children, headed east for a rocky hiding place at the Dalles of the Wisconsin, whither some Winnebagoes offered to guide them.[1]   The next day the heart of the old man smote him for having left his people to their fate, and he returned in time to witness from a neighboring bluff the con- clusion of the Battle of the Bad Axe, that struck the death-blow to the British Band. With a howl of rage, he turned back into the forest and fled.

The aged warrior had left excellent instruc- tions to his braves, in the event of the arrival of the white army by land. Twenty picked Sauks were ordered to stand rear guard on one of the high, ravine-washed bluffs which here line the east bank of the Mississippi; and when engaged, to fall back three miles up the river, thus to deceive the whites as to the

[1] Wakefield, pp. 97, 98.

location of the main band, and gain time for the flight of the latter across the stream, which was progressing slowly with but two canoes now left for the purpose.

Atkinson's men were on the move by two o'clock in the morning of the second. When within four or five miles of the Sauk position, the decoys were encountered. The density of the bottom timber obstructing the view, and the twenty braves being widely separated, it was supposed that the main force of the enemy had been overtaken. The army accordingly spread itself for the attack, Alexander and Posey forming the right wing, Henry the left, and Dodge and the regulars the centre. When, as directed by their chief, the braves retreated up the river, the white centre and right wing followed quickly, leaving the left wing — with the exception of one of its regiments detailed to cover the rear — without orders. This was clearly an additional affront to Henry, Atkinson's design being doubtless to crowd him out of what all anticipated would be the closing engagement of the campaign, and what little glory might come of it.

But the fates did not desert the brigadier. Some of Ewing's spies, attached to his command, accidentally discovered that the main

trail of the fugitive band was lower down the
river-bank than whither the decoys were leading the army. Henry, with his entire force,
thereupon descended a bluff in the immediate
neighborhood, and after a dash on foot through
the open wooded plateau between the base of
the bluff and the shore, found himself in the
midst of the main body of three hundred warriors, which was about the number of the attacking party. A desperate conflict ensued,
the bucks being driven from tree to tree at the
point of the bayonet, while women and children plunged madly into the river, many of
them being immediately drowned. The air
quivered with savage yells and whoops, with
the hoarse cry of the troopers as they cheered
one another on, and with the shrill notes of the
bugle directing the details of the attack.

A full half-hour after Henry had made his
descent upon the Sauk centre, Atkinson, hear-
ing the din of battle in his rear, came hasten-
ing to the scene with the centre and right wing,
driving in the decoys and stragglers before
him, thus completing the corral. The carnage
now proceeded more fiercely than ever. The
red men fought with intense desperation, and,
though weak from hunger, died like braves.
A few escaped through a broad slough to a

willow island, which the steamer "Warrior," now reappearing on the river, raked from end to end with canister. This was followed by a wild charge through mud and water by a detachment of regulars, with a few of Henry's and Dodge's volunteers, who ended the affair by sweeping the island with a bayonet charge. Some of the fugitives succeeded in swimming to the west bank of the Mississippi, but many were drowned on the way, or coolly picked off by sharpshooters, who exercised no more mercy towards squaws and children than towards braves — treating them all as though rats rather than human beings.[1]

The Battle of the Bad Axe — massacre would be a better term — lasted for three long, horrible hours. Few if any contests between red men and white men have been less creditable to our race. In the course of the carnage,

---

[1] "Although the warriors fought with the courage and valor of desperation, yet the conflict resembled more a carnage than a regular battle." — Reynolds, p. 265.

"Our braves, but few in number, finding that the enemy paid no regard to age or sex, and seeing that they were murdering helpless women and little children, determined to fight until they were killed." — *Autobiography*, p. 135.

Wakefield says, p. 85, "It was a horrid sight to witness little children, wounded and suffering the most excruciating pain. . . . It was enough to make the heart of the most hardened being on earth to ache."

a hundred and fifty Indians were slaughtered
outright, while as many more of both sexes
and all ages and conditions were drowned —
some fifty only being taken prisoners, and
they mostly women and children. About
three hundred of the band successfully crossed
the river, before and during the struggle. The
whites lost but seventeen killed and twelve
wounded.[1]

Those few of the Sauks who safely regained
the west bank were soon set upon by a party

*A dis-
honorable
chapter*

of a hundred Sioux, under Wabasha,
sent out for that purpose by Atkinson; and a half of these helpless,
nearly starved non-combatants were cruelly
slaughtered, while many others died of exhaus-
tion and wounds before they reached those of
their friends who had been wise enough to
abide by Keokuk's peaceful admonitions and
stay at home. Thus, out of the band of nearly
a thousand persons who crossed the Mississippi at the Yellow Banks in April, not more,
all told, than a hundred and fifty, lived to tell
the tragic story of the Black Hawk War — a

---

[1] I follow Reynolds, p. 265. He says apologetically,
years after the event, " Some squaws were killed by mistake
in the battle. They were mixed with the warriors, and some
of them dressed like the males."

dishonorable chapter in the history of the border.

The rest can soon be told. On the seventh of August, when the victors had returned to Prairie du Chien, General Winfield *The cost* Scott arrived and assumed command, discharging the volunteers the following day. Cholera among his troops had detained him first at Detroit, then at Chicago, and lastly at Rock Island, nearly a fourth of his detachment of a thousand regulars having died of the pestilence. Independent of this, the American loss in the war, including volunteers and settlers killed in the irregular skirmishes and in massacres, was not over two hundred and fifty. The financial cost to the nation and to the State of Illinois aggregated nearly two millions of dollars.

On the twenty-seventh of August, Chætar and One-eyed Decorah, two Winnebago braves *Black* who were desirous of displaying their *Hawk a* newly-inspired loyalty to the Amer- *prisoner* icans, delivered Black Hawk and the Prophet into the hands of Agent Street, at Prairie du Chien. They had found the conspirators at the Dalles of Wisconsin River, above the site of Kilbourn City.[1]

---

[1] See McBride's "Capture of Black Hawk," in *Wis. Hist. Colls.*, v., pp. 293, 294; *id.*, viii., p. 316, *note;* Wakefield, pp.

On the twenty-first of September, a treaty
of peace was signed at Fort Armstrong; under
its terms, Black Hawk, the Prophet, and Neapope — who had been captured later — were,
with others, kept as hostages for the good behaviour of the small remnant of the British
Band and their Winnebago allies.[1]   They were
kept through the winter at Jefferson Barracks
(St. Louis),[2] and in April, 1823, taken to
Washington; thence being sent as prisoners
of war to Fortress Monroe, where they were
discharged on the fourth of June.   After visiting the principal cities of the East, in which
Black Hawk was much lionized, and came for
the first time to appreciate the power and re-

95–101.   There have been many traditions of the capture,
differing from the above, but there is no documentary evidence to substantiate them.   The account here followed is
based upon Street's official report.   Decorah received from
Atkinson, at Dixon, twenty horses as his reward for the
delivery.   The originals of much of Street's correspondence
as Indian Agent are in the Iowa and Wisconsin historical
archives.

[1] *Treaties*, p. 508.

[2] Lieutenant Jefferson Davis took charge of the transfer
of the prisoners from Fort Armstrong to Jefferson Barracks.
The Davis biography previously cited, says, " He entirely
won the heart of the savage chieftain, and before they
reached Jefferson Barracks there had sprung up between the
stern red warrior and the young pale face a warm friendship
which only terminated with the life of Black Hawk."

sources of the whites, the party returned to Fort Armstrong, where they arrived about the first of August. Here the pride of the Sauk leader was completely crushed, he being formally transferred by the military authorities to the guardianship of his hated rival, Keokuk. This ceremony the fallen Black Hawk regarded as an irreparable insult, which he nursed with much bitterness through the remainder of his days.

The broken-hearted warrior, with the weight of seventy-one years upon his whitened head, *Death of* passed away on the third of October, *the Hawk* 1838, at his home on a small reservation which had been set apart for him and his few remaining followers, on the Des Moines River, in Davis County, Iowa.[1]   In July of the following year, an Illinois physician rifled his grave. Complaint being made by Black Hawk's family, Governor Lucas of Iowa, in the spring of 1840, caused the skeleton to be delivered to him at Burlington, then the capital of that Territory. Later in the year the seat of government being moved to Iowa City, the box

[1] Cornelius Buckley writes, in the Beloit *Weekly Free Press*, October 15, 1891: "He was buried in the northeast corner of Davis County, on section 2, township 70, range 12, ninety rods from where he died, and near the present village of Eldon."

containing the remains was deposited in a law office in that town, where it remained until the night of January 16, 1853, when the building was destroyed by fire.[1]

Black Hawk was an indiscreet man. His troubles were, in the main, the result of lack *His character* of mental balance, aided largely by untoward circumstances. He was of a highly romantic temperament; his judgment was warped by sentiment; and tricksters easily played upon this weakness. But he was honest, — more honorable, often, than those who were his conquerors. He was, above all things, a patriot. In the year before his death, he made a speech to a party of whites who were making a holiday hero of him, and thus forcibly defended his motives: "Rock River was a beautiful country. I liked my town, my cornfields, and the home of my people. I fought for them." No poet could have penned for him a more touching epitaph.

Forbearance, honorable dealing, and the exercise of sound policy upon the part of the whites might easily have prevented the war,

---

[1] It had been designed to place the warrior's bones in the museum of the Iowa Historical and Geological Institute, but the fire occurred before the removal could take place. — Burlington (Iowa) *Gazette*, August 25, 1888.

with its pitiful expenditure of blood and treasure. Squatters had been allowed with impunity to violate the spirit of treaty obligations, in harassing the Sauks in their ancient village long before the government had sold the land ; for six thousand dollars — a beggarly price for securing peace with a formidable band of starving savages, grown desperate from ill usage — Black Hawk would, in 1831, have removed his people to the west of the Mississippi, without any show of force ;[1] at Sycamore Creek, an observance of one of the oldest and most universally-established rules of war would have procured a peaceful retreat of the discouraged invaders ; on the night of the Battle of Wisconsin Heights, reasonable prudence in keeping an interpreter in camp, in a hostile country, would have enabled Neapope's peaceful mission to succeed ; at the Bad Axe, as at Sycamore Creek, a decent regard for the accepted amenities of civilized warfare, on the part of the reckless soldiers on the steamer " Warrior," would have secured an abject surrender of the entire hostile band, which was, instead, ruthlessly butchered ; while the sending out of Sioux bloodhounds upon the trail of the few worn-out fugitives, in the very

---

[1] *Autobiography*, pp. 99, 100.

country beyond the great river to which the Sauks had been persistently ordered, capped the climax of a bloody and costly contest characterized on our part by gross mismanagement, bad faith, and sheer heartlessness.

It is generally stated in the published histories of those commonwealths that the defeat *What was* of Black Hawk opened to settlement *accom-* northern Illinois and the southern *plished* portion of what is now Wisconsin. Unqualified, this statement is misleading. Indirectly, it is true that the war proved a powerful agent in the development of that region. The British Band was in itself no obstacle to legitimate settlement, the frontiers of which were far removed from Black Hawk's village, and need not to have crowded it for several years to come. Although the natural outgrowth of the excitable condition of the border, the war was not essential as a means of clearing the path of civilization. What it did accomplish in the way of territorial development, was to call national attention, in a marked manner, to the attractions and resources of an important section of the Northwest. The troops acted as explorers of a large tract concerning which nothing had hitherto definitely been known among white men. The

Sauks themselves were, previous to their invasion, unacquainted with the Rock River valley above the mouth of the Kishwaukee, and had but vague notions of its swamps and lakes, gathered from their Winnebago guides, who alone were well informed on the subject. From Wisconsin Heights to the Bad Axe, every foot of the trackless way was as unknown to the Sauks and their pursuers as was the interior of Africa to Stanley, when he first groped his way across the Dark Continent. During and immediately following the war, the newspapers of the Eastern States were filled with descriptions, more or less florid, of the scenic charms of, and the possibilities for, extractive industries in, the Rock River valley, of the groves and prairies on every hand, of the park-like region of the Four Lakes, of the Wisconsin River highlands, and of the picturesque hills and dense forests of Western Wisconsin. From the press were issued books and pamphlets by the score, giving sketches of the war and accounts of the newly discovered paradise — for the most part crude publications abounding in gross errors, and to-day practically unknown save to bibliographers and collectors. But in their own way and season they advertised the country and set flowing thither a tide of immigration. There necessarily followed, in due time, the opening to sale of public lands heretofore reserved, and the purchase of what territory remained in the possession of the Indian tribes of the district. Quite as important, the decisive ending of this war with the Sauks completely humbled the spirit of the mischief-making Winnebagoes, so that they never resumed their old-time arrogant tone, and were quite content to allow the affair to remain the last of the Indian uprisings in either Illinois or Wisconsin.

This incidental subduing of the Winnebagoes, and the broad and liberal advertising given to the theatre of disturbance, were therefore the two practical and immediate results of the Black Hawk War, the consequence of which was at once to give an enormous impetus to the development of both the State of Illinois and the Territory of Wisconsin.[1]

---

[1] Wisconsin Territory was erected in 1836.

IV

THE STORY OF MACKINAC

THE STORY OF MACKINAC

MACKINAC has played a considerable part on the stage of Western history. Early recognized as a vantage-point, commanding the commerce of the three uppermost *A struggle* lakes of the great chain, — Huron, *for mastery* Michigan, and Superior, — red men and white men have struggled for its mastery, tribe against tribe, nation against nation. The fleur-de-lis, the union jack, and the stars and stripes, have here each in their turn been symbols of conqueror and conquered; councils have been held here, and treaties signed, which settled the political ownership of fertile regions as wide as all Europe; and when at last armed hostilities ceased through the final surrender to the Republic, when the tomahawk was buried and the war-post painted white, a new warfare opened at Mackinac — the commercial struggle of the great fur-trade companies, whose rival banners contested the sway of lands stretching from Athabasca to the Platte, from the Columbia to Georgian Bay. It is a far cry from the invasion of Chippewa Michillimackinac by the long-haired coureurs de bois of New France, to the invasion of Mackinac Island by modern armies of summer tourists from New York and New England. In attempting, within this narrow compass, to tell the story of Mackinac, it will be impracticable to take more than a bird's-eye view.

In the first place, let us understand that the term Mackinac, as used in our earliest *Three* history, is the title of the entire dis-*Mackinacs* trict hereabout, as well as that of a particular settlement.   There have been, in chronological succession, at least three distinct localities specifically styled Mackinac: (1) Between 1670 and 1672, Mackinac Island, near the centre of the strait, was the seat of a French Jesuit mission.   (2) From 1672 to 1706, the Mackinac of history was on the north side of the strait, upon Point St. Ignace, and wholly under the French régime.   (3) From 1712 to 1781 Mackinac was on the south side of the strait — until 1763, just west of the present Mackinaw City, and possibly between 1764 and 1781 at some point farther west along the coast of Lake Michigan; this south-side Mackinac

was at first French and then English, and the
site near Mackinaw City has come to be known
in history as "Old Mackinaw." Finally, the
Mackinac settlement was in 1781 once more
placed upon the island, and while at first under
English domination at last became American.
A remembrance of these facts will help to
dispel the fog which has often obscured our
historical view of Mackinac.

That indefatigable explorer of high seas and
pathless forests, Samuel de Champlain, planted
the first permanent French colony in
Champlain
hears of Canada on the rock of Quebec, in
Lake 1608 — only a twelvemonth later than
Superior
the establishment of Jamestown, and
full twelve years before the coming to Plymouth
of the Pilgrim Fathers. It was seven years before Champlain saw Lake Huron, his farthest
point west in the limitless domain which the
King of France had set him to govern. Twenty-
one years had passed — years of heroic strug-
gling to push back the walls of savagery which
hemmed him in; when one day there came
to Quebec, in the fleet of Indian canoes from
this far northwest, — which annually picked
its way over fifteen hundred miles of rugged
waterways beset with a multitude of terrors, —
a naked Algonkin, besmeared with grease and

colored clays, who laid at the feet of the great white chief a lump of copper mined on the shores of Lake Superior. A shadowy region this, as far removed from the ordinary haunts of the adventurous woodsmen of New France as were the headwaters of the Nile from the African explorers of a generation ago, and quite as dangerous of access.

It was five years later (1634) before Champlain could see his way to sending a proper *Jean* emissary into the Northwest. Finally *Nicolet* one was found in the person of young Jean Nicolet, whom Champlain had had trained in the forest for tasks like this. Conveyed by Indian oarsmen engaged by relays in the several tribes through which he passed, Nicolet pushed up the St. Lawrence, portaged around the rapids at Lachine, ascended the trough of the turbulent Ottawa with its hundred waterfalls, portaged over to Lake Nipissing, descended French Creek to Georgian Bay, and threading the gloomy archipelago of the Manitoulins, sat at last in a Chippewa council at Sault Ste. Marie. Doubtless he here heard of Lake Superior, not many miles away, but it does not appear that he saw its waters. Intent on finding a path which led to the China Sea, supposed not to be far beyond this point, he turned south again, and pushing on through the straits of Mackinac found and traversed Lake Michigan. He traded and made treaties with the astonished tribesmen of Wisconsin and Illinois, who in him saw their first white man, and thus brought the Northwest within the sphere of French influence.[1]

Seven years later the Jesuit missionaries, Jogues and Raymbault, following in the path *The earliest French* of Nicolet, said mass before two thousand breech-clouted savages at Sault Ste. Marie. Affairs moved slowly in the seventeenth century, upon these far-away borders of New France. Jogues and Raymbault had long been ashes before the Northwest again appeared on the pages of history; nearly a generation had passed before the daring forest traders and explorers, Radisson and Groseilliers, arrived upon the scene (1658–62), discovered the Upper Mississippi, discovered Lake Superior, and first

---

[1] Authorities on Nicolet are: Butterfield's *History of the Discovery of the Northwest by John Nicolet* (Cincinnati, 1881); Gosselin's *Les Normands au Canada — Jean Nicolet* (Evreux, 1893); Jouan's "Interprète voyageur au Canada, 1618–1642," in *La Revue Canadienne*, Février, 1886; Sulte's *Mélanges d'histoire et de littérature* (Ottawa, 1876); articles by Garneau, Ferland, Sulte, etc., in *Wis. Historical Collections;* and a bibliography by Butterfield in *ibid.*, xi., pp. 23, 25.

made known to the English the fur-trading capabilities of the Hudson Bay region. The Hudson's Bay Company was organized in London, with these renegade Frenchmen as their pilots, in 1670; the following year, at Sault Ste. Marie, where the Jesuits had a fairly prosperous mission, Saint-Lusson formally took possession of the great Northwest for the French king.[1] I suppose that Saint-Lusson, when he floated the banner of France at the gateway of Lake Superior, knew nothing of his English neighbors, the Hudson's Bay Company; unconsciously he made an important play for France on the American chess-board; but a century later England won the game.

Those who have read Parkman's *Jesuits*[2] will remember that the Hurons, whose habitat *Flight of* had long been upon the eastern shores *the Hurons* of Georgian Bay, retreated northward and westward before the advance of the all-conquering Iroquois. At first taking refuge with starving Algonkins on the Manitoulin Islands, and on the mainland hereabout, they

[1] See Saint-Lusson's procès-verbal (June 14, 1671), in *Wis. Hist. Colls.*, xi., pp. 26–29.

[2] The present article, however, is in this respect based upon Thwaites's *The Jesuit Relations and Allied Documents* (Cleveland, 1896–1902).

were soon driven forth by their merciless foe, and made their stand in the swamps and tangled woods of far-away Wisconsin. Many of them centred upon Chequamegon Bay, the island-locked estuary near the southwest corner of Lake Superior, the ancient home of the Chippewas. Here Radisson and Groseilliers visited and traded with them.[1] The Jesuit Ménard, who had accompanied these adventurers, — the first missionary to follow in the wake of Jogues and Raymbault, — had stopped at Keweenaw Bay to minister to the Ottawas, and later lost his life while trying to reach a village of Hurons, crouching, fear-stricken, in the forest fastnesses around the headwaters of the Black River.[2]

Then came, three years later (1665), Father At Chequa- Alloüez, to reopen at Chequamegon megon Bay Bay the Jesuit mission on our greatest inland sea. Alloüez being ordered, after

[1] Radisson's "Journal" first appeared in *Prince Soc. Pubs.*, xvi. (Boston, 1885). Portions were published with notes, in *Wis. Hist. Colls.*, xi. See the following monographs on this subject: Campbell's "Exploration of L. Superior," *Parkman Club Pubs.*, No. 2 (Milw., 1896), and Moore's "Discoveries of L. Superior," in *Mich. Polit. Sci. Ass. Pubs.*, ii., No. 5 (Ann Arbor, 1897).

[2] See Campbell's "Père Rêné Ménard," *Parkman Club Pubs.*, No. 11 (Milw., 1897).

four years of arduous and I fear unprofitable labor at Chequamegon, to found a mission at Green Bay, was succeeded (1669) by the youthful Marquette. But Marquette was not long at Chequamegon before his half-naked parishioners provoked to quarrel their powerful western neighbors, the Sioux, the result being (1671) that the Chequamegon bands, and Marquette with them, were driven like leaves before an autumn blast eastward along the southern shore of the great lake; the Ottawas taking up their homes in the Manitoulin Islands, the Hurons accompanying Marquette to the island of Mackinac, where, the previous year, the Jesuits had founded the mission of St. Ignace.

Mackinac Island was then noted throughout this region for its abundance of fish, in both *Hurons return to Mackinac* summer and winter; also because it stood in the path to and from the southwest. In former days the island and the neighboring mainland had been thickly populated by several tribes of Indians who had been driven westward by the Iroquois. Now that peace with the Iroquois had been established, with hopes of its being permanent, the tribesmen had again flocked to the straits, making the region highly desirable as a mission resi-

dence.   It was therefore to their old homes on
the island that the Hurons now returned with
Marquette.   Here the young priest ministered
to the miserable savages about him, and to the
handful of nomadic fur-trade employés who
in spring and autumn gathered at this isolated
frontier station of New France on their way
to and from the great wilderness beyond.

Soon after his arrival, apparently within a
year, the mission was moved to the mainland,
Removal to on the site of the present village of
St. Ignace St. Ignace.   There is abundant ground
for belief that the St. Ignace monument, which
is visited each summer by thousands of tourists,
represents the place where stood the " rude
and unshapely chapel, its sides of logs and its
roof of bark," in which Marquette thereafter
conducted the offices of the Church.   Under
what circumstances the removal took place,
we know not.   Quite likely the island, at first
resorted to because of its safety from attack
by foes, was found too small for the villages
and fields of the Indians who now centred here
in large numbers ; and moreover was found
difficult of approach in time of summer storm,
or when the ice was weak in spring and early
winter.   The long continuance of peace with
the Iroquois removed for the time all danger

from that quarter, and events proved that they had made their last attack upon the tribesmen of these far Western waters.

Louis Jolliet, a coureur de bois, was sent forth by the authorities at Quebec (1672) to explore *Jolliet and* the Mississippi River, about which so *Marquette* much had been heard, and by that route to reach, if may be, the Great Western Ocean — for the road to India, either through the continent or by way of the Northwest Passage, was still being sought in those days. He arrived in December at Point St. Ignace, bringing orders to Marquette to accompany him. The conversion of the Indians went hand in hand, in New France, with the extension of commerce; no trading-post was complete without its missionary, no exploring expedition without its ghostly counsellor. Marquette, a true soldier of the cross, obeyed his marching orders, and on the seventeenth of May following, handed his spiritual task over to Father Philippe Pearson, and went forth to help discover unknown lands and carry to their peoples the word of Christ. With Jolliet he entered the Upper Mississippi at Prairie du Chien, and proceeded far enough down the great river to establish the fact that it emptied into the Gulf of Mexico and not the Pacific Ocean.   It is possible that Radisson and Groseilliers were on the Mississippi thirteen years before them; but Radisson's Journal, written in England long after, was not published until our own time, and it is not at all likely that Jolliet and Marquette, or any one else of importance in New France, ever heard of this prior claim.   The merit of carefully planned, premeditated discovery certainly rests with Jolliet and his companion.

It so happened — the story of the swamping of Jolliet's home-returning canoe in the wild

Mar-
quette's
Journal

rapids of Lachine is a familiar one — that the detailed journals and maps of the chief were lost; whereas the simple story which Marquette wrote at the Green Bay mission and transmitted by Indian courier to his father superior at Quebec, reached its destination and was published to the world for the glory of the church.   Thus it was that the gentle, unassuming Marquette became unwittingly its only historian; fate willed that his name should be more commonly associated with the great discovery than that of his secular companion.   Four years later the weary bones of this missionary-explorer, who had died on his way thither from the savage camps of the Illinois, were laid to rest " in a little vault in the middle of the chapel" at St. Ignace. In September, 1877, when antiquarians could but ingeniously guess at the site of this early mission in the wilderness, the bones of Father Marquette were discovered in the rude grave wherein they had rested for two centuries, and to-day are visible relics for inspiration to deeds of holiness.[1]

Throughout the seventeenth century the outpost of Mackinac at Point St. Ignace — *A French outpost* Michillimackinac, in those easy-going days when there was more time in which to pronounce the name — remained the most important French military and trading station in the upper lakes, for it guarded the gateway between Huron, Michigan, and Superior; and every notable expedition to the Northwest waters had perforce to stop here. We must not think of this Mackinac of the

[1] A detailed account, in German, of the discovery (said to have been written by Father Edward Jacker, then the Catholic missionary at St. Ignace) appeared first in the St. Louis *Pastoral-Blatt;* an English translation was published in the Green Bay (Wis.) *Advocate,* August 29, 1878. The site of the old mission was discovered May 4, but the remains of Marquette were not exhumed until September 3. See controversial articles in the St. Louis *Sunday Messenger,* June 24, 1877, and in the Chicago *Times,* August 14 and 29, and September 13, 1879. For details of Marquette's career, see Thwaites's *Father Marquette* (New York, 1902).

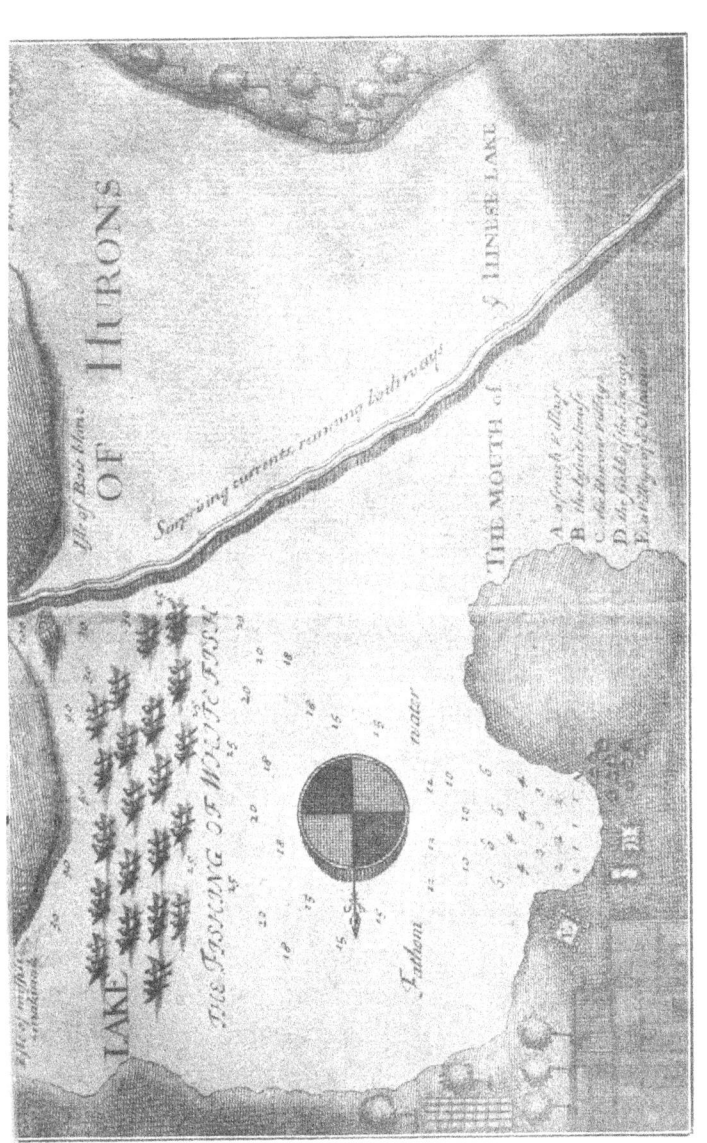

LAHONTAN'S MAP OF MACKINAC STRAIT

From Labontan's "Voyages" (Amsterdam, 1741)

seventeenth century, strategetically important though it was, as a settlement in any modern sense. The policy of the rulers of New France was to maintain the interior of the continent as a fur-bearing wilderness. Unlike Anglo-Saxons, they had no desire to plant settlements simply as settlements. They had not the colonizing spirit of Englishmen. To carry the fur-trade to the uttermost limits, to bring the savages to at least a nominal recognition of the cross, were their chief aims; to this end, palisaded trading-posts, which they rather grandiloquently called forts, were established throughout the country, the officers of which were rare diplomatists, and bullied and cajoled the red men as occasion demanded. Around each of these little forts, and Mackinac was one of them, were small groups of habitants, voyageurs, and coureurs de bois, who could hardly be called colonists, for few of them expected to lay their bones in the wilderness, but eventually to return to their own people on the Lower St. Lawrence, when enriched or their working days were over. It was rather an army of occupation than a body of settlers. The little log fort at Mackinac, calculated only to withstand a fusillade of savage arrows and musket-balls, was the principal feature of the

place, and the commandant the chief person-
age.   After him, the long-robed Jesuit, and
then the swarm of folk dependent on the spas-
modic fur-trade.

In the year of grace 1701, the little group
upon Point St. Ignace received word one day

Establish-   that a new post, called Detroit, had
ment of   been established away down in the
Detroit   unknown country at the narrow mouth
of Lake Huron, which was henceforth, under
one Cadillac, to be the centre of commerce in
these Western parts.   Heretofore, owing to the
Iroquois stoutly holding the lower lakes against
the French, progress to the far Northwest had
been altogether by way of the raging Ottawa.
But now, after seventy-five long years of
journeying by that toilsome route, it had from
various reasons become possible to come to
Mackinac through Lakes Ontario and Erie.
This new post, Detroit, was to command a still
wider range than that of Mackinac; the garrison was soon withdrawn thither; the fur-
traders, both white and Indian, for the most
part soon followed — it was easy for a population like this to pull up stakes and hie away
at beat of drum.   Nearly everybody went to
the new Mecca, save the Jesuit missionaries,
who were not wanted by this new man Cadillac,

a hater of the " black robes." For five years
the good fathers — there were then three
of them — maintained their little chapel and
school here on Point St. Ignace; but they
ministered to an ever-decreasing, disorderly
flock, and at last, burning their crude build-
ings, with a few white followers retired dis-
comfited to Quebec.

For six years there does not appear to have
been any French establishment hereabout. But
" Old in 1712 Governor-General Vaudreuil
Mackinaw" sent De Louvigny, a noted frontier
captain, to restore the abandoned post on the
upper waters. This he did, but upon the south
shore of the strait, not far west of the present
Mackinaw City; and over there on the mainland, at what came in time to be known as
" Old Mackinaw,"[1] — although it was, as we

[1] Note the orthographic change. The historic name is
Mackinac, an abbreviation of Michillimackinac, and such is
to-day the legal designation of Fort Mackinac, Strait of
Mackinac, and Mackinac Island; but the pronunciation
is Mack'inaw. The spelling has been made phonetic in the
cases of Old Mackinaw and Mackinaw City, to distinguish
them from the island, and many writers prefer to use the
phonetic form whenever mentioning any of the several
Mackinacs. A cultured native of Mackinac Island has told
me that, so far as he knew, but one person pronounced it
Macki*nack*; and he was Samuel Abbott, of the American
Fur Company, who in his day was regarded as an eccentric.

have seen, not the oldest Mackinac, — occurred such historic events as are spread upon the records to the credit of this name between 1712 and 1763. It was on the log ramparts of Old Mackinaw that, in token of the fall of New France, the fleur-de-lis was at last hauled down on September 28, 1761, and the union jack proudly lifted to the breeze. Here, upon the fourth of June, 1763, occurred that cruel massacre of the English garrison, which Parkman has so vividly described for us in his *Conspiracy of Pontiac.*

A year or more later the English rebuilt their fort, but whether or not upon the site of the *The* massacre is a moot question. There *English* appears to be good reason for the belief that it was among the sand-dunes farther west along the coast ; for in the official correspondence of the next fifteen years there is much complaint upon the part of commandants that their " rickety picket is commanded by sand hills " — a condition which does not exist at the old site near Mackinaw City.

To this rickety picket there came one October day, in the year 1779, Patrick Sinclair, lieutenant-governor of Michillimackinac and its dependencies, charged with the rebuilding and enlarging of his Majesty's post in these

parts. The Revolutionary War was in progress.
George Rogers Clark had captured Kaskaskia
and Vincennes; his emissaries were treating
with Indian chiefs away off in Wisconsin; there
were rumours of Clark's intended foray on
Detroit; and some suspicions that the "Bos-
tonnais," as the French Canadians called these
leather-shirted Virginians, had designs of putting a war vessel upon Lake Michigan. Sinclair saw at once that the old site was untenable
and the fort beyond repair.

In advance of orders he made a bold step.
Seven miles away to the northeast of Old
The island Mackinaw, in the midst of the strait,
reoccupied lay the comely island whereon had
first been established, a hundred and nine years
before, the Jesuit mission of St. Ignace — "La
Grosse Isle," the Canadians called it, although
smaller than its neighbor, Bois Blanc. The
Indians deemed it a sort of shrine, where at
times they gathered at their medicine feasts,
and to which, as to a sanctuary, they fled in
periods of extreme danger. Frenchmen were
more considerate of the superstitions of the
dusky tribesmen than were the intolerant
English. This now untenanted island Sinclair
appropriated to the king's use, although some
eighteen months later he formally bought it

from the Indians for £5000, New York currency. A month after his arrival the lieutenant-
governor began to erect a durable fort on the
island, and thither, upon receiving tardy permission from his superiors, he finally removed
in the spring of 1781, with him going the now
revived Catholic mission and the entire fur-trade
colony from the south shore. The new fort
still bore the name of Fort Mackinac, and La
Grosse Isle of the French henceforth was
known in the English reports as Mackinac
Island.

By the treaty of Paris (1783), Mackinac
came within the boundary of the United States;
Arrival of but the English still held the whip-
Americans hand in these parts, and upon sundry
pretexts continued to hold this and other lake
posts until the Jay treaty set matters right.
In October, 1796, American troops first took
possession of the post, and this gateway to the
upper lakes was at last ours. The English,
however, were still hopeful that they would
some day win this part of the country back
again, and their garrison retired to Isle St.
Josephs, only some forty miles to the northeast, where in 1795 they had built a fort.

The French and half-breeds did not at first
relish Yankee interference in their beloved

Northwest. They had maintained harmonious relations with the English, who fostered the fur-trade and employed the French with liberality. Then, too, among the Creoles the reputation of these Americans was not of the best. They were known to be a busy, bustling, driving people, quite out of tune with the easy-going methods of the French, and were, moreover, an agricultural race that was fast narrowing the limits of the hunting-grounds. The Frenchmen felt that their interests in this respect were identical with those of the savages, hence we find in the correspondence of the time a bitter tone adopted towards the new-comers, who were regarded as intruders and covetous disturbers of existing commercial and social relations.

When war broke out between England and the United States, in 1812, naturally the Creoles *English* of the Northwest were against us, and *capture the* freely entered the service of their old *island* and well-tried friends, the English. Fort Mackinac was then garrisoned by " 57 effective men, including officers." There had been no news sent here of the declaration of war, although the American lieutenant in charge, Porter Hanks, was expecting it. July 17, 1812, a British force of a thousand whites and Indians from Fort St. Josephs secretly effected a landing at the cove on the north-west shore of the island, — known to-day as " British Landing," — took possession of the heights overlooking the fort, and then coolly informed the commandant that hostilities had been declared between the two nations, and a surrender would be in order. The Americans were clearly at the mercy of the enemy, and promptly capitulated.

The old fort had from the first been in poor condition. The English, once more in posses-sion, built a new and stronger fort upon the higher land to the rear, which they had occu-pied, and named it Fort George, in honor of their sovereign. This stronghold was stormed on the fourth of August, 1814, by United States troops under Colonel George Croghan, who also disembarked at British Landing. The English position, however, was too strong for the assailants, who lost heavily under the galling fire of the French and Indian allies, and Croghan was obliged to retire. Among his dead was Major Holmes, a soldier of con-siderable reputation.

The treaty of Ghent resulted in the forti-fication being restored to the United States, the transfer being actually made on July 18,

1815. Colonel McDouall, the British commander at Mackinac, was loath to leave. His
Americans despatches to headquarters plainly
regain their indicate that he thought his govern-
footing ment weak in surrendering to the
Americans, for whom he had a decided con-
tempt, this Malta of the Northwest. When at
last obliged to depart, he went no farther than
necessary — indeed not quite so far, for he
built a fort upon Drummond Island, at the
mouth of River St. Mary, territory soon thereafter found to belong to the United States. It
was not until thirteen years later (1828) that
the English forces were finally and reluctantly
withdrawn from Drummond Island,[1] and English agents upon our northern frontier ceased
craftily to stir our uneasy Indian wards to
bickerings and strife.

When the United States resumed possession
of Mackinac Island the name of the fort built
by the English on the highest ground was
changed from Fort George to Fort Holmes, in
honor of the victim of the assault of the year
before; but later this position was abandoned,
and old Fort Mackinac, built by Sinclair and

[1] In his *Drummond Island* (Lansing, Mich., 1896), Samuel
F. Cook has given the history of the British occupation
thereof, with numerous illustrations of the ruins and sur-
roundings of the old fort.

capitulated by Hanks, was rehabilitated, and remains to this day as the military stronghold of the district.

The name of Mackinac will always be intimately associated with the story of the fur-trade. We have seen that the first settlement *Centre of the* upon the shores of these straits had *fur-trade* its inception in the primitive commerce of the woods; and chiefly as a protection to this trade the several forts were maintained under changing flags unto our own day. In 1783 the North West Fur Company opened headquarters here; later, the Mackinac Company and the South West Fur Company were formidable competitors; in 1815, with the re-establishment of the American arms, came the American Fur Company, of which John Jacob Astor was the controlling spirit.

We cannot fully understand the course of history in this region unless we remember that despite the treaty of Ghent (1783), Jay's treaty (1794), Wayne's Indian treaty at Greenville (1795), and the occupation of Fort Mackinac by United States troops between 1796 and 1812, the fur-trade upon the upper lakes and beyond was not really under American control until after the War of 1812–15; indeed, the territory itself was not until that time within the sphere of American influence, beyond the visible limits of the armed camps at Mackinac and Green Bay. After the Jay treaty, British traders, with French and half-breed clerks and voyageurs, were still permitted free intercourse with the savages of our Northwest, and held substantial domination over them. The Mackinac, North West, and South West companies were composed of British subjects — Scotchmen mainly — with headquarters at Montreal, and distributing points at Detroit, Mackinac, Sault Ste. Marie, and Grand Portage. Their clerks and voyageurs were wide travellers, and carried the forest trade throughout the Far West, from Great Slave Lake on the north to the valleys of the Platte and the Arkansas on south, and to the parks and basins of the Rocky Mountains. Goods were sent up the lakes from Montreal, either by relays of sailing vessels, with portages of men and merchandise at the Falls of Niagara and the Sault Ste. Marie, or by picturesque fleets of bateaux and canoes up the Ottawa River and down French Creek into Georgian Bay, from there scattering to the companies' various entrepôts of the South, West, and North.[1]

[1] See Turner's " Fur Trade in Wisconsin," *Wis. Hist. Soc. Proc.*, 1889.

The Creole boatmen were a reckless set.
They took life easily, but bore ill the mildest
The restraints of the trading settlements;
Creoles their home was on the lakes and rivers
and in Indian camps, where they joyously par-
took of the most humble fare, and on occasion
were not averse to suffering extraordinary
hardships in the service of their bourgeois.
Their pay was light, but their thoughts were
lighter, and the vaulted forest rang with the gay
laughter of these heedless adventurers; while
the pent-up valleys of our bluff-girted streams
echoed the refrains of their rudely melodious
boating songs, which served the double purpose
of whiling the hours away and measuring progress along the glistening waterways.

In Irving's *Astoria* is a charming description
of fur-trading life at the Grand Portage of
Lake Superior, over which boats and cargoes
were carried from the eastward-flowing Pigeon
to the tortuous waters which glide through
a hundred sylvan lakes and over a hundred
dashing rapids into the wide-reaching system
of Lake Winnipeg and the Assiniboin.[1] The
book records the heroic trans-continental expe-

[1] For historical sketch of Grand Portage, see *Wis. Hist.
Colls.*, xi., pp. 123–125. See N. Y. *Nation*, Dec. 23, 1897, pp.
499–501, for corrections of *Astoria.*

dition of Wilson and Hunt, which started from Mackinac one bright morning in August, 1809, and wended its toilsome way along many a river and through mountain-passes, beset by a thousand perils, to plant far-distant Astoria.

With the coming of peace in 1815, English fur-traders were forbidden the country, and American interests, represented by Astor's great company, were at last dominant in this great field of commerce. New and improved methods were introduced, and the American Fur Company soon had a firm hold upon the Western country; nevertheless, the great corporation never succeeded in ridding itself of the necessity of employing the Creole and mixed-blood voyageurs, engagés, and interpreters, and was obliged to shape its policy so as to accommodate this great army of easy-going subordinates.

The fur-trade of Mackinac was in its heyday about the year 1820. Gradually, with the in-
Modern life   rush of settlement and the consequent cutting of the timber, the commerce of the forest waned, until about 1840 it was practically at an end, and the halcyon days of Mackinac were over. For years it was prominent as the site of a Protestant mission to the modernized Indians of Michigan and Wis-

consin; [1] finally, even this special interest was removed to new seats of influence, nearer the vanishing tribes, and Mackinac became resigned to the hum-drum of modern life — a sort of Malta, now but spasmodically garrisoned; a fishing station for the Chicago trade; a port of call for vessels passing her door; a resort for summer tourists; a scene which the historical novelist may dress to his fancy; a shrine at which the historical pilgrim may worship, thankful, indeed, that in what many think the Sahara of Western history are left a few romantic oases like unto this.

[1] For an account of this experiment, see Williams's *The Old Mission Church of Mackinac Island* (Detroit, 1895).

V

THE STORY OF LA POINTE

V

THE STORY OF LA POINTE

IN 1634, when the child born upon the
"Mayflower" was but fourteen years of
Jean age, Jean Nicolet, a daring young
Nicolet explorer, was despatched by the
enterprising Champlain upon a journey of
discovery as far as Wisconsin, a thousand miles
of canoe journey west from Quebec. In that
far distant region, Nicolet made trading con-
tracts, such as they were, with a half-score of
squalid tribes huddled in widely-separated
villages throughout the broad wilderness lying
between Lakes Superior and Michigan. It
was a hazardous, laborious expedition, far
more notable in its day than, in our time, is
a journey through Thibet. Its results were
slow of development, for in the seventeenth
century man was still cautiously deliberate;
nevertheless this initial visit of the forest am-
bassador of New France to the country of the
Upper Lakes broke the path for a train of

events which were of mighty significance in American history.

Let us examine the topography of Wisconsin. That State is situated at the head of the chain of Great Lakes. It is touched

Topographical significance of Wisconsin

on the east by Lake Michigan, on the north by Lake Superior, on the west by the Mississippi, and is drained by interlacing rivers which so closely approach each other that the canoe voyager may with ease pass from one great water system to another. He may enter the continent by the Gulf of St. Lawrence, and by utilizing numerous narrow portages in Wisconsin emerge into the south-flowing Mississippi, eventually returning to the Atlantic through the Gulf of Mexico. From Lake Michigan, the Fox-Wisconsin river system was the most feasible of the several highways to the great river. Into Lake Superior there flow numerous turbulent streams from whose sources short portage trails lead over to the headwaters of feeders of the Mississippi. From the western shore of Lake Superior, Pigeon River invites to exploration of the Winnipeg country, whence the canoeist may by a half-hundred easy routes reach the distant regions of Athabasca and the Polar Sea, and — as Mackenzie found — even the Pacific Ocean.

In their early voyages to the head of lake navigation, it was in the course of nature that the French should soon discover Wisconsin, and having discovered it, learn that this was the key-point of the Northwest, — the principal waterway to the continental interior. Through Wisconsin's interlacing streams, to which Nicolet led the way, New France largely prosecuted her far-reaching forest trade and missionary explorations, securing a nominal control of the basin of the Mississippi at a time when Anglo-Saxons had gained little more of the Atlantic Slope than could be seen from the mast-head of a caravel. Thus, early in the history of New France, the geographical character of Wisconsin became an important factor. The trading posts and Jesuit missions on Chequamegon Bay[1] of Lake Superior, like those on Green Bay[2] of Lake Michigan, soon played a prominent part in American exploration.[3]

[1] In his authoritative "History of the Ojibway Nation," in *Minn. Hist. Colls.*, v., Warren prefers the spelling "Chagoumigon," although recognizing "Shagawaumikong" and "Shaugahwaumikong." "Chequamegon" is the current modern form. Edward P. Wheeler, of Ashland, an authority on the Chippewa tongue and traditions, says the pronunciation should be "Sheh-gu-wah-mi-kung."

[2] See Neville and Martin's *Historic Green Bay* (Milwaukee, 1894), and various articles in the *Wisconsin Historical Collections.*

[3] See *Minn. Hist. Colls.*, v., pp. 98, 99, *note*, and *Wis.*

After Nicolet's journey to Wisconsin, there followed a long period in which the energies of New France were devoted to fighting back the Iroquois, who often swarmed before the very gates of Quebec and Montreal. Exploration was for the time wellnigh impossible. Twenty-one years elapse before we have evidence of another white man treading Wisconsin soil. In the spring of 1655, the Indians of the Fox River valley were visited by two French fur-traders from the Lower St. Lawrence, — Pierre d'Esprit, Sieur Radisson, and his sister's husband, Médard Chouart, Sieur des Groseilliers. There are no characters in American history more picturesque than these two adventurous traders, who, in their fond desire to "travell and see countries," and "to be known w^h the remotest people," roamed at will over the broad region between St. James's Bay and the Wisconsin River, having many curious and perilous experiences. They made several important geographical discoveries — among them, pos-

Radisson and Groseilliers on the Fox

Hist. Colls., xvi. and xvii., for accounts of early copper mining on Lake Superior by Indians. In the summer of 1892, W. H. Holmes, of the Smithsonian Institution, found on Isle Royale no less than a thousand abandoned shafts which had been worked by them; and "enough stone implements lay around, to stock every museum in the country."

sibly, the discovery of the Mississippi River, eighteen years before the visit of Jolliet and Marquette; while from a trading settlement which they proposed to the English, when ill-treated by their fellow-countrymen, developed the great establishment of the Hudson's Bay Company. The unconsciously-amusing narrative which Radisson afterwards wrote, for the edification of King Charles II. of England, is one of the most interesting known to American antiquaries.[1]

Five years after Radisson and Groseilliers were upon Fox River, they were again in *At Chequa-* the Northwest, this time upon Lake *megon Bay* Superior, which they had approached, in the company of a party of Huron refugees, by carrying around the Sault Ste. Marie. Skirting the southern shore of the lake,

---

[1] See *Jesuit Relations*, xlv., pp. 235–237, for Father Lallemant's report of the discoveries of the "two Frenchmen," who had found "a beautiful River, large, wide, deep, and worthy of comparison, they say, with our great river St. Lawrence."

In Franquelin's map of 1688, what is now Pigeon River, a part of the international boundary between Minnesota and Canada, is called Groseilliers. An attempt was made in the Wisconsin Legislature, during the session of 1895, by members of the Wisconsin Historical Society, to have a proposed new county called Radisson; the name was adopted by the friends of the bill, but the measure itself failed to pass.

past the now famous Pictured Rocks, the traders and their savage companions carried across Keweenaw Point, visited a band of Christino Indians[1] not far from the mouth of Montreal River, now the far western boundary between upper Michigan and Wisconsin, and, portaging across the base of Point Chequamegon, — then united to the mainland, but now insular, — entered beautiful Chequamegon Bay. Just where the Frenchmen made their camp, it is impossible from Radisson's confused narrative to say; but that it was upon the mainland, no Wisconsin antiquary now doubts. We have reason to believe that it was upon the southwest shore, between the modern towns of Ashland and Washburn.[2]

Writes our chronicler, with a homeliness of detail suggestive of De Foe: " We went about to make a fort of stakes, wch was in this manner. Suppose that the watter-side had ben in one end; att the same end there should be mur-

[1] Now called Crees.

[2] Father Verwyst's " Historic Sites on Chequamegon Bay," in *Wis. Hist. Colls.*, xi., pp. 426–440, is accompanied by notes on the site of Radisson's fort, by Sam. S. Fifield and Edward P. Wheeler. Verwyst thinks the location to have been " somewhere between Whittlesey's Creek and Shore's Landing;" Fifield and Wheeler are confident that it was at Boyd's Creek.

therers, and att need we made a bastion in a triangle to defend us from assault. The doore was neare the watter-side, our fire was in the

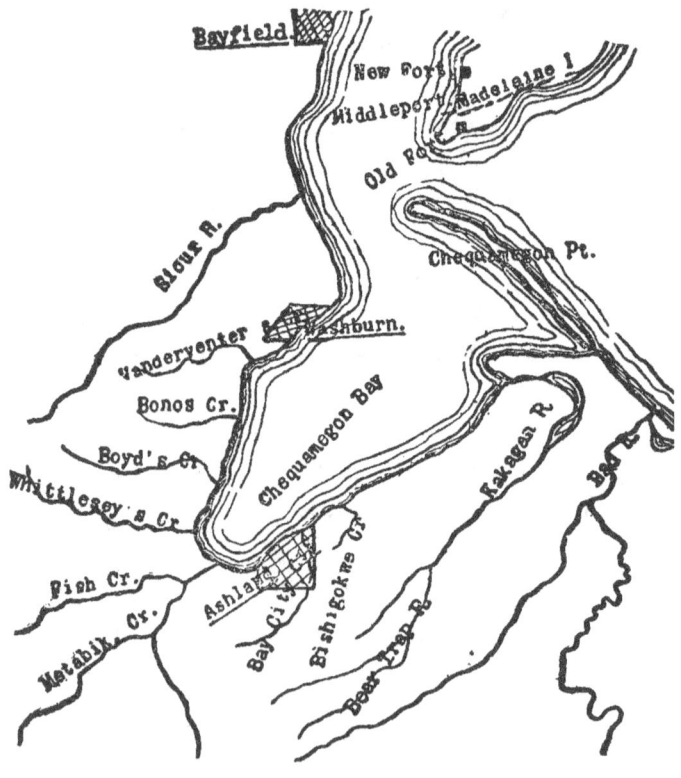

CHEQUAMEGON BAY

midle, and our bed on the right hand, covered. There were boughs of trees all about our fort layed acrosse, one uppon an other. Besides those boughs, we had a long cord tyed wth some small bells, wch weare sentereys. Finally, we made an ende to that fort in 2 dayes' time."

First habi- Modernize this statement, and in im-
tation of agination we can see this first dwell-
white men ing reared by white men on the shores of Lake Superior: a small log hut, built possibly on the extremity of a small rocky promontory; the door opens to the water front, while the land side, to the rear of the hut, is defended by a salient of palisades stretching from bank to bank of the narrow promontory; all about the rude structure is a wall of pine boughs piled one upon the other, with a long cord intertwined, and on this cord are strung numbers of the little hawk-bells then largely used in Indian trade for purposes of gift and barter. It was expected that in case of a night attack from savages, who might be willing to kill them for the sake of their stores, the enemy would stir the boughs and unwittingly ring the bells, thus arousing the little garrison. These ingenious defences were not put to the test, although no doubt they had a good moral effect in keeping the thieving savages at a respectful distance.

Winter was just setting in. The waters of the noble bay were taking on that black and sullen aspect peculiar to the season. The beautiful islands, later named for the Twelve *A gloomy* Apostles,[1] looked gloomy indeed in *winter* their dark evergreen mantles. From the precipitous edges of the red sandstone cliffs, which girt about this estuary of our greatest inland sea, the dense pine forests stretched for hundreds of miles westward and southward. Here and there in these gloomy depths was a cluster of starveling Algonquians, or a band of Hurons from east of Georgian Bay, still trembling from fear of a return of the Iroquois, who had chased them from Canada into this land of swamps and tangled woods, where their safety lay in hiding. At wide intervals, uncertain trails led from village to village, and in places the rivers were convenient highways; these narrow paths, however, beset with danger in a thousand shapes, but emphasized the unspeakable terrors of the wilderness.

Radisson and Groseilliers, true coureurs de bois, were undaunted by the dangers which daily beset them. Securely hiding their goods in skilful caches, they passed the winter with their Huron and Algonquian neighbors upon a prolonged hunt, far into the Mille Lacs region

---

[1] Apparently by Jonathan Carver, in the map accompanying his volume of *Travels*.

of Minnesota. The season was phenomenally
severe, and the Indians could not find game
enough to sustain life. A famine ensued in the
camp, the tragical details of which are vividly
painted by Radisson. In the spring of 1662,
the traders were back again at Chequamegon,
and built another fortified shelter, this time
possibly on the sand-spit of Shagawaumikong,[1]

[1] Says Warren (*Minn. Hist. Colls.*, v., p. 102): "Shag-a-
waum-ik-ong is a narrow neck or point of land about four
miles long, and lying nearly parallel to the island of La
Pointe, toward the western end of which it converges, till the
distance from point to point is not more than two miles." In
first entering the bay, the previous autumn, Radisson describes
Shagawaumikong, and adds: "That point should be very fitt
to build & advantageous for the building of a fort, as we did
the spring following." But later on in his journal, in describ-
ing the return to the bay from their winter with the Sioux of
the Mille Lacs, he does not mention the exact location of the
new " fort." While here, they "received [news] that the
Octanaks [Ottawas] [had] built a fort on the point that forms
that Bay, wch resembles a small lake. We went towards it
with all speede," — and had a perilous trip thither, across
thin ice. This would indicate that the French camp was not
on the point. As with many other passages in the journal,
it is impossible to reconcile these two statements. Verwyst
thinks that the traders were stationed on Houghton Point.
Warren, who had an intimate acquaintance with Chippewa
traditions, believed that that tribe, driven westward by degrees
from the shores of the Gulf of St. Lawrence, reached Lake
Superior about the time of the Columbian discovery, and
came to a stand on Shagawaumikong Point. "On this spot
they remained not long, for they were harassed daily by their

from which place they once more wandered in search of adventures and peltries, going as far northwest as Lake Assiniboin, and later in the season returning to their home on the Lower St. Lawrence.

Returning to Montreal in August (1660), the well-laden canoes of these adventurous

Ingratitude fur-traders were accompanied thither by a large party of Hurons from the Lac Courte Oreille country, which lies just over the Lake Superior watershed several days to the south of Chequamegon Bay.   Radisson and Groseilliers were obliged to suffer the con-fiscation of the greater part of their valuable

warlike foes, and for greater security they were obliged to move their camp to the adjacent island of Mon-ing-wun-a-kauning ["place of the golden-breasted woodpecker," now known as La Pointe].   Here, they chose the site of their ancient town, and it covered a space about three miles long and two broad, comprising the western end of the island." (*Minn. Hist. Colls.*, v., p. 96.)   They remained in this large town "for the space of three generations, or one hundred and twenty years," but for various reasons evacuated the place, and settling on the adjacent mainland came to regard La Pointe Island (now Madelaine) as an abode of evil spirits, upon which, it is said, until the days of Cadotte, no Indian dare stay over night alone.   Gradually, as the beaver grew more scarce, the Chippewas radiated inland; hence at the time of Radisson's visit, the shores of the bay were almost unoccupied, save during the best fishing season, when Chippewas, Ottawas, Hurons, and others congregated there in considerable numbers.

peltries, because of trading in the upper waters without a license, and were nearly ruined by this unfortunate outcome of their enterprise. Such ungenerous treatment of the explorers, who had brought tidings of a vast stretch of new territory, led to their desertion to the English and the ultimate formation of the Hudson's Bay Company.

While in Montreal, the Hurons were met by Jesuit missionaries who persuaded them to

Father Ménard

request the presence of a " black-gown " in their far-away camps in the Wisconsin woods. Father René Ménard was assigned to the task by his superior, and in September returned with the tribesmen, accompanied by his servant and seven other Frenchmen. After a deplorable winter at Keweenaw Bay, on the south shore of Lake Superior, where he had been abandoned by his hosts, Ménard started overland to find them. It was a toilsome journey of some two hundred miles to the southwest, partly by water, but much of it through a tangled forest. While making a portage around Bill Cross Rapids, in the upper reaches of the Wisconsin River, the unfortunate priest appears to have lost the path and perished of exposure. He was never after seen by his companion.

It was not until August of 1665, four years later, that Father Claude Allouez, another *Father Allouez* Jesuit, was sent to re-open the Lake Superior mission. He chose his site on the southwestern shore of Chequamegon Bay, possibly at the mouth of Vanderventer's Creek, doubtless not far from the spot on which Radisson's hut had been built, four years previously. The mission and the locality were called *La Pointe du Saint Esprit*, which in familiar speech was soon shortened to La Pointe.[1]

---

[1] Neill (in *Minn. Hist. Colls.*, v., p. 116) is of the opinion that Allouez "built a bark chapel on the shores of the bay, between a village of Petun Hurons and a village composed of three bands of Ottawas." That Allouez was stationed upon the mainland, where the Indians now were, is evident from his description of the bay (*Jesuit Relations* for 1666-67, l., p. 273): "It is a beautiful Bay, at the head of which is situated the great Village of the Savages, who there cultivate fields of Indian corn and lead a settled life. They number eight hundred men bearing arms, but are gathered from seven different nations, living in peace, mingled one with another." Verwyst, whose local knowledge is thorough, thinks that Allouez's mission was at the mouth of Vanderventer's Creek, and I have followed him in this regard.

In christening his mission "La Pointe," Allouez had reference, doubtless, to the neighboring sandy point of Shagawaumikong, hemming in the bay on the east. In this he must have had a poetic interest, for tradition told him that it was the landfall of the Chippewas, and the place where, perhaps a century before, had been fought a great battle be-

At the time of Radisson's visit, the shores of Chequamegon Bay were uninhabited save by a few half-starved Hurons, who came periodically to fish, from the larger villages on inland lakes to the south.   But soon thereafter it became the centre of a considerable Indian population, residents of several tribes — Chippewas, Potawatomis, Kickapoos, Sauks, and Foxes, native to Wisconsin, together with Hurons and Ottawas from the Huron country — having been attracted thither: first, by the fisheries; second, by a fancied security in

tween them and the Dakotas (or Sioux), relics of which were to be found in our day, in the human bones scattered freely through the shifting soil; doubtless in his time, these were much in evidence.

The map in the *Jesuit Relations* for 1670–71 (lv., p. 94) styles the entire Bayfield peninsula, forming the west shore of the bay, " La Pointe du St. Esprit," which of course was map-making from vague report.   Franquelin's map of 1688, more exact in every particular, places a small settlement near the southwestern extremity of the bay.   See also Verwyst's *Missionary Labors of Fathers Marquette, Ménard, and Allouez* (Milwaukee, 1886), p. 183.

In 1820, Cass and Schoolcraft visited Chequamegon Bay, and the latter, in his *Narrative*, says : " Passing this [Bad] river, we continued along the sandy formation to its extreme termination, which separates the Bay of St. Charles [Chequamegon] from that remarkable group of islands called the Twelve Apostles by Carver.   It is this sandy point which is called La Pointe Chagoimegon by the old French authors, a term now shortened to La Pointe."

so isolated a region against the Iroquois of the East and the wild Sioux of the West. When Allouez arrived in this polyglot village, the first of October, he found here Chippewas, Potawatomis, Kickapoos, Sauks, and Foxes, all of them Wisconsin tribes; besides these were Hurons, Ottawas, Miamis, and Illinois — victims of Iroquois hate who had fled in droves before the westward advances of their merciless tormentors.

Despite his large congregations, Allouez made little headway among these people, being *Father* consoled for his hardships and ill-*Marquette* treatment by the devotion of a mere handful of followers. For four years did he labor alone in the Wisconsin wilderness, hoping against hope, varying the monotony of his dreary task by occasional canoe voyages to Quebec, to report progress to his father superior. Father Jacques Marquette, a more youthful zealot, was at last sent to relieve him, and in September, 1669, arrived at La Pointe from Sault Ste. Marie, after spending a full month upon the journey — so hampered was he, at that early season, by snow and ice. Allouez, thus relieved from a work that had doubtless palled upon him, upon invitation of the Potawatomis proceeded to Green Bay,

where he arrived early in December, and
founded the second Jesuit mission in Wisconsin, St. Francis Xavier, on the site of the
modern town of De Pere.[1]

Marquette had succeeded to an uncomfort-
able berth. Despite his strenuous efforts as
a peacemaker, his dusky parishioners soon un-
wisely quarrelled with their western neighbors,
the Sioux,[2] with the result that the La Pointe
bands, and Marquette with them, retreated
eastward along the southern shore of the great
lake: the Ottawas taking up their home in the
Manitoulin Islands of Lake Huron, and the
Hurons accompanying Marquette to the Island

[1] By this time, fear of the Iroquois had subsided and
many Hurons had lately returned with the Potawatomis,
Sauks, and Foxes, to the old haunts of the latter, on Fox
River. Cadillac, writing in 1703 from Detroit, says (*Margry*,
v., p. 317): "It is proper that you should be informed that
more than fifty years since [about 1645] the Iroquois by
force of arms drove away nearly all of the other Indian
nations from this region [Lake Huron] to the extremity of
Lake Superior, a country north of this post, and fright-
fully barren and inhospitable. About thirty-two years ago
[1671] these exiled tribes collected themselves together at
Michillimakinak."

[2] "The cause of the perpetual war, carried on between
these two nations, is this, that both claim, as their exclusive
hunting-ground, the tract of country which lies between them,
and uniformly attack each other when they meet upon it."—
Henry's *Travels and Adventures* (N. Y., 1809), pp. 197, 198.

of Mackinac, where the Jesuits had recently established the mission of St. Ignace.

With La Pointe mission abandoned, and Lake Superior closed to French enterprise by the "raging Sioux," the mission at De Pere now became the centre of Jesuit operations in Wisconsin; and it was a hundred and sixty-four years later (1835) before mass was again said upon the forest-fringed shores of Chequamegon Bay.

Although the missionary had deserted La Pointe, the fur-trader soon came to be much in *Lords of* evidence. The spirit of Radisson and *the fur-* Groseilliers long permeated this out-*trade* of-the-way corner of the Northwest. We find (1673), two years after Marquette's expulsion, La Salle's trading agent, Sieur Raudin, cajoling the now relentent Sioux at the western end of Lake Superior. In the summer of 1679, that dashing coureur de bois, Daniel Graysolon du Luth,[1] ascended the St. Louis River, which divides Wisconsin and Minnesota, and penetrated with his lively crew of voyageurs to the Sandy Lake country, being probably the first white trader upon the headwaters of the Mississippi. The succeeding winter he spent in profitable commerce with

[1] From whom the city of Duluth, Minn., was named.

the Assiniboins, Crees, and other northern
tribes in the neighborhood of Grand Portage,
on the present boundary between Minnesota
and Canada. In June, probably unaware of
the easier portage by way of the Mille Lacs
and Rum River, Du Luth set out at the head
of a small company of employés to reach
the Mississippi by a new route. Entering
the narrow and turbulent Bois Brulé, halfway along the southern shore of Lake Superior,
between Red Cliff and St. Louis River, he
with difficulty made his way over the fallen
trees and beaver dams which then choked its
course. From its headwaters there is a two-
mile portage to the Upper St. Croix; this
traversed, Du Luth was upon a romantic stream
which swiftly carried him, through foaming
rapids and deep, cool lakes, down into the
Father of Waters. Here it was that he heard
of Father Louis Hennepin's captivity among
the Sioux, and with much address and some
courage rescued that doughty adventurer, and
carried him, by way of the Fox-Wisconsin
route, in safety to Mackinac.[1]

An adventurous forest trader, named Le
Sueur, was the next man to imprint his name

[1] See Thwaites's edition of Hennepin's *New Discovery*
(Chicago: A. C. McClurg & Co., 1903).

on the page of Lake Superior history. The
Fox Indians, who controlled the valleys of the
Fox and Wisconsin rivers, had for various
reasons become so hostile to the French that
those divergent streams were no longer safe
as a gateway from the Great Lakes to the
Great River. The tendency of the prolonged
Fox War was to force the fur-trade travel to
the portages of Chicago and St. Josephs on
the south, and those of Lake Superior on the
north.[1] It was with a view to keeping open
the Bois Brulé-St. Croix route, that Le Sueur,
who had been in the West for several years,
was despatched by the authorities of New
France in 1693. He built a stockaded fort
on Madelaine Island, convenient for guarding
the northern approach,[2] and another on an
island in the Mississippi, below the mouth
of the St. Croix, and near the present town

[1] See Parkman's *Half-Century of Conflict*, Hebberd's
Wisconsin under French Dominion (Madison, 1890), and
Wis. Hist. Colls., xvi., xvii.

[2] Neill, in *Minn. Hist. Colls.*, v., p. 140, says that soon
after St. Lusson's taking possession of the Northwest for
France, at Sault Ste. Marie (1671), French traders built a
small fort set about with cedar palisades, on which a cannon
was mounted, "at the mouth of a small creek or pond midway between the present location of the American Fur Company's establishment and the mission-house of the American
Board of Foreign Missions."

of Red Wing, Minnesota. The post in the Mississippi soon became "the centre of commerce for the Western parts." The station in Chequamegon Bay also soon rose to importance, for the Chippewas, who had drifted far inland into Wisconsin and Minnesota with the growing scarcity of game, — the natural result of the indiscriminate slaughter which the fur-trade encouraged, — were induced by the new trading facilities to return to their old haunts, massing themselves in an important village on the southwestern shore.

This incident strikingly illustrates the important part which the trader early came to play

The Indian and the trader in Indian life. At first, the tribesman was an agriculturist in a small way, and hunted and fished only to meet the daily necessities of food and clothing. The white man, however, induced him to kill animals solely for their furs, luxuries ever in great demand in the marts of civilization. The savage now wholly devoted himself to the chase, and it became necessary for the white man to supply him with clothing, tools, weapons, and ornaments of European manufacture, — the currency, as well as the necessities, of the wilderness.[1] These articles the

[1] *Minn. Hist. Colls.*, v., p. 125. Originally, the Indians of Lake Superior went to Quebec to trade; but, as the whites

savage had heretofore laboriously fashioned
for himself at great expenditure of time; but
now he was not content with native manu-
factures, and indeed he quickly lost his old-
time facility for making them. Soon he was
almost wholly dependent on the white trader
for the commonest conveniences of life. No
longer tied to his fields, he became more and
more a nomad, roving restlessly to and fro in
search of fur-bearing game, and quickly popu-
lating or depopulating a district according to
the conditions of trade. Without his trader,
he quickly sank into misery and despair; with
the advent of the trader, a certain sort of prosperity once more reigned in the tepee of the
red man. In the story of Chequamegon Bay,
the heroes are the fur-trader and the missionary: and of these the fur-trader is the greater,
for without his presence on this scene there
would have been no Indians to convert.

Although Le Sueur was not many years in
command upon Chequamegon Bay,[1] we there-

penetrated westward by degrees, these commercial visits were
restricted to Montreal, Niagara, Detroit, Mackinac, Sault
Ste. Marie, as each in turn became the outpost of French influence; finally, trading-posts were opened at La Pointe, St.
Louis River, and Pigeon River, and frequently traders even
followed the savages on their long hunts after the ever-
decreasing game.

[1] In July, 1695, Chingouabé, chief of the Chippewas,

after catch frequent glimpses of stockaded fur-
Fur-trade trade stations here, — French, English,
stockades and American, in turn, — the most
of them doubtless being on Madelaine Island,
which not only commands the bay but is
easily defensible from mainland attacks.[1]   We

voyaged with Le Sueur to Montreal, to "pay his respects
to Onontio, in the name of the young warriors of Point
Chagouamigon, and to thank him for having given them
some Frenchmen to dwell with them; and to testify their
sorrow for one Jobin, a Frenchman killed at a feast.   It occurred accidentally, not maliciously."   In his reply (July 29),
Governor Frontenac gave the Chippewas some good advice,
and said that he would again send Le Sueur "to command at
Chagouamigon " — *Minn. Hist. Colls.*, v., p. 421.

[1] It is evident that hereafter Madelaine Island was the
chief seat of French power in Chequamegon Bay, but it was
not until the present century that either the name La Pointe
or Madelaine was applied to the island.   Franquelin's map
(1688) calls it " Isle Detour ou St. Michel."   Bellin's French
map of Lake Superior (in Charlevoix's *Histoire et Description Générale de Nouvelle France*, Paris, 1744) calls the long
sand-point of Shagawaumikong, " Point de Chagauamigon,"
and styles the present Madelaine Island, " Isle La Ronde."
after the trader La Ronde.   What is now Basswood Island,
he calls "Isle Michel," and at the southern extremity of the
bay indicates that at that place was once an important Indian
village.   In De l'Isle's map of 1745, a French trading house
(*Maison Françoise*) is shown on Shagawaumikong Point itself.   Madelaine Island has at various times been known
as Monegoinaiccauning (or moningwunakauning, Chippewa for " golden-breasted woodpecker "), St. Michel, La
Ronde, Woodpecker, Montreal, Virginia (Schoolcraft, 1820),
Michael's (McKenney, 1826), Middle (because midway be-

know that in 1717 there was a French trader at La Pointe, — now the popular name for the entire bay district, — for he was asked by Lieutenant Robertel de la Noüe, who was then at Kaministiqua,[1] to forward a letter to a certain Sioux chief. In September of the following year, Captain Paul le Gardeur St. Pierre, whose mother was a daughter of Jean Nicolet, Wisconsin's first explorer, was sent to command at Chequamegon, assisted by Ensign Linctot, the authorities of the lower country having been informed that the local Chippewa chief was, with his fellow-chief at Keweenaw, going to war with the Foxes. St. Pierre was at Chequamegon for at least a year, and was succeeded by Linctot, who effected an important peace between the Chippewas and Sioux.[2]

Whether a garrisoned stockade was maintained at Chequamegon Bay, from St. Pierre's time to the close of the French domination, it is impossible to say; but it seems probable, for the geographical position was one of consider-

tween the stations of Sault Ste. Marie and Fort William, at Pigeon River), Cadotte's, and La Pointe (the latter, because La Pointe village was situated thereon).

[1] On the site of the present Fort William, Ont., near Thunder Bay.

[2] *Wis. Hist. Colls.*, xvi., p. 380; *Minn. Hist. Colls.*, v., pp. 423–425.

able importance in the development of the fur-
trade, and the few records extant mention the
fort as one of long standing.[1]

In 1730 it is recorded that a nugget of
copper was brought to the post by an Indian,

A copper and search at once made for a mine.
nugget But a year later, the authorities of
New France wrote to the home office in Paris
that, owing to the superstitions of the Indians, which led them to conceal mineral
wealth from the whites, no copper mine had
thus far been found in the neighborhood of
Chequamegon Bay.

The commandant of Chequamegon at this
time was Louis Denys, Sieur de la Ronde —

The first like most of his predecessors, a con-
bark siderable trader in these far Western
parts, and necessarily a man of enterprise
and vigor. La Ronde, who was reported as
"knowing the savage languages better than
the savages, as they themselves admit," [2] was
for many years the chief trader in the Lake
Superior country, his son and partner being
Denys de la Ronde. In order to search for

[1] It was during this period the only fur-trading station on
the south shore of Lake Superior, and was admirably situated for protecting not only the west end of the lake, but the
Bois Brulé-St. Croix trade route.

[2] Beauharnois to the French Minister, Oct. 11, 1732.

copper mines, as well as to conduct their growing fur-trade, they built a bark of forty tons,
which was without doubt "the first vessel on
the great lake, with sails larger than an Indian
blanket."[1]   On account of the great outlay
incurred by him in this and other wilderness
enterprises, the post of Chequamegon, with its
trading monopoly, had, according to a de-
spatch of that day, been given to the elder La
Ronde, "as a gratuity to defray expenses."
Other allusions to the La Rondes are not
infrequent: in 1736,[2] the son is ordered to
investigate a report of a copper mine at Iron
River, not far east of the Bois Brulé; in the
spring of 1740, the father is at Mackinac, on
his return to Chequamegon from a visit to the

---

[1] James D. Butler's "Early Shipping on Lake Superior,"
in *Wis. Hist. Soc. Proc.*, 1894, p. 87. The rigging and other
materials were taken in canoes from the lower country to Sault
Ste. Marie, the vessel being built at Point aux Pins, on the
north shore, seven miles above the Sault. Butler shows that
Alexander Henry was interested with a mining company in
launching upon the lake in May, 1771, a sloop of 70 tons.
After this, sailing vessels were regularly employed upon
Superior, in the prosecution of the fur-trade and copper
mining. The Hudson's Bay Company's "Speedwell" was
upon the lake as early as 1789; the North West Company's
principal vessel was the "Beaver."

[2] In this year there were reported to be 150 Chippewa
braves living on Point Chagouamigon. — *N. Y. Colon.
Docs.*, ix.

lower country, but being sick is obliged to return to Montreal, where he died;[1] and in 1744,
Bellin's map gives to what we now know as
Madelaine, the name "Isle de la Ronde" —
fair evidence that the French post of this period
was on that island.

We hear nothing more of importance concerning Chequamegon until about 1756, when
Allies of   Hertel de Beaubàssin, the last French
the French commandant there, was summoned to
Lower Canada with his Chippewa allies, to do
battle against the English.[2]   For several years
past, wandering English fur-traders had been
tampering with the powerful Chippewas of Lake
Superior, who in consequence frequently maltreated their old friends, the French;[3] but
now that the tribe were summoned for actual
fighting in the lower country, with extravagant
promises of presents, booty, and scalps, they
with other Wisconsin Indians eagerly flocked

---

[1] Martin MSS., Dominion Archives, Ottawa — letter of
Beauharnois. For much of the foregoing data, see Neill's
"History of the Ojibways," *Minn. Hist. Colls.*, v.

[2] *N. Y. Colon. Docs.*, x., p. 424.

[3] Says Governor Galissonière, in writing to the colonial
office at Paris, under date of October, 1748: "Voyageurs
robbed and maltreated at Sault Ste. Marie, and elsewhere on
Lake Superior; in fine, there appears to be no security anywhere." — *N. Y. Colon. Docs.*, x., p. 182.

under the French banner, and in painted swarms appeared on the banks of the St. Law-rence, with no better result than to embarrass the French commissariat and thus unwittingly aid the ambitious English.

New France was tottering to her fall. The little garrison on Madelaine Island had, with *A tragic* many another like it, been withdrawn *tale* from the frontier to help in the de-fence of the lower country; and the Upper Lakes, no longer policed by the fur-trade monopoly, were free plunder for the unlicensed coureurs de bois. Doubtless such were the party who encamped upon the island during the autumn of 1760. By the time winter had set in upon them, all had left for their wintering grounds in the forests of the far West and Northwest, save a clerk named Joseph, who remained in charge of the stores and the local traffic. With him were his little family, — his wife, who was from Montreal, his child, a small boy, and a man-servant, or voy-ageur. Traditions differ as to the cause of the servant's action — some have it, a desire for wholesale plunder; others, detection in a series of petty thefts, which Joseph threatened to re-port; others, an unrequited passion for Joseph's wife. However that may be, the servant mur-

dered first the clerk, and then the wife; and
in a few days, stung by the piteous cries of
the child, the lad himself. When the spring
came, and the traders returned to Chequamegon, they inquired for Joseph and his family; but the servant's reply was unsatisfactory,
and he finally confessed to his terrible deed.
The story goes, that in horror the traders dismantled the old French fort as a thing accursed,
sunk the cannon in a neighboring pool, and so
destroyed the palisade that to-day certain mys-
terious grassy mounds alone remain to testify
of the tragedy. Carrying their prisoner with
them on their return voyage to Montreal, he
is said to have escaped to the Hurons, among
whom he boasted of his deed, only to be killed
as too cruel a companion even for savages.[1]

New France having now fallen, an English
trader, Alexander Henry, spent the winter of
Alexander 1765–66 upon the mainland opposite
Henry the island.[2] Henry had obtained

[1] See the several versions of this tale, *Wis. Hist. Colls.*,
viii., pp. 224 *et seq.*, and *Minn. Hist. Colls.*, v., pp. 141–145, 431,
432. Warren says that some Chippewa traditions ascribe
this tragedy to the year 1722, but the weight of evidence is
as in the text above.

[2] " My house, which stood in the bay, was sheltered by an
island of fifteen miles in length, and between which and the
main the channel is four miles broad. On the island there
was formerly a French trading-post, much frequented; and

from the English commandant at Mackinac
the exclusive trade of Lake Superior, and at
Sault Ste. Marie took into partnership Jean
Baptiste Cadotte,[1] a thrifty Frenchman, who
for many years thereafter was one of the most
prominent characters on the Upper Lakes.
Henry and Cadotte spent several winters together on Lake Superior, but only one upon
the shores of Chequamegon, which Henry
styles "the metropolis of the Chippeways."[2]

The next dweller at Chequamegon Bay,
John of whom we have record, was John
Johnston Johnston, a Scotch-Irish fur-trader of
some education. Johnston established himself

in its neighborhood a large Indian village." — Henry's
Travels, p. 199. Henry doubtless means that formerly there
was an Indian village on the island ; Warren says that until
after the coming of Cadotte the island was thought by the
natives to be bewitched.

[1] Jean Baptiste Cadotte (formerly spelled Cadot) was the
son of one Cadeau, who is said to have come to the Northwest in the train of Sieur de Saint-Lusson, who in 1671
took possession of the region centring at Sault Ste. Marie.
Jean Baptiste, who was legally married to a Chippewa woman,
had two sons, Jean Baptiste and Michel, both of whom were
extensive traders and in their turn married Chippewas. See
Minn. Hist. Colls., v., index.

[2] "On my arrival at Chagouenig, I found fifty lodges of
Indians there. These people were almost naked, their trade
having been interrupted, first by the English invasion of
Canada, and next by Pontiac's war." — *Travels*, p. 193.

on Madelaine Island, not far from the site of
the old French fort. Some four miles across
the water, on the mainland to the west, near
where is now the town of Bayfield, was a
Chippewa village with whose inhabitants he
engaged in traffic. Waubojeeg (White Fisher),
a forest celebrity in his day, was at this time
the village chief, and possessed of a comely
daughter whom Johnston soon sought and
obtained in marriage. Taking her to his
island home, Johnston appears to have lived
there for a year or two in friendly commerce
with the natives, at last retiring to his old
station at Sault Ste. Marie.[1]

Mention has been made of Jean Baptiste
Cadotte, who was a partner of Alexander
The Cadottes   Henry in the latter's Lake Superior
trade, soon after the middle of the
century. After his venture with Henry, Ca-

---

[1] McKenny, in *History of the Indian Tribes* (Phila., 1854),
i., pp. 154, 155, tells the story. He speaks of Johnston as
"the accomplished Irish gentleman who resided so many
years at the Sault de Ste. Marie, and who was not better
known for his intelligence and polished manners than for his
hospitality." Johnston died (aged sixty-six) at Sault Ste.
Marie, September 22, 1828. His widow became a Presbyterian, and built a church of that denomination at the Sault.
Her daughter married Henry B. Schoolcraft, the historian
of the Indian tribes of the Upper Lakes. Waubojeeg died
at an advanced age, in 1793.

dotte, whose wife was a Chippewa, returned to Sault Ste. Marie, from which point he conducted an extensive trade through the Northwest. Burdened with advancing years, Jean retired from the traffic in 1796 and divided the business between his two sons, Jean Baptiste and Michel.

About the opening of the nineteenth century,[1] Michel took up his abode on Madelaine Island, and from that time to the present there had been a continuous settlement there. He had been educated at Montreal, and marrying Equaysayway, the daughter of White Crane, the village chief of La Pointe,[2] at once became a person of much importance in the Lake Superior country. Upon the old trading site at the southwestern corner of the island, by this time commonly called La Pointe, — borrowing the name, as we have seen, from the original La Pointe, on the mainland, and it in turn from Point Chequamegon, — Cadotte lived at his

---

[1] Warren thinks he settled there about 1792 (*Minn. Hist. Colls.*, v., p. 111), but there is good evidence that it was at a later date.

[2] "The Cranes claim the honor of first having pitched their wigwam, and lighted the fire of the Ojibways, at Shaug-ah-waum-ik-ong, a sand point or peninsula lying two miles immediately opposite the Island of La Pointe." — Warren, in *Minn. Hist. Colls.*, v., p. 86.

ease for over a quarter of a century. Here he cultivated a " comfortable little farm," commanded a fluctuating but often far-reaching fur-trade, first as agent of the North West Company, and later of Astor's American Fur Company, and reared a considerable family. His sons, educated, as he had been, at Montreal, became the heads of families of Creole traders, interpreters, and voyageurs whom antiquarians now confidently seek when engaged in resurrecting the French and Indian traditions of Lake Superior.[1]

[1] "Kind-hearted Michel Cadotte," as Warren calls him, also had a trading-post at Lac Courte Oreille. Like the other Wisconsin Creole traders, he was in English employ during the War of 1812–15, and engaged in the capture of Mackinac (1812). He died on the island, July 8, 1837, aged seventy-two years, and was buried there. As with most of his kind, he made money freely and spent it with prodigality, partly in high living, but mainly in supporting his many Indian relatives; as a consequence, he died poor, the usual fate of men of his type. — *Minn. Hist. Colls.*, v., p. 449. Warren says (*ibid.*, p. 11) the death occurred " in 1836," but the tombstone gives the above date.

Cass, Schoolcraft, and Doty visited Chequamegon Bay in 1820. Schoolcraft says, in his *Narrative*, pp. 192, 193: " Six miles beyond the Mauvaise is Point Che goi-me-gon, once the grand rendezvous of the Chippeway tribe, but now reduced to a few lodges. Three miles further west is the island of St. Michel (Madelaine), which lies in the traverse across Chegoimegon Bay, where M. Cadotte has an establishment. This was formerly an important trading-post, but is

VILLAGE OF LA POINTE, MADELAINE ISLAND

In the year 1818 there came to the Lake Superior country two sturdy, fairly educated [1] *The Warrens* young men, natives of the Berkshire hills of Massachusetts—Lyman Marcus Warren, and his younger brother, Truman Abraham. They were of the purest New England stock, being lineally descended from Richard Warren, one of the "Mayflower" company. Engaging in the fur-trade, the brothers soon became popular with the Chippewas, and in 1821 still further intrenched themselves in the affections of the tribesmen by marrying the two half-breed daughters of old Michel Cadotte — Lyman taking unto himself Mary, while Charlotte became the wife of Truman. At first the Warrens worked in opposition to the American Fur Company. But John Jacob Astor's lieutenants were shrewd men, and understood the art of overcoming commercial rivals; Lyman was made by them a

now dwindled to nothing. There is a dwelling of logs, stockaded in the usual manner of trading-houses, besides several outbuildings, and some land in cultivation. We here also found several cows and horses, which have been transported with great labour."

[1] Alfred Brunson, who visited Lyman Warren at La Pointe, in 1843, wrote: "Mr. Warren had a large and select library, an unexpected sight in an Indian country, containing some books that I had never before seen." — *Western Pioneer* (Cincinnati, 1879), ii., p. 163.

partner in the lake traffic, and in 1824 established himself at La Pointe as the company's agent for the Lac Flambeau, Lac Court Oreille, and St. Croix departments, an arrangement which continued for some fourteen years. The year previous, the brothers had purchased the interests of their father-in-law, who now, much reduced in means, retired to private life after forty years' prosecution of the forest trade.[1]

The brothers Warren were the last of the great La Pointe fur-traders.[2]   Truman passed away early in his career, having expired in 1825, while upon a voyage between Mackinac and Detroit.   Lyman dwelt at La Pointe until 1838, when his connection with the American Fur Company ceased; he then received an appointment as United States sub-agent to the Chippewa reservation on Chippewa River, where he died on the tenth of October, 1847, aged fifty-three years.[3]

[1] *Minn. Hist. Colls.*, v., pp. 326, 383, 384, 450.   Contemporaneously with the settlement of the Warrens at La Pointe, Lieutenant Bayfield of the British navy made (1822–23) surveys from which he prepared the first accurate chart of Lake Superior; his name is preserved in Bayfield peninsula, county, and town.

[2] Borup had a trading-post on the island in 1846; but the forest commerce had by this time sadly dwindled.

[3] He left six children, the oldest son being William Whipple Warren, historian of the Chippewa tribe. See

Lyman Marcus Warren was a Presbyterian, and, although possessed of a Catholic wife, *First Prot-* was the first to invite Protestant mis-*estant mis-* sionaries to Lake Superior. Not since *sionaries* the days of Allöuez had there been an ordained minister at La Pointe. Warren was solicitous for the spiritual welfare of his Chippewa friends, especially the young, who were being reared without religious instruction, and subject to the demoralizing influence of a rough element of white borderers. The Catholic Church was not just then ready to re-enter the long-neglected field; and his predilections were in favor of the Protestant faith. In 1830, while upon his annual summer trip to Mackinac for supplies, he secured the co-operation of Frederick Ayer, of the Mackinac mission, who returned with him in his batteau as lay preacher and school-teacher, and opened at La Pointe what was then the only mission upon the shores of the great lake. In August the following year, Warren brought out from Mackinac Rev. Sherman Hall and wife, who served respectively as missionary and teacher, and Mrs. John Campbell, an interpreter.[1]

Williams's " Memoir of William W. Warren," in *Minn. Hist. Colls.*, v.

[1] See Davidson's excellent " Missions on Chequamegon Bay," in *Wis. Hist. Colls.*, xii., to which I am chiefly indebted

La Pointe was then upon the site of the old French trading-post at the southwest corner of Madelaine Island; and there, on the first Sunday afternoon after his arrival, Mr. Hall preached " the first sermon ever delivered in this place by a regularly ordained Christian minister." The missionaries appear to have been kindly received by the Catholic Creoles, several of whom were now domiciled at La Pointe. The school was patronized by most of the families upon the island, red and white, who had children of proper age. By the first of September there was an average attendance of twenty-five. Instruction was given almost wholly in the English language, with Sunday-school exercises for the children, and frequent gospel meetings for the Indian and Creole adults.

We have seen that the first La Pointe village was at the southwestern extremity of the island. This was known as the "Old Fort" site, for here had been the original Chippewa village, and later the fur-trading posts of the French and English. Gradually, the old harbor became

---

for information concerning the modern La Pointe missions. Mr. Davidson has since given us, in his *Unnamed Wisconsin* (Milwaukee, 1895), ampler details of this interesting mission.

shallow, because of the shifting sand, and unfit for the new and larger vessels which came to be used in the fur-trade. The American Fur Company therefore built a " New Fort " a few miles farther north, still upon the west shore of the island; and to this place, the present village, the name La Pointe came to be transferred. Halfway between the " Old Fort " and the " New Fort," Mr. Hall erected (probably in 1832) " a place of worship and teaching," which came to be the centre of Protestant missionary work in Chequamegon Bay.

The Presbyterians and Congregationalists were at that time, through the American Home

A denominational controversy
Missionary Society and the American Board, respectively united in the conduct of Wisconsin missions; it is, therefore, difficult for a layman to understand to which denomination the institution of the original Protestant mission at La Pointe may properly be ascribed. According to Neill, Warren was a Presbyterian; so also, nominally, were Ayer and Hall, although the last two were latterly rated as Congregationalists. Davidson, a Congregational authority, says: " The first organization of a Congregational church within the present limits of Wisconsin took place at La Pointe in August, 1833, in con-

nection with this mission; "[1] and certainly the
missionaries who later came to assist Hall were
of the Congregational faith; these were Rev.
Leonard Hemenway Wheeler and wife, Rev.
Woodbridge L. James and wife, and Miss
Abigail Spooner. Their work appears to
have been as successful as such proselyting
endeavors among our American Indians may
hope to be, and no doubt did much to stem
among the Wisconsin Chippewas the tide of
demoralization which upon the free advent
of the whites overwhelmed so many of our
Western tribes.

James's family did not long remain at La

[1] *Wis. Hist. Colls.*, xii., p. 445.   Mr. Davidson writes to
me that in his opinion Ayer leaned to independency, and was
really a Congregationalist ; Hall is registered as such in the
Congregational Year Book for 1859.   "As to the La Pointe
Odanah church," continues Mr. Davidson in his personal
letter, "its early records make no mention of lay elders —
officers that are indispensable to Presbyterian organization.
In manner of organization it was independent, rather than
strictly Congregational.   This could not well be otherwise,
with no church nearer than the one at Mackinac.   That was
Presbyterian, as was its pastor, Rev. William M. Ferry.
The La Pointe church adopted articles of faith of its own
choosing, instead of holding itself bound by the Westminster
Confession.   Moreover, the church was reorganized after the
mission was transferred to the Presbyterian board.   For this
action there may have been some special reason that I know
nothing about.   But it seems to me a needless procedure if
the church were Presbyterian before."

Pointe. Wheeler was soon recognized as the
leading spirit there, although Hall
An early
Western did useful service in the field of pub-
book lication, his translation of the New
Testament into Chippewa (completed in 1836)
being among the earliest of Western books.
Ayer eventually went to Minnesota. In May,
1845, owing to the migration of the majority
of the La Pointe Indians to the new Odanah
Reservation, on the mainland upon the banks
of Bad River, Wheeler removed thither and
remained their civil as well as spiritual counsellor until October, 1866, when he retired from
service, full of years, and conscious of a record
of noble deeds for the uplifting of the savage.
Hall tarried at La Pointe until 1853, when
he was assigned to Crow Wing Reservation,
on the Mississippi, thus ending the Protestant
mission on Chequamegon Bay. The new
church building, begun in 1837 near the present La Pointe landing, had fallen into sad decay,
when, in July, 1892, it became the property of
the Lake Superior Congregational Club, who
purpose to preserve it as an historic treasure,
considering it the first church-home of their
denomination in Wisconsin.

Not far from this interesting relic of Protestant pioneering at venerable La Pointe is a

rude structure dedicated to an older faith.
Widely has it been advertised, by poets,
romancers, and tourist agencies, as "the identical log structure built by Père Marquette";
while within there hangs a picture which we
are soberly told by the cicerone was "given
by the Pope of that time to Marquette, for his
mission church in the wilderness." It is strange
how this fancy was born; stranger still that it
persists in living when so frequently proved
false. It is as well established as any fact in
Western history — by the testimony of living
eye-witnesses, as well as by indisputable records
— that upon July 27, 1835, five years after
Warren had introduced Ayer to Madelaine
Island, there arrived at the hybrid village of
La Pointe, with but three dollars in his pocket,
Father a worthy Austrian priest, Father
Baraga (afterwards Bishop) Frederick Baraga.
By the side of the Indian graveyard at Middleport, he at once erected "a log chapel, 50 x
20 ft. and 18 ft. high," and therein he said mass
on the ninth of August, one hundred and sixty-
four years after Marquette had been driven
from Chequamegon Bay by the onslaught of
the Western Sioux.[1]   Father Baraga's resus-

[1] See Verwyst's *Missionary Labors*, pp. 146–149. This
chapel was built partly of new logs, and partly of material

citated mission — still bearing the name La
Pointe, as had the mainland missions of Allouez
and Marquette — throve apace. His " child-
like simplicity," kindly heart, and self-sacrificing
labors in their behalf won to him the Creoles
and the now sadly impoverished tribesmen;
and when, in the winter of 1836–37, he was in
Europe begging funds for the cause, his simple-
hearted enthusiasm met with generous response
from the faithful.

Returning to La Pointe in 1837, he finished
the little chapel, built log-houses for his half-
starved parishioners, and lavished attentions
upon them. Says Father Verwyst, himself an
experienced missionary among the Chippewas,
" In fact, he gave them too much altogether —
so to say — spoiled them by excessive kindness." Four years later, his chapel being ill-
built and now too small, he constructed a new
one at the modern village of La Pointe, some
of the materials of the first being used in the
second. This is the building, blessed by Father
Baraga on the second Sunday in August, 1841,
which to-day is falsely shown to visitors as that
of Father Marquette. It is needless to say
that no part of the ancient mainland chapel of

from an old building given to Father Baraga by the American
Fur Company.

the Jesuits went into its construction; as for
the picture, a " Descent from the Cross," alleged
to have once been in Marquette's chapel, we
have the best of testimony that it was im-
ported by Father Baraga himself from Europe
in 1841, he having obtained it there the preceding winter, when upon a second tour to
Rome to raise funds for the new church.[1]   This
remarkable man, promoted later to a missionary bishopric, continued throughout his
life to labor for the uplifting of the Indians of
the Lake Superior country, exhibiting a self-
sacrificing zeal which is rare in the annals of
any church, and establishing a lasting reputation as a student of aboriginal philology.   He
left La Pointe mission in 1853, to devote himself to the Menominees, leaving his work
among the Chippewas of Chequamegon Bay to
be conducted by others.   About the year 1877,
the town of Bayfield, upon the mainland opposite, became the residence of the Franciscan
friars who were now placed in charge.   Thus,

---

[1] See *Wis. Hist. Colls.*, xii., pp. 445, 446, *note ;* and Verwyst's *Missionary Labors*, pp. 183, 184.   Father Verwyst also
calls attention to certain vestments at La Pointe, said to be
those of Marquette: "That is another fable which we feel it
our duty to explode.   The vestments there were procured by
Bishop Baraga and his successors; not one of them dates
'from the seventeenth century."

while the Protestant mission, after a relatively
brief career of prosperity, has long since been
removed to Odanah, the Catholics to this day
retain possession of their ancient field in Chequamegon Bay.

In closing, let us briefly rehearse the changes
in the location of La Pointe, as a
Changes in location geographical term, and thus clear our
minds of some misconceptions into
which several historians have fallen.

1. As name-giver, we have Point Chequamegon (or Shagawaumikong). Originally a long
sand-spit hemming in Chequamegon Bay on
the east, it is now an island. The most conspicuous object in the local topography, it
gave name to the district; and here, at the
time of the Columbian discovery, was the
Chippewa stronghold.

2. The mission of La Pointe du St. Esprit,
founded by Alloüez, was, it seems well established on the mainland at the southwestern
corner of the bay, somewhere between the
present towns of Ashland and Washburn, and
not far from the site of Radisson's fort. The
point which suggested to Alloüez the name of
his mission was, of course, the neighboring
Point Chequamegon.

3. The entire region of Chequamegon Bay came soon to be known as La Pointe, but early within the nineteenth century the name was again localized by being popularly attached to the island which had previously borne many names, but which to-day is officially designated " Madelaine."

4. Cadotte's little trading village on the southwestern extremity of the island, on the site of the old Chippewa village and the early French forts, came soon especially to be designated as La Pointe. Thus still further was localized this historic name, which first had reference to a picturesque point of land, then to a Jesuit mission within sight of the point, then to the entire environs of Chequamegon Bay, then to an island within the bay, and now to a village upon that island.

5. When the American Fur Company established a new fort, a few miles north of the old, the oft-moved name La Pointe was transferred thereto. This northern village was in popular parlance styled " New Fort " and the now almost-deserted southern village " Old Fort "; while the small settlement around the Indian graveyard midway, where Father Baraga built his first chapel, was known as " Middleport."

VI

A DAY ON BRADDOCK'S ROAD

A DAY ON BRADDOCK'S ROAD

A BUSY little corner of the world is the Pennsylvania town of Brownsville, on the Monongahela. The lover of nature notes its *Browns-* existence, because beginning here *ville* the works of man have caused the river to change its character. The beautiful Monongahela, from flowing with broad and placid current between steep, wooded hills, deep dented with ravines, — a sore temptation to adventurous angler and canoeist and botanist, — becomes henceforth a commercial stream, lined with noisy, busy, grimy, matter-of-fact manufacturing towns literally abutting one upon the other, all of the sixty miles down to Pittsburg, and fast defiling the once picturesque banks with the grewsome offal of coal mines and iron plants.

To the student of Western history, however, Brownsville is a sort of shrine, albeit a smoky, dusty shrine, with the smell of lubricators and the noise of hammers, and much talk thereabout of the glories of Mammon. It is the Redstone of the eighteenth century : the centre of the first English settlement west of the Alleghanies, prominent in the annals of the French-English struggle for the mastery of the Ohio, and long the point of departure for expeditions down that river. It was, too, the terminus of one of two great pioneering paths across the Alleghanies, the other being Boone's trail through Cumberland Gap.

Doubtless the comparative ease by which the Alleghanies can be crossed, between the waters of the Potomac at Cumberland (" Will's Creek," of frontier history), and those of the *Redstone*   Monongahela at the junction of Red-*Old Fort*   stone Creek, was appreciated by the aborigines centuries ago : for extensive earthwork fortifications of the mound-building epoch were found by English settlers upon the riverside hill within the present city limits of Brownsville, these giving to the region its historic name, " Redstone Old Fort." It is presumable, also, that the Indians had had, for a long period, a well-defined trail between Will's Creek and Redstone.

In 1749, the Ohio Company was chartered by

the English crown for fur-trading in the Ohio
valley, and built a fort and storehouse at Will's

Nema- Creek. Nemacolin, a Delaware In-
colin's dian, whose village was at Redstone,
Path was employed to show the company's
agent, Christopher Gist, the native route over
the mountains ; and it was " Nemacolin's Path "
that was in great part followed by young
Major Washington in 1753 in his visit to the
French at Venango, that was improved for
wagon traffic by Washington on his Fort Necessity campaign the following year, and that
was followed much of the way by Braddock in
1755. For sixty-five years " Nemacolin's Path "
— later developed into " Braddock's Road " —
was travelled as the great northern highway to
the West, until the present National Road was
built (1795 till about 1820) between Cumberland and Brownsville. This latter closely and
often actually follows the Braddock route from
Cumberland until near Uniontown, whence it
diverges westward to Brownsville — practically
along the old Indian trail, leaving the Braddock
Road to verge northeastward to Gist's planta-
tion at Mount Braddock, and thence westward
to the mouth of Turtle Creek, where is now the
modern iron-making town of Braddock.

It was with the view of visiting the scenes of

Washington's service along Nemacolin's Path, a century and a half ago, that we set out from *Redstone Creek* Brownsville, one morning early in May. The railway journey of some eighteen miles to Uniontown abounds in interest. The line makes its ascent to the foot of the Laurel Hills, up the rugged little valley of Redstone Creek, hugging the serpentine banks with a persistence resulting in sharp curves which bounce the traveller about in his seat to a degree more lively than agreeable. There is a strange mixture upon the Redstone — dreary little coal-mine towns, with hillocks of shale sprawling over the landscape, and red-bedaubed, unhomelike homes of operatives; banks of coke ovens, hideously lurid; soft brown fields, pricked with springing grain; stretches of rectangular market-gardens; and pretty farm-steads, half hid in apple orchards, closely nestled by hillside shafts. Between jerks, you get charming vistas from the car-windows — of the swift little mountain stream flowing with alternating noisy cascades and placid pools between banks in which are outcroppings of the reddish stone which gives name to the locality; of grassy slopes, spangled with trillium, violets, and dandelions; of forest trees rustling into leaf; of the quaint log cabins of the pioneers, now falling into decay; and of picturesque side ravines where disused, dilapidated water-wheels serve as relics of the crude milling industries of generations gone before.

At Uniontown, a smart, well-built little town of some eight thousand inhabitants, dependent *The National Road* chiefly on the coking industry, we took carriage for Fort Necessity, ten miles distant to the southeast, on the National Road — locally styled "the pike." White, dusty, and rather stony, the old highway leads straight over the foot-hills through the pleasant rustic suburb of Hopwood, and soon begins its zigzag climb over the Laurel Hills. The road is often carved out of the side of a rugged slope, and then we have below us sharp descents, heavily forested with chestnuts, maples, oaks, and lindens, already well in leaf. Great grapevines hang from the topmost boughs in rich festoons; masses of ferns and the glossy may-apple are luxuriating in the moist depths; flowering dogwoods lift their clusters of white bloom into gay relief on opposite hill slopes; shining masses of the great laurel give an air of luxuriance to the crests of road-side banks, and everywhere are flitting butterflies panoplied in rainbow tints, rejoicing in the scents and splendors of early summer.

We have also backward views of the rolling country from which we have risen, of the hills scattered about us like haycocks, their sunny sides checkered with rectangular fields of yellow, brown, and gray, and of whitewashed hamlets dotting the green depths.

At the summit of the range, where a by-road, to be followed later in the day, leads off northward to Jumonville's Camp and Washington's Springs, an enterprising farm-wife conducts a summer resort, with cottages for guests who may, during the stifling summer days yet to come, desire to be up in the air, out of the dust of the coke ovens. A tall, angular, harsh-visaged woman, in a blue sunbonnet and with sockless feet, stood leaning over a stile hard by, her eyes more intent on our approach than on the far-stretching mountain view.

"We fit fire last night, on Ches'nut Ridge, jest over yon," she volunteered, pointing with her thumb to the north, where a thin bank of smoke hung dreamily over the dark forest which here mantles the hills. She had no knowledge of Fort Necessity by that name, but "'lowed as thar was an ol' fort over on Facenbaker's farm, yon way, up the pike." As to how far it was, as expressed in miles, she "'lowed she could n't tell, but it was a bit

furder — yon way furder, now "; and the peak
of her sunbonnet flapped in the direction of
the southeast, where the white line of turnpike
dipped down into a little valley and ran up over
the next hill, and then appeared to jump off
into space.

When we had climbed thither, there was a
dreary little frame tavern on the top of the hill,
with a lager-beer sign conspicuously posted, a
watering trough, and a half-dozen farm hands
sousing their heads at the tavern pump, pre-
paratory to dinner. The aspect was not inviting. In further search of dinner, we descended
into the next valley, where an old stone hos-
telry stood by a shallow run in which hogs
wallowed, and waddling geese craned their
necks and hissed defiance to the new guests.
The generous hall and dining-room, with their
large open fireplaces and the commodious gal-
leries, are eloquent of the old coaching days
of the '20's and '30's, when the National Road
from Cumberland to Redstone was the great
trans-mountain highway, over which rolled a
motley throng of immigrants, tourists, traders,
and speculators, on foot, on horseback, and in
every imaginable conveyance, bound for the
unfolding West.

This old stone pile, built in 1820, when

the Westering tide was at its flood, was one
of several established along the way, every
A coaching twenty miles or so apart — veritable
tavern   coaching taverns, at which man and
beast in this restless stream might obtain re-
freshment, solid and liquid.   But few of these
coaching houses now remain; there is one six
miles east of Brownsville, another in Uniontown,
and this one at Braddock's Run.   No more
are they the scenes of nightly uproar — the
crack of drivers' whips, the shouts and imprecations of a rushing throng eager to reach the
Western goal; to-day they are peaceful spots
much affected by summer boarders from Pittsburg and Uniontown, and existing but in the
shadow of their old-time glory.

Upon the banks of this noisy little run, now a
muddy barnyard rivulet, the famous Braddock
Where   is said to have died and been interred.
Braddock It will be remembered that the
fell   general was mortally wounded in the
slaughter-pen at the mouth of Turtle Creek,
that fateful ninth of July, but was borne by his
soldiers upon the retreat, and on the fourteenth
died in camp.   In the journal of Colonel James
Burd, sent out through this district by Bouquet
in 1759, to establish a base of supplies for the
defence of the frontier, it is said that " two

miles from here [Fort Necessity] we found General Braddock's grave, about twenty yards from a little hollow, in which there is a small stream of water, and over it a bridge." This locality answers fully to Burd's description, and just up there on the hillside, — now an open pasture, a few yards north of the present National Road, and immediately within the plainly marked Braddock Road, which here crosses the former, — is a clump of tall evergreens, surrounded by a whitewashed board fence, which tradition establishes as the site of Braddock's burial. The evidence, I think, is acceptable, that Braddock was buried at about this spot, although the measures taken by his soldiers to obliterate the grave against possible Indian desecration were so thorough that the precise locality can never be known.

It quickens one's historical imagination to stand by Braddock's resting-place, able with the eye to trace plainly through the hollow and up over the wooded hill to the west the path which the English engineers hewed out for the intrepid general. Brave and well-meaning he certainly was, and not so bad a man as many have pictured, else Washington would never have loved him and mourned his loss. Braddock was but the victim of the traditions of his school; and that these have lasted unto our own day, the Boer War affords ample evidence.

Two miles to the southeast, along the turn-pike, which follows the crest of a low-lying *Great* spur dipping towards the Youghio-*Meadows* gheny (pronounced *Yock'-i-o-ga-ney*), is Geoffrey Facenbaker's farm, which includes Great Meadows and Fort Necessity. Descending through a fenced cattle-way for three hundred yards, one emerges upon the meadow, a low, almost marshy tract of some fifty acres, surrounded by low, gently-sloping hills which once were heavily forested, but now are for the most part open fields. A small creek flowing southeasterly towards the Youghiogheny, and styled East Meadow Run, courses through the centre of the valley, and on its northern bank Washington built his fort.

The first English fur-traders, in their journey along Nemacolin's Path, found here a springy, treeless basin much grown to bushes, but abounding in sweet grasses. They called it Great Meadows, in contradistinction to Little Meadows, a similar basin thirty-one miles to the east, and but twenty from Cumberland. In these meadows, Great and Little, they were accustomed in over-mountain trips to pasturing

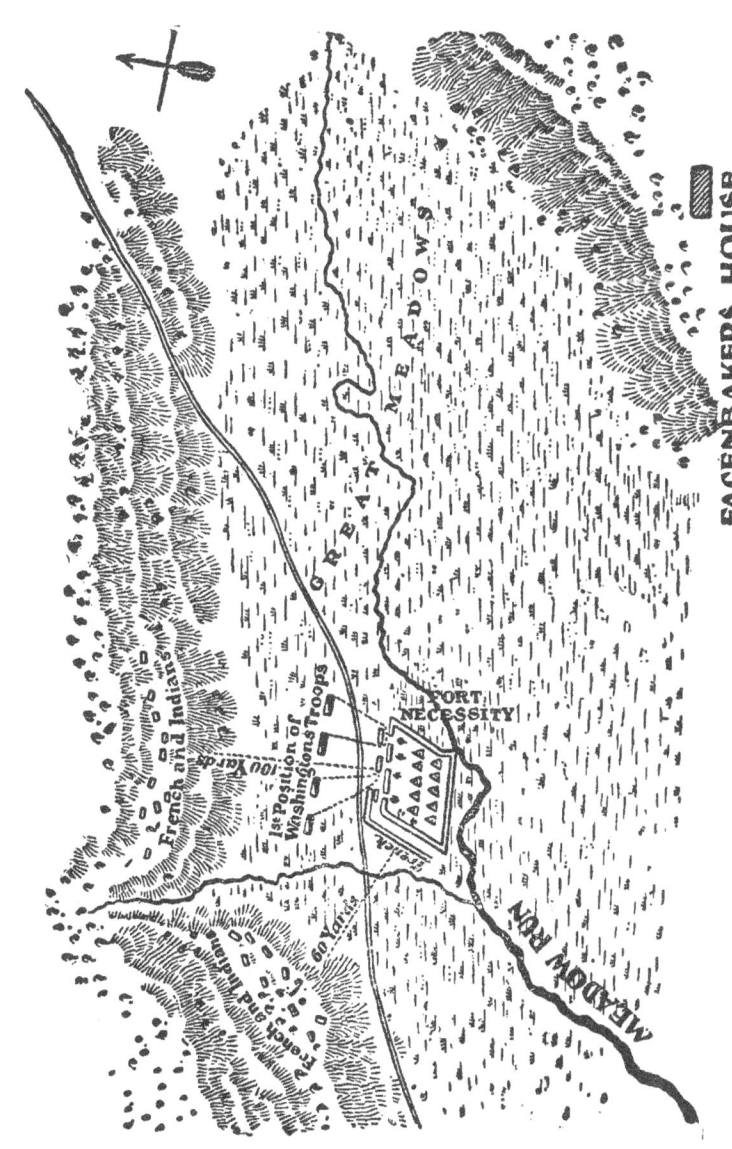

FACENBAKERS HOUSE

PLAN OF BATTLE AT FORT NECESSITY

their horses and cattle, and Washington also found them serviceable in this regard, in his expedition of 1754. It will be remembered that on his way to support the Virginian occupation of the Forks of the Ohio (Pittsburg), he made the Great Meadows a base of operations, although his recognition of its unfitness for the purpose was recognized in the name he gave to his stockade.

The French had driven off the English fort-makers at Pittsburg, before Washington's *The first* arrival. Jumonville, sent out by way *shot* of Redstone to watch the Virginians, hid in an obscure ravine a half-dozen miles to the northwest, and five hundred yards east of Nemacolin's Path, at the base of a lofty hill from which he had a wide view of the country. Washington, with his advance party, here came upon Jumonville, and the encounter which ensued led to the death of the latter and the opening of the French and Indian War.

Washington, too weak to meet the avenging French force from Fort Duquesne, under *Siege of* Jumonville's brother, De Villiers, who *Fort* had ascended the Monongahela in *Necessity* boats and was rapidly approaching up the valley of the Redstone, fell back to Fort Necessity, strengthened it as best he might, and there stood siege with his half-starved band through that dreary third of July. In a rude stockade surrounded on three sides by hills, one of them so close that the enemy could approach within sixty yards under cover of the woods, and with the besieged crippled for lack of stores, the result was inevitable. The " buckskin general" was obliged to capitulate, and at daybreak of the fourth marched out over Nemacolin's Path towards Will's Creek, a toilsome journey of fifty miles across the mountains, upon a mere apology for a road, the heart-sick officers and men bearing their burdens on their backs, and their wounded on stretchers. They were suffered to carry one swivel with them, for defence against the Indians who hung upon their flanks, and to spike the eight left behind them in the fort. The injury inflicted upon these latter was apparently but nominal, for the following year several of the guns were taken to Fort Cumberland. Years after this, emigrants to the West, following the old over-mountain route, discovered and used others at Great Meadows, and eventually these found their way into Kentucky, where they did service in the defence of savage-harassed settlers on the " dark and bloody ground."

It was surprising to find the remains of Fort Necessity so well preserved. Great *Remains of the fort* Meadow Run, originally a lazy, weed-grown stream some ten feet wide, has been straightened by the present proprietor into a drainage ditch, but its ancient windings are readily distinguishable. The change in the course of the run destroyed an outlying work, but the embankment of the fort itself is traceable through the greater part of its length. The line of earthwork is still some eight or ten inches above the surrounding level; while on the inner side, counting the excavation ditch, it has a height of about fifteen inches.

The accounts of visitors to the fort differ materially as to its shape. In his Journal of 1759, Colonel Burd says, under date of September 10: " Saw Colonel Washington's fort, which was called Fort Necessity. It is a small, circular stockade, with a small house in the centre." In 1816 Freeman Lewis made a survey, and declared that the embankments were then nearly three feet high, and had the shape of an obtuse-angled triangle of one hundred and five degrees, with the base of two hundred and seventy-two feet on the stream (then unchanged in its course), and the sides one hundred and fifteen and ninety-nine feet respectively. Sparks visited the place in 1830, and tells us that it occupied "an irregular square, the dimensions of which were about one hundred feet on each side," and his engraving gives it a diamond shape. The author of the *History of Fayette County* (1822) thinks the outlines are those of a right-angled triangle. I cannot agree with any of these, for our measurements with compass and line gave us an equilateral triangle with sides of about a hundred and twenty feet. Of the side nearest the run (from northwest to southeast) seventy feet are now distinguishable; upon that extending from the still perfect northwest corner towards the southern angle there remains the upper portion, a hundred and ten feet in length; the third side is broken at both ends, owing to the utter destruction of the southern and southeastern angles, but has ninety feet left in the curtain. There are of course no remaining evidences of the palisade, on top of the embankment, for this was at the time destroyed by the French, and all relics have long since been gathered up by curiosity-seekers.

Two hawthorn-trees are growing on the western embankment, one of them fifty-four

inches in circumference; and Mr. Facenbaker
reports that some forty years ago, on coming
into the property, he eradicated a young
locust grove then occupying the site of the fort.
In the centre of the fort still rests, although
upheaved by frost, a hewn block of limestone,
two feet square, the only surviving memento
of a movement inaugurated in 1854 — the
centennial year — for the erection here of a
Washington monument.   This corner-stone
was laid with much ceremonial by Fayette
Lodge, A. Y. M., the Fourth of July of that
year; but nothing has since been done about
the matter, and the outlines of the fort alone
remain as visual evidence of the momentous
affair of the Great Meadows.   Washington
himself was conscious of the historic importance of the spot, and did his best to protect
it from change.   In 1767 he acquired claim to
two hundred and thirty-four acres hereabout,
including the meadow, and mentions the tract
in his will.   Sold by his executors, the site of
Fort Necessity passed through several hands,
but has been untouched by the plough unto this
day; although thousands of crayfish, piling up
little mounds of clay, are just now doing their
best to disturb the surface.

Leaving Great Meadows, with its sloping

brown sides being ploughed and harrowed for
field crops, we ascended to the turnpike once

Jumon-
ville's
Camp

more, through the cattle-way, and
an hour later were back at Summit
House, turning off to the northeast on
the by-road towards Jumonville's Camp. It is
the roughest sort of mountain road, the hubs
of the carriage one moment bumping trees and
stumps, and the other wallowing in deep ruts
which are still filled with the residuum of yes-
terday's rain. Up and down steep grades,
swishing around sharp curves, rattling over
stony hillsides, toiling laboriously through
alternate beds of sand and clay, we reach an
understanding of what Braddock's Road must
have been before the turnpike came. In three
miles we pass Washington's Springs, a romantic glen where the Virginia major is supposed
to have camped the night before he met Jumonville. There is, in this isolated spot, a
small summer hotel with an outlying cottage
or two. As we passed, a tall mountaineer and
his women-folk were busied in whitewashing
and repapering the establishment in preparation for the " season," soon to open.

A half mile or so farther, we found the rocky
hillside hollow in which Jumonville made his
camp, and where was fired the first shot in the

final struggle between French and English for the control of the continent. The sides are now hung thick with laurel, and great beds of ferns carpet the ground; while all about, the dark mountain forest is perhaps quite as tangled and dreary as it was in Washington's day. Towering aloft, a steep climb, is the hill which was Jumonville's outlook over Nema-colin's Path, and from which he could, himself unseen, readily observe the movements of the Virginians. Not far away, on the bank of the outlet of this spring, and at the foot of a huge boulder, is the spot styled Jumonville's Grave, although there is less evidence that here was the actual grave than there is concerning the identity of Braddock's resting-place.

A half mile to the north was, the following year, the camp of Colonel Dunbar, in charge *Dunbar's* of Braddock's heavy reserves. It was *Camp* to Dunbar's camp that the survivors of the ambuscade at Turtle Creek fled in terror; and from here commenced that shameful retreat at a time when the victorious but apprehensive French and Indians were themselves in flight towards Fort Duquesne. Dunbar's Spring, in which Braddock's great stores of powder were spoiled, is still pointed out to strangers, and the story is told that twelve years after Braddock's defeat there were still visible "some six inches of black nitrous matter all over the basin of the spring" — the residuum of the English powder so freely poured into it.

Upon a lofty elevation near Dunbar's camp, with its stirring memories of border warfare, *The mean-* and a half-dozen miles east of Union-*ing of it* town, is one of the admirable soldiers' orphans' schools, of which there are several in Pennsylvania. Just as the sun was sinking, we emerged from the rough forest road which passes the eastern gate of the institution, and drove through the grounds as a cut-short to the Uniontown "pike." The smartly-uni-formed school-lads were drawn up in platoons on the parade-ground, saluting the flag of the country for which Washington, less than a mile distant, virtually fired the first shot, a century and a half ago. That for which Washington stood, at Jumonville's hiding-place, was the guarantee to all white dwellers in North America of the perpetuity of free English institutions, as against the mediæval despotism of the French dominion; the fathers of these homeless boys extended the benefits of those institutions to the blacks within our borders, thus completing the task so well begun.

VII

EARLY LEAD MINING ON THE UPPER MISSISSIPPI

VII

EARLY LEAD MINING ON THE UPPER MISSISSIPPI [1]

IT is not probable th⁀t the aboriginal inhabitants of the Upper Mississippi valley, aside
from using it to ornament their pipes and other
utensils, made any considerable use of lead

Aboriginal previous to the appearance among
use of them of French missionaries, ex-
lead plorers, and fur-traders.   The French
continually searched for metallic deposits, and
questioned the Indians closely regarding their
probable whereabouts.   Although superstitious
with regard to minerals, the latter appear to
have early made known to the whites the veins
of lead in the tract which now embraces the

[1] Not a formal treatise upon this interesting subject.   I
have here but thrown together in outline, as useful material
for those who may wish to develop it, these notes on early
lead mining in the Fever (or Galena) River region, the result
of a somewhat protracted investigation, which, however, I
have not had the opportunity to carry to its utmost
possibilities.

counties of Grant, Iowa, and La Fayette, in Wisconsin; Jo Daviess and Carroll counties in Illinois; Dubuque County, in Iowa, and portions of Eastern Missouri. This is one of the richest of lead-bearing regions, and when once brought to the notice of the explorers of New France its fame became widespread. The French introduced fire-arms among the Northwestern Indians, and induced them to hunt, on a large scale, fur-bearing animals; thus lead at once assumed a value in the eyes of the latter, both for use as bullets in their own weapons, and as an article of traffic with the traders.

The Wisconsin and Illinois Indians were visited in 1634 by Nicolet, who doubtless was *Taught by whites* the first to teach them the use of lead in connection with fire-arms. Radisson and Groseilliers followed in 1658–59, and heard of lead mines among the Bœuf Sioux, apparently in the neighborhood of Dubuque.[1]

Jolliet and Marquette, when in 1673 returning from the Lower Mississippi, must *Early traffic in ore* have instructed the Illinois in the use of fire-arms and the utility of lead — if, indeed, this tribe had not already had some

1 *Wis. Hist. Colls.*, xi., p. 93.

traffic in the ore with wandering traders and coureurs de bois operating the upper waters of the Mississippi River or on Lake Michigan, of whose presence in the region we catch faint glimpses in the earliest records of exploration.[1]

The journals of Marquette and of La Hontan (1689) speak of the mineral wealth of the Upper Mississippi country; but they appear never to have seen the mines themselves, and, misunderstanding their informants, concluded that the deposits were of gold, silver, and copper. Hennepin's map of 1687[2] places a lead mine in the neighborhood of the present Galena, showing that he had definite information regarding it. Joutel, who was in the country that year, says[3] that "travelers who have been at the upper part of the Mississippi

---

[1] "There cannot be a doubt ·that many of the French voyageurs besides M. Perrot and the Du l'Huts had explored a large part of the country * * * at a very early day, but of their adventures we have no account, because they were not sufficiently educated to record them. We have occasionally incidental allusions in public documents, in works on geography, and in memoirs, which prove this to have been the case" — Mills, *Report on the Boundaries of the Province of Ontario* (Ottawa, 1877), p. 6.

[2] Breese, *Early History of Illinois;* and Winchell, *Geological Survey of Minnesota, Final Report.*

[3] Joutel, *Journal* (1713).

affirm that they have found mines of very good lead there."

It is alleged[1] that some French traders stationed in the vicinity of Peoria Lake, on the Illinois River, purchased a quantity of lead in 1690 from certain Indian mines on what afterwards came to be known as Fever or Galena River.

After having made an expedition up the Mississippi in 1690, Nicholas Perrot, then *Perrot's* French commandant of the West, on *mines* being presented by a Miami chief with a lump of lead ore, promised that within twenty days he would establish a post below the Wisconsin River.[2] La Potherie says[3] that the chief gave Perrot information as to the locality of the mines, and the latter accordingly visited them. Perrot, we are told, found " the lead hard to work, because it lay between rocks and required blasting; it had very little dross, and was easily melted." His post, built at this time, was doubtless on the east side of the river, apparently opposite the Dubuque mines.

[1] *Hunt's Merchants' Magazine*, xviii., p. 285.

[2] *Wis. Hist. Colls.*, xvi., pp. 146, 151, 157.

[3] Edition of 1753, ii., p. 251; *Wis. Hist. Colls.*, pp. 301, 331.

As early as 1693 Le Sueur was commandant at Chequamegon Bay, and appears to have *Le Sueur's* made extended explorations through-*operations* out the Upper Mississippi valley, thereby "acquiring renown."[1] In 1695 he built a fort on a large island in the Mississippi River between Lake Pepin and the mouth of the St. Croix,[2] which became for the French, says Charlevoix, "the centre of commerce for the Western parts." While occupying this position, it appears that Le Sueur discovered "mines of lead, copper, and blue and green earth,"[3] and went to France to solicit the court's permission to work them. After many delays, he returned in 1699, in D'Iberville's second expedition to Louisiana, which arrived at its destination in December. Having been commissioned by the king to explore and work "the mines at the source of the Mississippi," he had thirty miners assigned to him. His reporter and companion, Pénicaut, after speaking of the rapids in the Mississippi at Rock Island, says: "We found both on the right and left bank the lead mines, called to

[1] Shea, *Early Voyages up and down the Mississippi* (Albany, 1861), pp. 89 *et seq.*

[2] Neill, *History of Minnesota* (1882), p. 148; Thwaites, *Story of Wisconsin* (Boston, 1890), p. 79.

[3] *Wis. Hist. Colls.*, xvi., p. 178.

this day the mines of Nicholas Perrot, the name of the discoverer.   Twenty leagues [thirty-nine English miles, by U. S. land survey] from there on the right, was found the mouth of a large river, the Ouisconsin."[1]   It was the thirteenth of August, 1700, when they arrived opposite Fever River, which Pénicaut calls " Rivière à la Mine."   He reports that up this little river, a league and a half, there was " a lead mine in the prairie."   Passing up the Mississippi, Pénicaut mentions two streams which correspond to the Platte and Grant rivers, in Wisconsin, and says that Le Sueur " took notice of a lead mine at which he supplied himself" — supposed to be what afterwards came to be known as " Snake diggings," near Potosi, Wisconsin.   After making note of the Black, Buffalo, Chippewa, and St. Croix rivers, in Wisconsin, Le Sueur passed the winter on the Blue River, in what is now Minnesota. He does not appear, except for his immediate necessities, to have utilized the lead mines he had discovered, and the following summer abandoned his post, returning to France.[2]

[1] Margry, v., p. 412.

[2] In this same year (1700), Father Gravier made a trip down the Mississippi, and wrote : " I do not know what our court will decide about the Mississippi, if no silver mines are found, for our government does not seek land to cultivate.

On William de l'Isle's chart of Louisiana (1703), in which he was assisted by the observations of Le Sueur, the Galena lead mines are plainly indicated, as are also the Dubuque mines on the west side.[1]

September 14, 1712, Louis XIV. granted to Sieur Anthony Crozat, for a term of fifteen *Crozat's* years, a monopoly of trade and min-*monopoly* ing privileges in Louisiana. The mines were granted in perpetuity, subject to a royalty, and to forfeiture if abandoned. While Crozat's men found none of the precious metals, they appear to have discovered considerable lead deposits in what is now Southeastern Missouri;[2] and no doubt the English traders, who seriously encroached on the French domain, and the wandering coureurs de bois, had more or less traffic with the Indians for ore, to meet both present needs and home demand.

In 1715, La Mothe Cadillac, governor of Louisiana, and founder of Detroit, went up to the Illinois country in search of reputed silver

They care little for mines of lead, which are very abundant near the Illinois." — Winsor, *Cartier to Frontenac* (Boston, 1894), p. 365.

[1] Neill, *Minnesota*, p. xlv.

[2] Wallace, *Illinois and Louisiana under French Rule* (Cincinnati, 1893), pp. 239, 240.

mines, but carried back only lead ore "from the mines which were shown him fourteen miles west of the river." [1]

Crozat resigned his monopoly to John Law's Company of the West, chartered September 6, 1717; and two years later Louisiana — to which the Illinois country had now been attached — entered upon the brief period of "boom" which was inaugurated by that ill-timed enterprise.

In 1719 there arrived in the Illinois, Philippe François de Renault, newly appointed "director-general of the mines of the Royal India Company in Illinois." [2]

De Renault's discoveries

He despatched prospecting parties to various points on both sides of the Mississippi River, and during the four years which he spent in the district discovered lead mines on the Meramec River and north of what is now Potosi, in Missouri; while M. de la Motte found paying leads on the St. François River, also in Missouri. July 21, 1722, one Le Gardeur de l'Isle writes from Fort Chartres, near Kaskaskia,

[1] Winsor, *Narr. and Crit. Hist. of Amer.*, v., p. 50.

[2] The term Illinois was then applied to a large district lying on the Mississippi and centring at the mouth of the Illinois River — practically all of the present State of that name, and the eastern half of Missouri and Iowa.

that he was in command of a detachment of twelve soldiers to accompany M. de Renault to the Illinois River, to look after some alleged copper and coal mines, and found what he claimed to be silver and gold.[1] No doubt these deposits were but lead and coal, for the French explorers were prone to deceive their patrons as to the value of their mineral discoveries. Charlevoix refers to alleged silver discoveries by Cadillac, but doubtingly. Shea says[2] that De Renault " extracted silver from Illinois lead ore in 1722." Silver is certainly combined with the lead, in this district, but is not present in quantity sufficient for profitable working. In June, 1723, De Renault was granted a square league of territory in the northwestern part of what is now Monroe County, Illinois, and also a tract at Peoria containing about fourteen thousand acres. Upon the former grant he planted a small village named St. Philippe ; but by 1765 the place was deserted, the French residents having removed to the west bank of the Mississippi.[3]

The next reference we find to the lead mines is in 1743, when a M. le Guis gives an ac-

---

[1] E. B. Washburne's letter to Chicago Hist. Soc.
[2] In his edition of Charlevoix, vi., p. 25.
[3] E. B. Washburne's letter to Chicago Hist. Soc.

count [1] of the methods of " eighteen or twenty "
miners then operating in the Fever River re-
Primitive   gion — a fast lot, he says, every man
methods   working for himself at surface operations, and extracting only enough to secure
a bare existence for the rest of the year.   Le
Guis makes the following report of wasteful
smelting methods employed by these miners,
which were strikingly similar to those in vogue
among American miners of later days until the
introduction of the Drummond blast furnace,[2]
about 1836: " They cut down two or three big
trees and divide them in logs five feet long;
then they dig a small basin in the ground and
pile three or four of these logs on top of each
other over this basin: then they cover it with
the same wood, and put three more logs,
shorter than the first, on top, and one at each
end crossways.   This makes a kind of box, in
which they put the mineral, then they pile as
much wood as they can on top and around it.
When this is done, they set fire to it from
under; the logs burn up and partly melt the
mineral.   They are sometimes obliged to re-
peat the same operation three times in order

[1] Wallace, pp. 274, 275.
[2] Invented by Robert A. Drummond, of Jo Daviess
County, Ill.

to extract all the matter. This matter, falling into the basin, forms a lump, which they afterward melt over again into bars weighing from sixty to eighty pounds, in order to facilitate the transportation to Kaskaskia. This is done with horses, who are quite vigorous in the country. One horse carries generally four or five of these bars. It is worthy of remark, gentlemen, that in spite of the bad system these men have to work, there has been taken out of the La Motte mine 2,500 of these bars in 1741, 2,228 in 1742, and these men work only four or five months in the year at most."

Up to November 3, 1762, France held possession of both sides of the Mississippi, and *France* then ceded the eastern half of the *and Spain* valley to Great Britain. In the same year, France made a secret treaty with Spain by which the country west of the river was transferred to the latter power, which, however, allowed six years to elapse before she assumed charge.

In 1763, Francis Benton made finds of lead near Potosi, Missouri, and for a time had extensive workings there.

The map made by Jonathan Carver, as a result of his extended Northwestern travels in 1766, places lead mines at Blue Mounds, just

south of the Wisconsin River. He found ore in
the streets of " the Great Town of the Saukies,"
about the site of the present Prairie du Sac,
and appears to have ascended the principal
mound, which he says " abounded in lead." [1]

In Captain Henry Gordon's Journal, written
the same year (1766),[2] occurs the following
passage, showing that there was at
A con- that time a considerable lead industry
siderable
industry in progress among the French on the
west side of the Mississippi: " The French
have large boats of 20 tons, rowed with 20
oars, which will go in *seventy odd days* from
New Orleans to the Ilinois. These boats go to
the Ilinois twice a year, and are not half loaded
on their return; was there any produce worth
sending to market, they could carry it at no
great expence. They, however, carry lead, the
produce of a mine on the French side of the
river, which yields but a small quantity, as they
have not hands to work it. These boats, in
times of the floods, which happen only in May
and June, go down to New Orleans from the
Ilinois in 14 and 16 days."

The first application for a concession of lead-

[1] Carver, *Travels* (London, 1778), pp. 47, 48.
[2] In Pownall, *Topographical Description of North America*
(London, 1776).

mine land in the valley of the Upper Mississippi was made in 1769 by Martin Miloney
Duralde's Duralde, who signed his application
grant at St. Louis, July 5, 1769. The day
following, the grant was issued by Louis St.
Ange de Bellerive, captain-commandant of the
Illinois, and Joseph Labuxière, " attorney of
the attorney general, judge, etc., of the royal
jurisdiction of the Illinois, for the French."
This tract embraced land " three arpents in
front, by the ordinary depth,"[1] on Le Sueur's
River of the Mines (Fever River), " 160 leagues,
more or less, above" St. Louis. From the
tone of his petition, Duralde appears to have
been a ne'er-do-well, and there is no record
extant to show that he ever settled upon his
grant or opened any mines, although the
Spaniards confirmed all French grants.

Captain Philip Pittman, writing in 1770 of

[1] French claims in Michigan were usually forty arpents in
depth; at Green Bay these claims were merely possessory,
and allowed by the government to extend eighty arpents from
front to rear. The old Spanish common-field lots, in and
around St. Louis, were from one to four arpents wide on the
river, by forty in depth. This appears to have been " the
usual depth " of grants during this period, although in special
cases they were much more ample. The Spanish and French
grants in Upper Louisiana are fully discussed in Scharf's
St. Louis, chap. xiii. The arpent is equal to about 192 feet,
English linear measure.

Ste. Genevieve,[1] which had become a notable market for lead, says: " A lead mine about fif-

A notable market teen leagues distant, supplies the whole country with shot." It appears that at this time lead was, next to peltries, the most important and valuable export of the country, and served as currency. The lead trade was afterwards transferred to St. Louis, when that town began to control the commerce of the region.[2]   One of the largest lead-dealers of the day was Joseph A. Sire, an associate of Chouteau & Sarp's fur company.   Under the Spanish régime, which now ensued, we are told by Stoddard,[3] a careful annalist, that lead miners working for themselves often took out " thirty dollars per day, for weeks together." The traders who dealt in the material also made large profits, the returns being " cent per cent for the capital invested."[4]

[1] *Present State of European Settlements on the Mississippi* (London, 1770).

[2] In Ogden, *Letters from the West* (New Bedford, Mass., 1823), p. 58, is this entry, showing that Ste. Genevieve was still flourishing in his time : " St. Genevieve, in particular, is a fine flourishing town.   Here, back of the river, lead ore is found in great abundance, which has become a traffic of great profit to the inhabitants."

[3] Major Amos Stoddard, *Sketches Hist. and Descrip. of Louisiana* (Philadelphia, 1812).

[4] Scharf, *St. Louis*, p. 308 ; *Mich. Pion. Colls.*, ix., p. 548. In his notes to Forman's *Narrative* (Cincinnati, 1888), L. C.

Julien Dubuque was the next character of note upon the scene. He was a man of re-
Dubuque's mines markable energy, and influential with the Indians. In 1788 he obtained from a full council of Sauk and Fox Indians, held at Prairie du Chien, formal permit "to work lead mines tranquilly and without any prejudice to his labors." He had previously made rich discoveries of this ore on the west bank of the Mississippi, in the bluffs and ravines adjoining the site of the present Iowa town which bears his name. In the immediate neighborhood of his mines, if not one of them, was a rich lead discovered in 1780 by the squaw of Peosta, a Fox warrior.[1] Tradition has it that

Draper says: "About the first of June, 1790, Colonel Vigo, an enterprising trader of the Illinois country, consigned to him [Michael Lacassangue, a Louisville trader] 4,000 pounds of lead, brought by Major Doughty [who built the fort at Cincinnati] from Kaskaskia."

In 1796, John James Dufour, afterwards founder of the Swiss colony at Vevay, Ind , came to America and made his start here by buying lead at Kaskaskia, St. Louis, etc., and taking it up the Ohio River to Pittsburg, where he disposed of the cargo at a profit. With the proceeds he bought 630 acres of land for a vineyard, at the Big Bend of Kentucky River.

[1] Schoolcraft, *Discovery of Sources of Mississippi River* (Phila., 1855), pp. 174, 175. Schoolcraft visited the Dubuque mines in 1820, and gives an entertaining account of them and the native manner of working them — *ibid.*, pp. 169–173. He

when Dubuque made his first location, a man
named Du Bois was living at a mine on the
eastern bank, nearly opposite — probably just
south of the present village of Dunleith.
Dubuque, in honor of the Spanish possessors
of the soil, styled his diggings "The Spanish
Mines." Undoubtedly some Spaniards had
before his time conducted operations in the
neighborhood, for when he went into the country he found substantial roads built for the
transportation of ore; these, the Indians told
him, had been made by Spaniards.[1] Dubuque
does not appear to have restricted himself to
the west side of the river. It is believed that
his prospectors and miners, who all enjoyed
the full sympathy and confidence of the Sauks
and Foxes, roved at will on both sides, and
opened leads on Apple River, near the present

places the distance below Prairie du Chien at sixty miles, and
the extent of the tract, "seven leagues in front [along the
Mississippi] by three in depth." See also Schoolcraft, *View
of the Lead Mines of Missouri*, etc. (N. Y., 1819).

[1] In 1780, as appears from letters of Lieutenant-Governor
Patrick Sinclair to General Frederick Haldimand (*Wis. Hist.
Coll.*, xi., pp. 151, 152, 155, 156), the Sauks and Foxes, led
by MM. Calvé and Ducharme, were in active league with
Spanish and American miners against British influences in
the diggings. The Winnebagoes and Menominees assisted
the British in attacking the miners, and seventeen of the
Americans and Spaniards were taken prisoners to Mackinac.

village of Elizabeth; and as early as 1805 even operated the old Buck and Hog leads on Fever River.

It is fair to presume that the Indians had themselves crudely operated the mines fully *Aboriginal* a century before Dubuque's time. *smelting* But, as we have seen, this was doubtless only to obtain bullets for the guns which they had acquired through trade with the French, and to furnish the fur-traders with a commodity quite as desirable as peltries. It is presumable that the French first taught the natives how to mine and smelt the ore. There is no evidence that the American aborigines ever practised the arts of smelting and casting, before the advent of the whites. The methods in vogue among the Indians were practically such as the whites are known to have employed in the earlier days of lead-mining, and are thus described by an eye-witness, writing in 1819: "A hole was dug in the face of a piece of sloping ground, about two feet deep and as wide at the top. This hole was shaped like a mill-hopper and lined with flat stones. At the bottom or point of the hopper, which was eight or nine inches square, narrow stones were laid across, gratewise. A trench was dug from the sloping ground inward to the bottom of the hopper. This channel was a foot in width and height, and was filled with dry wood and brush. The hopper being filled with the ore and the fuel ignited, in a few minutes the molten lead fell through the stones at the bottom of the hopper, and thence was discharged through the trench over the earth. The fluid mass was then poured into an awkward mould, and as it cooled it was called a ' plat,' weighing about 70 lbs., very nearly the weight of the ' pig ' of later days."

There is no doubt, however, that this method was an improvement over that in vogue among the savages in the time of early French domination; for we read that in Crozat's day the Indians reduced the mineral by throwing it on top of large fires. " Large logs would be placed on the ground and smaller pieces of wood piled around and the ore heaped on. The fire would be set in the evening, and in the morning shapeless pieces of lead would be found in cakes, or in small holes scratched in the earth under the logs; or sometimes in shapeless masses. These pieces were sold to the traders." [1]

We are told by another writer [2] that the

[1] Cf. *Wis. Hist. Colls.*, ii., p. 228.
[2] *Hist. Jo Daviess Co., Ill.* (Chicago, 1878), p. 836.

Indians as a rule but only skimmed the surface; although occasionally they drifted into side-hills for some distance, and upon reaching *Aboriginal* " cap rock " would build a fire under *mining* it and then crack the ore by dashing cold water on the heated surface. In the earliest times, their tools were buck-horns, many of which were found in abandoned drifts by the early white settlers; but in Dubuque's day they obtained hoes, shovels, and crowbars from the traders to whom they sold lead. The Indians loaded their ore at the bottom of the shaft into tough deerskins, the bundle being hoisted to the surface or dragged up inclined planes by long thongs of hide.[1] Many of these Indian leads, abandoned by the aborigines when the work of development became too difficult for their simple tools, were afterwards taken possession of by whites, with improved appliances, and found to be among the best in the region. Early writers generally agree that the Indian mining was almost wholly conducted by old men and squaws, the bucks doing the smelting. However this may be, it is certain that in later days a good many bucks worked in these primitive mines, and many of them are known to have assisted Dubuque. The Sauks and Foxes

[1] *Hist. Grant Co.* (Chicago, 1881), p. 477.

were the owners of the lead-mine district during the eighteenth century, but by the treaty of 1804 they relinquished their lands east of the Mississippi, and the gypsy Winnebagoes then squatted in the district; although with them were mingled many Sauks and Foxes who had married into the Winnebago tribe, in addition to "the British Band" of Sauks, around Rock Island, who were afterwards (1832) implicated in the Black Hawk War.

Dubuque appears to have largely employed his Indian friends in prospecting for lead mines. When their discoveries were reported to him, he would send Canadians and half-*Dubuque's* breeds to prove the claims and some-*Indian* times to work them; although in *prospectors* many cases, he was content with proving the claim and allowing the Indians to work it themselves, the product being brought to his large trading-house on the west side of the river. In this manner the entire lead region of Iowa, Wisconsin, and Illinois became more or less occupied by Dubuque's men before any permanent American settlement.[1]

Conciliating the Spaniards by naming his

[1] In 1826, at Ottawa (Allenwrath diggings), two miles from Galena, there was found, under the ashes of a primitive furnace, a heavy sledge-hammer, undoubtedly left by Dubuque's miners.

west-side plant " The mines of Spain," Dubuque deemed it advisable to seek a formal recognition from the government of Louisiana. He obtained, November 10, 1796, from Baron de "*The* Carondelet, Spanish intendant and *Mines of* governor-general of the province, the *Spain* " grant of a tract seven leagues in length along the west bank of the Mississippi, by three in depth, but with certain restrictions as to trade, to be prescribed by " the merchant Don Andrew Todd," who had a monopoly of the commerce of the upper valley. Dubuque's friendship with the Indians and their dislike of the Spanish were a sufficient safeguard against interference from Don Andrew; although he appears to have met with no small opposition on the east side of the river from wandering representatives of the American Fur Company, whose Mackinac agents are said to have obtained considerable supplies of lead from the crafty Foxes, and indeed to have themselves smelted some ore.

Dubuque waxed wealthy from his lead and peltries, which he shipped to St. Louis, making semi-annual trips in a pirogue. In a formal statement made to Major Zebulon M. Pike (September 1, 1805),[1] he claimed that his mines

[1] Pike, *Expedition* (Philadelphia, 1810), appendix to part i., p. 5.

on the west side of the Mississippi extended over a tract of territory "twenty-eight or *Dubuque's* twenty-seven leagues long, and from *statement* one to three broad." He said that he made each year from twenty to forty thousand pounds of lead pigs; although it is probable that this was an underestimate, for evidently he did not view with favor this evidence of American curiosity about his affairs.

In 1800, France coerced Spain into retroceding Louisiana, and three years later sold it to the United States. It was, however, several years before Americans began operations in the lead region of the Upper Mississippi.

We incidentally learn that in 1811 George E. Jackson, a Missouri miner, had a rude log furnace on an island — now washed away — towards the east side of the Mississippi, not far below Dunleith and nearly opposite the mouth of Catfish Creek.[1] Jackson floated his lead to *Opening of* St. Louis by flatboat, and experi-*American* enced much trouble with the Indians, *régime* who had a thorough dislike for Englishmen and Americans. The reason for their aversion to the Anglo-Saxon race, which with few exceptions has been noticeable from our

[1] *Hist. La Fayette Co.* (Chicago, 1881), p. 394. Cf. *Wis. Hist. Colls.*, vi., p. 272.

earliest intercourse with the red man, is easily explained. The French have been more in sympathy with the savages, with whom their pioneers have readily intermarried; they settled among Indians for the purposes of the fur-trade, and their interests were identical with those of the Indians, being to keep the forests intact. The bearing of the Anglo-Saxon towards the savage has ever been of a domineering character; we are pre-eminently an agricultural and manufacturing people; our plan of colonization aims at the reduction of nature, with the view to making the land support a large population. Our aims, our methods, our manners, are diametrically opposed to a state of savagery. We are a covetous people, and it did not take long for the Indian to understand that the English or American borderer was the herald of a relentless system of conquest. In the presence of the Anglo-Saxon settler, there was no room for the Indian.

In 1812–13, John S. Miller joined fortunes with Jackson, but soon afterwards they abandoned their island furnace and returned down the river. Five years later, Miller returned with two companions, traded a boat-load of goods at Dubuque's old mines, and is supposed to have penetrated to the site of Galena and spent some time in the lead region. Miller and Jackson again visited the place in 1823.

The manufacture of shot near St. Louis dates from 1809, when J. Macklot ran his first cast through a tower which he had erected at *A shot* Herculaneum, thirty miles distant *tower* from St. Louis, on the Joachim River. Indians brought lead in small quantities in their canoes, but the bulk of the ore was transported from the mines by Frenchmen.

In the following February, Nicholas Boilvin, then United States agent for the Winnebagoes, passed through on foot from Rock Island to Prairie du Chien, with Indian guides who *The Buck* showed him a lead mine near Fever *lead* River — supposed to be what afterwards came to be known as the "Buck lead."[1] In a letter to the secretary of war, dated a year later,[2] Agent Boilvin reported that the Sauks and Foxes (on the eastern side of the river) and the Iowas (on the west side) had "mostly abandoned the chase, except to furnish themselves with meat, and turned their attention to the manufacture of lead, which they procure from a mine about sixty miles below Prairie du Chien," — undoubtedly the Fever River and

[1] *Hist. La Fayette Co.*, p. 396.
[2] *Wis. Hist. Colls.*, xi., p. 252.

Dubuque diggings. He reports that in 1810 they manufactured four hundred thousand pounds of the metal, which they exchanged for goods, mainly with Canadian traders, who were continually inciting them to opposition against Americans. Boilvin alludes to the fact that the Indians found lead-mining more profitable than hunting, and that the government would be wise to introduce among them a blacksmith and improved tools. He thinks that by thus encouraging the Indian miners, " the Canadian trade would be extinguished."

In the same year (1810) Henry Shreeve is said to have worked up the Mississippi as far as Fever River, and taken back from there to the towns on the lower Mississippi, a small cargo of Indian-smelted lead.

Between 1815 and 1820, Captain John Shaw made eight trips with a trading boat between St. Louis and Prairie du Chien, and several times visited the Fever River mines, where he saw the Indians smelting lead in rude furnaces. At one time he bought from them seventy tons of metal, " and still left much at the furnace." [1]

Boilvin does not appear to have broken up

---

[1] *Wis. Hist. Colls.*, viii., p. 250. See Shaw's personal narrative in *id.*, ii., pp. 197 *et seq.*

the French-Canadian trade in the lead district, for we find that up to 1819 several American

French- traders, who attempted to go among
Canadians the Sauk and Fox miners and run
ousted opposition to the Canadians, had been killed.

In the immediate neighborhood of where Galena came to be planted, there were, in 1815, about twenty rude Indian furnaces, the product being bought almost entirely by French-Canadian traders, who are reported to have rated a peck of ore as worth a peck of corn. The same year, a crew of American boatmen attempted to go up Fever River by water; but the Indians prevented them, fearing the cupidity of the Americans, who might become excited by the richness of the mines and attempt to dispossess the natives.

In 1816, Colonel George Davenport, agent of the American Fur Company, and engaged

Lead a in trade with the Sauks and Foxes,
currency erected a trading-post on the portage between the Mississippi and the Fever, near the mouth of the latter; but he soon after left and went to Rock Island, where he settled. Davenport is credited with shipping to St. Louis in 1816, the first flatboat cargo of lead ever avowedly emanating from the Fever

River mines; it was used in payment for Indian goods. Lead in those days was, like fur, quite as useful as currency in the financial operations of the Western country.

By a treaty concluded at St. Louis August 24, 1816, all lands lying north of a line drawn due west of the southern extremity of Lake Michigan to the Mississippi, were granted to the Indians,[1] except a tract on the Mississippi River five leagues square, to be designated by the President. This reservation was intended to include the lead mines, the exact location of which was as yet undefined.

In 1819 there appears to have been a more

---

[1] To the Ottawas, Chippewas, and Potawatomis. In a letter of Governor Ninian Edwards, of Illinois, dated Belleville, September 13, 1827 (Washburne, *Edwards Papers*, pp. 304–306), and addressed to President Adams, it is pointed out that the Sauks and Foxes relinquished, by the treaty of 1804, all the lands between the Illinois and Wisconsin rivers; and that by the treaty of 1816 the United States gave the greater part of this tract, with the lead-mine reservation, to the three tribes named. Thus the Sauks had no share in this gift to the Ottawas, Chippewas, and Potawatomis; neither did the Winnebagoes have any claim in it, "unless some right has been recognized to them inadvertently by the United States, since 1816, of which I know nothing, but which if it exists, was a clear and palpable violation of the treaty with the Ottawas, Chippewas, and Potawatomis aforesaid, unless their consent was previously obtained, which I do [not] suppose was the case."

general movement upon the lead regions. That year, Jesse W. Shull, François Bouthil- *A general* lier, Samuel C. Muir, and A. P. Van *movement* Metre were either trading or operating small smelters in the district, and had taken Fox women for wives.[1]

Colonel James Johnson of Kentucky [2] came to the lead mines of Fever River as early as 1819–20, and did some mining or smelting, and trading. A traveller on the Mississippi in 1821 speaks of meeting Johnson's flatboats, loaded with lead.[3]

The largest discovery of lead ore up to Johnson's time was made in 1819 by the Sauks and Foxes operating a mine about a mile above the site of Galena. Those Indians were members of a band led by " The Buck," who had long been encamped in the vicinity.[4] It is thought that the lead had originally been worked by Dubuque's men, but that after Dubuque's death (1810) the natives had taken possession and continued operations with the crude furnace plant erected by

[1] *Hist. La Fayette Co.*, p. 400.

[2] A brother of Col. Richard M. Johnson, who was said to have slain Tecumseh.

[3] J. G. Soulard, in *Hist. La Fayette Co.*, p. 402.

[4] *Wis. Hist. Colls.*, vi., p. 281.

the whites. It took the entire force of the band to raise the enormous nugget which they *An enormous nugget* had discovered, and they were very proud of it. The Indians expressed a strong desire that the find should be sent as a present to their Great Father at Washington; but as it was never so forwarded, it is presumable that the traders secured it in piecemeal, in the course of traffic, the rate of exchange still being a peck of corn for a peck of ore. The whites afterwards called this mine " Buck's lead," in honor of the chief who operated it; and a neighboring lead was styled " Doe's," in remembrance of the Buck's favorite squaw. The estimate was made, about 1820, that up to that time several millions of pounds had been extracted from the Buck lead, by the Indians and Dubuque's people — more than afterwards taken therefrom by the American miners, despite the fact that it was one of the richest mines in the region, and came to be worked in a scientific manner.

In June and July, 1819, Major Thomas Forsyth, United States Indian agent for the Sauks and Foxes, made a voyage from St. Louis to the Falls of St. Anthony, and in his journal gives us,[1] upon good authority, " the

[1] *Wis. Hist. Colls.*, vi., p. 194.

number, situation, and quality of all the lead
mines between Apple Creek and Prairie du
Chien." Contractors for army and Indian
supplies were at this time frequently passing
the mines, on their way between St. Louis and
Prairie du Chien, and Green Bay and Mississippi River points, and both Indian and white
miners found ready customers for their lead.

Congress had in 1807 reserved mineral lands
from sale, and ordered that leases thereof
The lease should be granted to individuals for
system terms of three and five years. But
owing to Indian opposition and the intrigues
of Canadians, operations under government
leases were confined chiefly to Missouri. Elsewhere, men operated on their own account,
and without system. The first lease in the
Fever River country was granted January 4,
1822, to T. D. Carneil and Benjamin Johnson, and Messrs. Suggett & Payne, all of
Kentucky. Lieutenant C. Burdine, U. S. A.,
was ordered to aid them in selecting a hundred
and sixty acres each in the lead region, and
to protect them with an armed force.[1] But
no report of the expedition, if it were ever
undertaken, appears to have been published.

As early as April 12 following, a lease for

[1] *Hist. La Fayette Co.*, p. 402.

three years was granted to Colonel James Johnson, who had for three years operated in the country without license. He immediately took to the mines a number of workmen, including some negro slaves, together with a supply of good tools. Encamping where Galena now stands, and under strong military protection,[1] Johnson began operations on the most extensive scale yet known in the lead country. At the time there were several French and Indian settlements on the Fever, the former being engaged in trade and the latter in mining and smelting.

There now flocked thither a horde of squatters and prospectors from Missouri, Kentucky, and Tennessee; while many came from Southern Illinois via Fort Clark (Peoria) and the old Indian trail which was afterwards developed into a wagon road and styled "Kellogg's trail." For the most part, the newcomers paid small attention to Congressional enactments. The lessees not being supported in their rights, protracted disputes ensued, many of them disastrous to all concerned. In 1822 there were, as we have seen, but four other lessees besides Johnson; and in 1823 but nine were added to the

A horde of squatters

[1] *Wis. Hist. Colls.*, vi., p. 272; viii., p. 250.

list — among them Dr. Moses Meeker, who established a considerable mining colony, which gave great impetus to the development of the region.[1] The unlicensed plants could, however, be numbered by the score. The leasing system was so unsatisfactory to all concerned, and yielded the government such scanty revenue, that, under act of Congress approved July 11, 1846, the lands were brought into the market and sold.

It appears from the report of Lieutenant M. Thomas, U. S. A., superintendent of lead *The great* mines, made to Congress in 1826,[2] *"boom"* that there were in the Fever River diggings, the first of July, 1825, about a hundred persons engaged in mining; which was increased to four hundred and fifty-three by the close of August the following year. The agent estimates that in Missouri, at the period of his report, there were two thousand men thus engaged — "miners, teamsters, and laborers of every kind (including slaves)"; but some of these were farmers who, with their slaves, spent only their spare time in the mines.

[1] In *Wis. Hist. Colls.*, vi., p. 271, Dr. Meeker gives an interesting statement of early affairs in the mines after his first visit in 1822. Another valuable account is in *Hist. Jo Daviess Co., Ill.*, pp. 448 *et seq.*

[2] *House Ex. Docs.*, 19th Cong., 2d sess., ii., No. 7.

In 1827 the name Galena was applied to the largest settlement on Fever River, six miles from its junction with the Mississippi.[1] The heaviest immigration began in 1829, and from that time forward the history of the lead country is familiar.

What had particularly assisted the later development of the Fever River region, after *Spanish* the Indians had been quieted, was the *claimants* fact that on the west side of the *ejected* Mississippi the mines were held to be private property, and prospectors were warned off. In 1832 the United States War Department asserted the right of the general government to the tract granted by Spain to Dubuque, and Lieutenant Jefferson Davis was sent from Fort Crawford with a detail of infantry to eject from "the Spanish mines" all settlers claiming title from Spain. There was much dispute as to the right of the government to so act, but Congress ignored the claims of the settlers, and the lands being placed on the market were regularly sold. Many years after, a test case was decided in the United States Supreme Court; and the appellants — the heirs of Auguste Chouteau and John Mullamphy of St. Louis,

---

[1] The river is not now navigable, owing to heavy deposits of soil worked down from the limestone bluffs.

who claimed to have, in 1804, purchased a certain part of Dubuque's tract — were defeated.
In 1833 mining began upon an extended scale
west of the river, the Spanish and the Indian
titles having at last been cleared.

VIII

THE DRAPER MANUSCRIPTS

THE DRAPER MANUSCRIPTS

D URING the past decade, the Draper
Manuscripts in the library of the
The Wisconsin Historical Society have
collector become so familiar to students of
Western history, who have cited them on
hundreds of their pages, that some account
of the man who collected them, and of the
manner in which he amassed this now cele-
brated storehouse of historical materials, would
seem a fitting conclusion to the present volume.

Lyman Copeland Draper was born in the
town of Hamburg (now Evans), Erie County,
New York, on the fourth of September, 1815.
His ancestors, five generations before him,
were Puritans in Roxbury, Massachusetts; his
paternal grandfather was a Revolutionary
soldier, and his maternal grandfather fell in the
defence of Buffalo against the British in 1813,
while his father Luke was twice captured by
the English during the same war.

When Lyman was three years of age, the

family removed to Lockport, on the Erie Canal.
Luke Draper was by turns grocer, tavern-
keeper, and farmer, and as soon as his son
Lyman could be of service about the house,
the store, or the land, he was obliged to assume
his full share of family labor.   Up to the age of
fifteen, the boy's experiences were those of the
average village lad of the period — the almost
continuous performance of miscellaneous duties,
including family shoe repairing, the gathering
and selling of wild berries, and occasional
"jobs" for the neighbors.   One summer was
spent in acting as a hod-carrier for a builder in
the village, at the daily wage of twelve-and-a-
half cents.   From his fifteenth year to his
eighteenth, he served as clerk in various village
shops.   During this time, after having exhausted the possibilities of the village school,
he added to that meagre curriculum the reading of what few books were obtainable by
purchase or loan in the then frontier settlement, and thereby established a local reputation as a youth of letters.

The lad's taste for Revolutionary history
A youthful was early developed.   He came natu-
passion   rally by it.   At Luke Draper's fire-
side, the deeds of Revolutionary heroes formed
the chief topic of conversation.   There were

yet living many veterans of the Continental Army, who were cordially welcomed to the hospitality of the Draper household, while the War of 1812–15 was an event of but a few years previous. The boy, eagerly listening, became steeped in knowledge of the facts and traditions of Anglo-American fights and Western border forays. It was in after years impossible for him to remember when he first became inspired with the passion for obtaining information as to the events in which his ancestors took part.

As a boy he neglected no opportunity to see and talk with distinguished pioneers and patriots. In 1825, when but ten years of age, he saw La Fayette during the latter's visit to the United States; and in his own last days declared he held a vivid recollection of the lineaments of that distinguished friend of the Revolutionary cause. Lewis Cass, DeWitt Clinton, and other celebrities of the day, he also heard speak at Lockport. Visits to the village, on various occasions, of the then noted Seneca chiefs, Tommy Jimmy, Major Henry O'Bail, and others, were to the young enthusiast in border history like visitations from a realm of fancy. La Fayette was the subject of young Draper's first school composition. His first article for the press, published in the Rochester *Gem* for April 6, 1833, was a sketch of Charles Carroll of Carrollton, the last of the " signers." One of the first historical works he read, was Campbell's *Annals of Tryon County ; or, Border Warfare of New York*, published in 1831. This and other publications of the time were replete with lurid accounts of border disturbances, well calculated to fire the imagination of youth.

Peter A. Remsen, a cotton factor at Mobile, Alabama, had married Draper's cousin (1833). *A patron of learning* Taking an interest in the lad, then eighteen years of age, he invited him to pass the winter at his home. While in Mobile, Draper chiefly occupied himself in collecting information regarding the career of the famous Creek chief, Weatherford, many of whose contemporaries lived in the neighborhood of the Alabama metropolis. These manuscript notes, laboriously written down seventy years ago, are, like the greater portion of his materials for history, still mere unused literary bricks and stone.

In 1834, during his nineteenth year, Draper *At college* entered the college at Granville, Ohio, now styled Denison University. Here he remained for over two years as an undergraduate. He appears to have been a good student, but was compelled from lack of money to leave before graduation. Remsen had now returned from the South to New York, and took up his new home in the neighborhood of Alexander, Genesee County. Draper's father was poor, and unable either to help his son towards an education or to support him in idleness; it is probable, also, that the elder Draper was lacking in appreciation of Lyman's unusual tastes. The young man was undersized, far from robust, and entertained aspirations which appeared only to fit him for the then unprofitable career of a man of letters. Remsen, sympathetic and having some means, offered him without cost a congenial home, and to this patron he again turned upon leaving Granville. For a time he was placed at Hudson River Seminary, in Stockport, his studies there being followed by an extended course of private reading, chiefly historical.

Doddridge, Flint, Withers, and afterwards Hall were the early historians of the border. *Doctors disagree* The young student of their works found that on many essential points, and in most minor incidents, there were great discrepancies between them. It was in 1838,

when twenty-three years of age, that Draper
conceived the idea of writing a series of biographies of trans-Alleghany pioneers, in which
he should aim by dint of original investigation
to fill the gaps and correct the errors then
marring all existing books upon this fertile
specialty.   This at once became his controlling
ambition.   He entered upon its execution with
an enthusiasm which never lagged through a
half-century spent in the assiduous collection
of material for what he always deemed the
mission of his life ; but in the end he had only
investigated and collected, and the biographies
were never written.

From the Remsen home, Draper began an
extensive and long-continued correspondence
Notable   with prominent pioneers all along the
corre-   Western frontier — with Drs. Daniel
spondents   Drake and S. P. Hildreth, and Colonel
John McDonald, of Ohio ; William C. Preston,
of South Carolina ; Colonel Richard M. Johnson, Charles S. Todd, Major Bland W. Ballard,
Dr. John Croghan, and Joseph R. Underwood,
of Kentucky ; ex-Governor David Campbell,
of Virginia ; Colonel William Martin and Hugh
L. White, of Tennessee, and scores of others of
almost equal renown.   Correspondence of this
character, first with the pioneers and later with

their descendants, he actively conducted until within a few days of his death.

In 1840 he began to supplement his correspondence with personal visits to the homes *An itinerant interviewer* of pioneers and the descendants of pioneers and Revolutionary soldiers. He had found that for his purpose the gaining of information through letters was slow and unsatisfactory, for in those days the mails were tardy, unreliable, and expensive; and many of those who possessed the material he most sought were not adepts with the pen. There were then practically no railroads in the country which he visited, and for many years the eager collector of historical material travelled far and wide, by foot, by horseback, by stage, by lumber wagon, and by steamboat, his constant companion being a knapsack well laden with note-books.

In these journeys of discovery, chiefly through sparsely settled regions, Draper *Pioneer hospi- tality* travelled, in all, over sixty thousand miles, meeting with hundreds of curious adventures and hairbreadth escapes by means of runaway horses, frightful storms, swollen streams, overturned stages, snagged steamboats, extremities of hunger, and the like, yet never injured nor allowing any untoward circumstance to thwart the particular mission at the time in view.

Especially before 1850, many of those he sought were far removed from taverns and other conveniences of civilization ; but pioneer hospitality was abundant, and a stranger at the hearth a welcome diversion to the dull routine of a frontiersman's home. The guest of the "interviewed," the inquisitive stranger, who was generally blessed with abundant leisure, often stopped weeks together at those crude homes in the New York, Ohio, Kentucky, Virginia, and Tennessee backwoods — long enough to extract, with the acquired skill of a cross-examiner, every morsel of historical information, every item of valuable reminiscence stored in the mind of his host; while old diaries, letters, account-books, or other family documents which might cast sidelights on the romantic story of Western settlement, were deemed objects worthy of acquisition by exercise of the most astute diplomacy.

It would be wearisome to give a list of those whom Draper visited in the course of these re-*Important* markable wanderings which, with but *interviews* few lapses, he made his chief occupation through nearly a quarter of a century, and resumed at intervals for many years after.

Only a few of the most notable can here be mentioned. Perhaps the most important interview he ever held was with Major Bland Ballard, of Kentucky, a famous Indian fighter under General George Rogers Clark in the latter's campaigns against the Ohio Indians. Other distinguished border worthies who heaped their treasures at Draper's feet were Major George M. Bedinger, prominent in Kentucky as a pioneer and Indian fighter; General Benjamin Whiteman, of Ohio, and Captain James Ward, of Kentucky, two of Kenton's trusted lieutenants; and General William Hall, a field officer under Jackson in the Creek War, and afterwards Governor of Tennessee. Draper also met in this manner fifteen of George Rogers Clark's fellow-Indian campaigners and many of the associates and descendants of Boone, Kenton, Sumter, Sevier, Robertson, Pickens, Crawford, Shelby, Brady, Cleveland, and the Wetzels — all of these, names to conjure with in Western and Southern history.

He also visited and took notes among aged survivors of several Indian tribes — Senecas, Oneidas, Tuscaroras, Mohawks, Chickasaws, Catawbas, Wyandots, Shawnees, Delawares, and Potawatomis. Not the least interesting

of these were the venerable Tawanears, or
Governor Blacksnake, one of the Seneca war
captains at Wyoming, who served as such with
the famous Mohawk chief, Joseph Brant, and
the scholarly Governor William Walker, of the
Wyandots. The descendants of Brant among
the Canada Mohawks, among whom Draper
visited at much length, gave him an Indian
name signifying "The Inquirer." Draper
once visited at the home of Andrew Jackson,
and had a long conversation with the hero
of New Orleans. At another time he was the
guest of his old-time correspondent, Colonel
Richard M. Johnson, who is thought to have
killed Tecumseh. Once when in Kentucky,
on a hunt for manuscripts, he saw Henry
Clay; and in Ohio laid eyes on General
William Henry Harrison, — but he had no
opportunity to speak to either of these.

The period of Draper's greatest activity in
the matter of personal interviews was between
A rich 1840 and 1879, although in his latter
harvest years he also frequently resorted to
that method of obtaining materials for history;
while the period of his active correspondence
in searching for information was ended only
by death. The result of this half-century
of rare toil was a rich harvest of collections.

Upon the shelves of the manuscript room in the Wisconsin Historical Library, the Draper Manuscripts now fill four hundred folio volumes.[1] The geographical field covered, is, in the main, from the Hudson River to the Wabash, from Charleston to Louisville; and the period, from the year 1742 — McDowell's fight in the Valley of Virginia — until the close of the War of 1812–15. Some of the material bears upon the trans-Mississippi region, such as the papers of William Clark and the journal of Sergeant Charles Floyd (Lewis and Clark expedition).

The classification is chiefly by the principal border heroes or pioneers concerned, for we have seen that Draper collected with a view solely to using the material for a series of biographies: George M. Bedinger, Daniel Boone, Samuel Brady, Joseph Brant, Daniel Brodhead, George Rogers Clark, Jonathan Clark, William Clark, George and William Croghan, Josiah Harmar, William Henry Har-

[1] In 1857, he computed that his material comprised " some 10,000 foolscap pages of notes of the recollections of warrior-pioneers, either written by themselves, or taken down from their own lips; and wellnigh 5,000 pages more of original manuscript journals, memorandum books, and old letters written by nearly all the leading border heroes of the West." It was somewhat added to in later years.

rison, William Irvine, Simon Kenton, Robert Patterson, James Potter, William Preston, David Shepherd, Thomas Sumter, John Cleves Symmes, Tecumseh, and Louis Wetzel. There are six volumes of data relative to the Mecklenburg declaration of independence; other volumes contain early manuscripts relative to Alabama, Georgia, Illinois, Kentucky, New York, Ohio, Pennsylvania, South Carolina, Tennessee, Virginia, and King's Mountain; numerous volumes are wholly devoted to Draper's interviews with pioneers or their descendants in many parts of the border States and the Middle West. It should, indeed, be explained that while this collection is rich in contemporary documents, in bulk these constitute the lesser part of the Draper Manuscripts, for the old frontier heroes were neither much addicted to the diary habit nor fond of writing letters. Much the larger proportion of the papers are the great collector's interviews and correspondence while seeking information, all of them freely interspersed and enriched with his critical notes. These laborious methods of investigation furnish an interesting and instructive study to historical specialists.

In 1841, while in the midst of his life-long task, Draper drifted to Pontotoc, in Northern

Mississippi, where he became part owner and
editor of a small weekly journal, the *Spirit of
the Times.*[1] This venture not proving

A Missis- financially successful, at the end of a
sippi year his partner considerately pur-
episode chased his interest, giving in payment the deed
to a tract of wild land in the neighborhood.
There came to Pontotoc, about this time, a
young lawyer named Charles H. Larrabee,
afterwards a prominent citizen of Wisconsin,
where he became a circuit judge and a congressman. Larrabee had been a student with
Draper at Granville. The legal outlook at
Pontotoc not being rich with promise, he
united his fortunes with those of his college-
mate, and together they moved upon Draper's
tract. For about a year the young men lived
in a floorless, windowless hut, a dozen miles from
Pontotoc, the nearest post-office, raising sweet
potatoes and living upon fare of the crudest
character. In the summer of 1842 Draper
received the offer of a clerkship under a relative who was an Erie Canal superintendent at

[1] He left Pontotoc in December, 1843. Journeying
leisurely northward, as usual visiting pioneers on the way,
he called in March on Andrew Jackson, at the Hermitage.
In a letter to The Perry (N. Y.) *Democrat*, dated Nashville, Tenn., March 16, 1844, he describes his visit and relates his conversation with the ex-President.

Buffalo, and retraced his steps to the North, leaving Larrabee in sole possession. But the latter soon had a call to Chicago, and followed his friend's example, leaving their crop of sweet potatoes ungarnered and their land at the mercy of the first squatter who chanced along.

The following year, however, Draper, ill fitted for a clerical life, was back again in *In a* Pontotoc, where he made some inter-*haven of* esting "finds" in the chests of the *refuge* Mississippi pioneers. In 1844, once more adrift in the world, he sought, as a haven of refuge, the Remsen household, then near Baltimore. The Remsens eventually moved to Philadelphia, whither their protégé accompanied them. For eight years thereafter, Draper's principal occupation was the prosecution of his search for historical data, always collecting and seldom writing up any of his material. Conscientious, as well as ambitious to leave nothing to be said by later writers upon his topics, he declared that he was not willing to begin until to his own satisfaction he had exhausted every possibility of finding more. Within reasonable limits his attitude is commendable; but as a matter of fact, Draper had by this time become so imbued with the zeal of collecting that he looked upon the digestion of his material as of secondary consideration.

During his life in Philadelphia, he added miscellaneous printed Americana to the objects *Alone* of his collection, and particularly old *in his* newspaper files, for he found that *specialty* these latter were, when obtainable, among the most valuable sources of contemporaneous information on any given topic in history. He thus gathered at the Remsen home a library of prints which came to attract almost as much attention among scholars as had his manuscript possessions. It was a time when in America there were few historical students engaged in original research; as a specialist in the trans-Alleghany field, Draper stood practically alone. George Bancroft, Hildreth, S. G. Drake, Parkman, Sparks, Lossing, and others displayed much interest in the Draper collections, which several of them personally examined and publicly praised. They sent him encouraging letters, urging him to enter upon his proposed work of writing biographies of heroes of the border.

In 1854, Lossing went so far as to enter upon a literary co-partnership with Draper for the joint production of a series of such life his-

tories — Boone, George Rogers Clark, Sevier,
Robertson, Brady, Kenton, Martin, Crawford,

Co-partner-ship with Lossing

Whitley, the Wetzels, Harmar, St.
Clair, Wayne, and some others being
selected for immediate treatment, each
work to be in several large volumes. The
titles of the several biographies were agreed
upon at a meeting in Madison between Lossing
and Draper. But while as a collector Draper
was ever in the field, eager, and abounding in
shrewd resource, as a writer he was a procras-
tinator, and nothing was at the time done.
Three years later, he developed renewed interest in the plan, and sent broadcast over the
country a circular informing the public that
the long-promised work was at last to be performed; and yet naught came of it.

Nineteen years had now elapsed since Draper
had entered upon the full tide of his career as
a collector. Up to this time, he had made a
collection of material perhaps in all essential
points nearly as valuable as it was at his death.
His accumulations in after years were chiefly
in the direction of minor details. Much of this
class of matter, in obtaining which he spent a
large part of the last thirty-five years of his
life, would be considered as unimportant by
historical writers imbued with the modern

spirit and practising modern methods. Draper, however, being by nature an antiquarian, considered no circumstance regarding his heroes as too trivial for collection and preservation. His design was to be encyclopædic; he would have his biographies embrace every scrap of attainable information, regardless of its relative merit. More than once, with some sadness he confessed to the present writer that he felt himself quite lacking in the sense of historical proportion, could not understand what men meant when they talked of historical perspective, and as for generalization he abhorred it. Yet his literary style was incisive, and sometimes he shone in controversy.

"I have wasted my life in puttering," he once lamented, "but I see no help for it; I *Fearing to "go to press"* can write nothing so long as I fear there is a fact, no matter how small, as yet ungarnered." Draper not only feared to "go to press," but even refrained from writing up his notes, literally — as he often admitted — from an apprehension that the next mail might bring information which would necessitate a recasting of his matter. At the time of his contract with Lossing, he had completed some twenty voluminous chapters of his proposed *Life of Boone* — perhaps a

third of the number contemplated.   It is probable that this manuscript was written before he
came to Madison; from its present appearance,
it seems certain that he added nothing to it
during the succeeding thirty-four years of his
life.   Of his other projected biographies, it
was discovered at his death that he had written
no more than a few skeleton chapters, here and
there.

In January, 1849, the Wisconsin Historical
Society had been organized at Madison.   It
Practically   had at first but a nominal existence,
founds the   for there was then no person at its
Wisconsin
Historical   service with the technical skill neces-
Society   sary to the advancement of an undertaking of this character.   Larrabee, Draper's
old friend, had drifted to Wisconsin, and was
now a circuit judge.   He was one of the
founders of the Society.   In full knowledge
of the quality of his friend's labors, he successfully urged upon his associates the importance
of attracting such a specialist to Madison.
About the middle of October, 1852, Draper
arrived upon the scene.   His patron Remsen
had died the spring before, and the following
year Draper married the widow, who was also
his cousin.   The historian was then thirty-seven
years of age, full of vigor and push, kindly of

disposition, persuasive in argument, devoted to his life-task of collecting, self-denying in the cause, and of unimpeachable character.

The story of his really magnificent work as secretary and executive officer of the Wisconsin Historical Society is familiar to all who are intimately concerned with the study of Western history. It has been told so often, in the publications of that institution and elsewhere, that it does not here require specific treatment. Thirty-three years of his life were in large measure consecrated to the service of the Society. He resigned at the close of the year 1886, turning over to the charge of his successor a reference library of national reputation; while the ten volumes of *Wisconsin Historical Collections* which he had edited, are generally recognized as ranking with the best American publications of this character. But not least important were his untiring labors in the face of sometimes bitter opposition, to secure an assured official support for the institution, which at last, after weary years of striving, he saw placed on a strong financial footing as the trustee of the State.

Although the author of numerous pamphlets, of articles in the *Wisconsin Historical Collections*, and in encyclopædias, of a mono-

graph upon collections of autographs of the
" Signers," and of scattering chapters of pro-
King's   jected biographies, and the editor of
Mountain   a few minor publications aside from
the *Collections*, Dr. Draper — the University
of Wisconsin had thus honored him — published but one important historical work:
King's Mountain and its Heroes (Cincinnati,
1881). Unfortunately for the publisher and
author, the greater part of the edition was soon
after its issue consumed by fire, so that few
copies are now extant. Aside from the border
forays of whites and Indians, the really romantic portion of the history of the Revolution in
the South is confined to the Whig and Tory
warfare of the Carolinas, which was first fully
treated in Draper's volume. It was well received at the time; but in later years Winsor
and others have very properly criticised it as
possessing the faults which were conspicuous
in the author's methods: a desire ·to be encyclopædic, and a lack of proper historical
perspective. But even with these faults, *King's
Mountain* is, as a bulky storehouse of information regarding the Revolutionary War in the
South obtained at first hand, a permanently
valuable contribution to American historical
literature.

The reason for Dr. Draper's retirement from
official life, at the age of seventy-one, was the
desire at last to write the numerous biographies
which he had projected so many years before.
His physical vigor was waning, but his literary
ambition was as strong as in youth. Unfortunately for himself, he had accumulated so
Material vast a flood of material that at last it
beyond his was beyond his control; and although
control ever hopeful of soon beginning in
earnest, it was plain that he contemplated his
task with awe. In his nearly five years of
leisure he made no important progress.

"Still puttering," he often mournfully re-
plied, whenever the present writer inquired as
to what he was doing. But his countenance
would lighten with boyish glee, as he continued,
"Well, I'm really going to commence on
George Rogers Clark in a few days, as soon as
I hear from the letters I sent to Kentucky this
morning; but I am yet in doubt whether I
ought to have a Boston or New York publisher
—what is your judgment?" It had ever been
the same story—always planning, never doing.
For his society he was one of the most practical of men, and his persistent energy was re-
warded by almost phenomenal success. But
the work of the institution was pressing; in his

own enterprises he could wait — until, like the patient cat in the fable, he waited too long.

On the fifteenth of August, 1891, the doctor suffered a paralytic stroke, which was the be-

The end   ginning of the end.   Nevertheless, when partially recovered, he bravely returned to his " puttering," still confident that his projected series of a dozen huge biographies would yet leap from his pen when he was at last ready.   Thus, full of hope, although physically feeble, he toiled on until again paralysis laid him low.   On the twenty-sixth he passed quietly to the hereafter, his great ambition unattained, his Carcassonne unreached.   Death had rung down the curtain on this tragedy of a life's desire.

Of stature short and slight, Dr. Draper was a bundle of nervous activity.   Almost to the last,

The man   his seventy-six years sat easily on his
himself   shoulders.   Light and rapid of step, he was as agile as many a youth, despite the fact that he was seldom in perfect health.   His delicately cut features, which exhibited great firmness of character and the powers of intense mental concentration, readily brightened with the most winning of smiles.   By nature and by habit he was a recluse.   His existence had largely been passed among his books and

manuscripts; he cared little for those social
alliances and gatherings which delight the
average man. Long abstention from general
intercourse with those with whom he had no
business to transact, made him slow to form
new acquaintances, and wrongly gained for him
a reputation of being unapproachable. He who
had a legitimate errand thither, found hanging
without the latch-string of the fire-proof library
and working "den," which was hidden in a
dense tangle of lilacs and crab-trees in the rear
of the bibliophile's home. Access gained, the
literary hermit was found to be a most amiable
gentleman, a charming and often merry con-
versationist; for few kept better informed on
current events, or had at command a richer
fund of entertaining reminiscence. To know
Dr. Draper was to admire him as a man of
generous impulses, who wore his heart upon
his sleeve, was the soul of purity and honor,
did not understand what duplicity meant,
loved children and flowers, and was sympathetic to a fault.

If not a great man, this gentle scholar was in
An emi- many directions eminently useful to
nently use- his generation. As the guiding spirit
ful career of an historical society which he made
great, he was in his day incomparable; as

an editor of historical material, he did most excellent service; and undoubtedly he was the most successful of all collectors of material for American border history. So jealously did he guard his treasures, however, that during his lifetime they literally were inaccessible to all save himself. Not unnaturally, from his point of view, he deemed this great mass of documents and notes as his own hard-won quarry, the working of which was to be done in due time. Upon his death, however, the great collection was found to have been willed to the archives of the Society which he loved so well — so many bricks and stones for future historical architects. Coming to the society in a sadly chaotic condition, — for the doctor's private library was a realm strictly guarded against womankind, and his own methods were the reverse of orderly, — in 1892 they were carefully classified, mounted, and bound, thus making them available for all comers.

No doubt students of Western history will always express regret that Draper found it im-

An en-during monument practicable to give to the world the important, many-volumed works for which from his youth he had so eagerly planned. For while contemporary documents are alike useful to all, at least he could himself have best interpreted the multitude of notes and interviews which form so large a proportion of his matter; the world has in his death lost forever a mine of information and a wealth of judgment on controverted points in Western history, which might have illumined his pages. But if more fruitful in printer's "copy," possibly he might have been less persistent as a collector; and of the two classes of public service, if we were to choose between them, we must admit that the Draper Manuscript Collection will prove through generations to come a far more useful and enduring monument to its founder than the shelfful of books which he had proposed to leave as his chiefest legacy.

INDEX

INDEX

ABBOTT, Samuel, American Fur Company employee, 217.
Alabama, manuscripts relating to, 346.
Alexander, Gen. Milton K., in Black Hawk War, 165, 166, 168–173, 183, 184, 189.
Algonquian Indians, 205, 208, 239.
Allouez, Claude, Jesuit missionary, 209, 243–246, 265, 271, 273.
American Fur Company, 172, 217, 224, 227, 249, 262–264, 267, 271, 274, 319, 324.
— Historical Association *Report*, 69.
American Historical Review, 27.
American Home Missionary Society, in Wisconsin, 267.
— Mission Board, 257.
Anderson, Lieut. Robert, in Black Hawk War, 145.
Armstrong, Perry A., *Sauks and Black Hawk War*, 144.
Ashland (Wis.), 12, 236, 273.
Assenisipia, proposed state of, 77, 78.
Assiniboin Indians, 248.
Astor, John Jacob, 224, 227, 262, 263.
Atkinson, Gen. Henry, commands troops against Black Hawk, 141–149, 156, 158, 164-174, 183, 184, 190-194.
Ayer, Frederick, Wisconsin missionary, 265, 267, 269, 270.

BAD AXE, battle of, 145, 188–192, 197, 199.
Bailey, Maj. David, in Black Hawk War, 147.
Ballard, Maj. Bland W., Kentucky pioneer, 340, 343.
Bancroft, George, commends Draper, 349.

Baraga, Frederick, Catholic missionary, 270, 274.
Bay, Chequamegon, 209, 210; discovered, 236; map, 273; described, 242; Indians, 240, 243–247, 259; posts at, 233, 252–256, 266, 274; historic sites, 236, 273, 274; fur-trade, 247, 250–254, 259–264; Catholic mission, 245–247, 270–273; Protestant mission, 265, 270, 273; French commandants, 252–254, 256, 303; French post dismantled, 258; Radisson and Groseilliers at, 234–240; Allouez, 243–246, 271, 273; Marquette, 245-247; Cadotte, 261–264; Warrens, 263-265.
—, Georgian, 204, 206, 208, 225, 239.
—, Green, 9, 102, 103, 233.
—, Keweenaw (Mich.), 209, 242.
—, St. Charles. *See* Chequamegon.
—, St. James, 234.
Bayfield, Lieutenant, 264.
— (Wis.), 260, 264, 272.
— peninsula (Wis.), 244.
Beardstown (Ill.), 142, 144, 158.
Beaubassin, Hertel de, French commandant, 256.
Beauharnois, Charles, Marquis de, governor of Canada, 254, 256.
"Beaver," Lake Superior vessel, 255.
Bedinger, Maj. George M., Kentucky pioneer, 343, 345.
Bellin's map of Lake Superior, 252, 256.
Beloit (Wis.), 166; *Free Press*, 166, 195.
Benton, Francis, discovers lead mines, 309.
—, Thomas H., proposes new territory, 98.
Big Foot, Potawatomi chief, 141.
Bill Cross Rapids (Wis.), 242.

Bismarck (N. Dak.), 96, 97.

Black Hawk (Makataimeshekia-kiak), Sauk Indian leader, birth, 118; in War of 1812–1815, 122; hostile to Americans, 122–125, 128; makes treaties, 125, 126; influenced by White Cloud, 127, 129; massacres Menominees, 131, 132; recruits forces, 134; invades Illinois, 139; attacks Stillman's detachment, 148–153; harries the border, 159–163; retreats to Lake Koshkonong, 167–173; flight, 174–178; attacks army, 179, 180; retires, 183–185; sues for peace, 187; taken captive, 193, 194; imprisoned, 194, 195; travels in East, 194; death, 195; characterized, 119–122, 196; *Autobiography*, 120, 122, 124–126, 129–131, 133, 134, 140, 143, 149, 153, 178, 182, 185, 191.

Blue Mounds (Wis.), 142, 160, 162, 164, 183; mines at, 309.

Boilvin, Nicholas, Indian agent, 322, 323.

Boone, Daniel, Kentucky pioneer, 11, 28, 343, 345, 350; Draper's *Life*, 351, 352.

Boone County (Ill.), 106.

Boonesborough (Ky.), 10.

Boone's road (Ky.), 6, 278.

Borup, ——, fur-trader, 264.

Bouquet, Gen. Henry, in expedition of 1758, 284.

Bouthillier, François, in lead mines, 326.

Bowman, Capt. Joseph, accompanies Clark, 20, 31, 38, 57, 62; *Journal*, 47, 51, 55, 58, 61.

Boyd, Charles S., Illinois pioneer, 135.

"Boyd Papers," in *Wis. Hist. Colls.*, 181.

Boyd's Grove (Ill.), 135.

Braddock, Gen. Edward, 284, 285, 294.

Braddock (Pa.), 279.

Braddock's Road, 277, 279–285, 293.

— Run (Pa.), 284.

Brady, Gen. Hugh, in Black Hawk War, 184.

—, Samuel, Kentucky pioneer, 28, 343, 345, 350.

Brant, Joseph, Mohawk chief, 29, 66, 344, 345.

Breese, Sidney, *Early History of Illinois*, 301.

Brodhead, Daniel, pioneer, 345.

Brownsville (Pa.), 22, 277-280, 283, 288.

Brunson, Alfred, visits La Pointe, 263.

Buck, Sauk and Fox chief, 326, 327.

Buckley, Cornelius, discusses Black Hawk War, 166, 195.

Buffalo Grove (Ill.), 142.

Burd, Col. James, identifies Braddock's grave, 284, 285; *Journal*, 290.

Burdine, Lieut. Clark, protects lead miners, 328.

Burlington (Ia.), 195; *Gazette*, 196.

Burnet, Jacob, *Notes on Northwest Territory*, 85.

Burr Oak Grove (Wis.), 162.

Butler, James Davie, "Early Shipping on Lake Superior," 255.

—, Mann, *History of Kentucky*, 41.

Butterfield, Consul W., *History of Nicolet*, 207.

Byron (Ill.), 138.

CADEAU. *See* Cadotte.

Cadillac, Antoine de Lamothe, Sieur de, founder of Detroit, 216, 246; governor of Louisiana, 305; searches for mines, 306, 307.

——, Jean Baptiste, Wisconsin pioneer, 241, 259-261.

—, Jean Baptiste, junior, 261.

—, Michel, 259, 261-264, 274; daughters of, 263, 265.

Cahokia (Ill.), 12-14, 34-39, 42, 46, 65.

Caldwell, Billy, Potawatomi chief, 122.

Calvé, Joseph, in War of 1812-1815, 314.

Campbell, David, governor of Virginia, 340.

—, Henry C., "Explorations of Lake Superior," 209; "Père Ménard," 209.

—, Mrs. John, Wisconsin missionary, 265.

—, William W., *Annals of Tryon County*, N. Y., 338.

Canada, founding of, 205; conquest of, 218, 257, 258; boundary of, 81, 83, 204, 234; archives of, 256.

Carneil, T. D., in lead trade, 328.

Carondelet, Spanish governor of Louisiana, 319.

Carroll, Charles, of Carrollton, signer, 338.
Carroll County (Ill.), 106; lead mines in, 300.
Carver, Jonathan, Western traveller, 239, 244; *Travels*, 309, 310; map, 309.
Cass, Lewis, at Chequamegon Bay, 244, 262; at Lockport, 337.
Cassville (Wis.), 142.
Catawba Indians, visited by Draper, 343.
Cave Hill Cemetery, Louisville, Clark's grave in, 71.
Chætar, Winnebago chief, 193.
Champlain, Samuel de, founder of Canada, 205, 206, 231.
Charlevoix, Pierre François Xavier de, *Histoire de Nouvelle France*, 252, 307.
Chequamegon Point, 236, 240, 243, 244, 252, 261, 262, 273.
Chersonesus, proposed State of, 77, 78.
Chestnut Ridge (Pa.), 282.
Chicago, 105, 135-137, 141, 193, 228; *Times*, 214.
— Historical Society, 307.
— & Northwestern Railway, 175.
Chickasaw Indians, visited by Draper, 343.
Chillicothe (Ohio), 66, 83-85, 88.
Chingouabé, Chippewa chief, 251, 252.
Chippewa, proposed territory of, 98; boundaries of, 99, 100.
— County (Mich.), 93.
— Indians, 8, 39, 132, 204, 206, 209, 244, 245, 250, 252, 259-262, 265, 266, 268, 272; number of, 255; language, 233, 269; early history of, 240-243, 253, 256, 273; treaty with, 325; removal to Odanah, 269.
Chouteau, Pierre, in fur-trade, 312, 331.
Christino Indians. *See* Crees.
Cincinnati, fort at, 313.
Clark, Gen. George Rogers, 1, 3, 6, 17, 72, 219; early life, 10, 11; plans expedition, 17, 18; in Virginia, 18; recruits forces, 19-25; Illinois march, 25-28; captures Kaskaskia, 28-32, 219; conciliates habitants, 31-33; treats with Spaniards, 36-38; conciliates Indians, 38-40; attempts to capture, 42-44; march to Vincennes, 47-

Clark, Gen. Geo. Rogers (*cont'd*). 54; letter to inhabitants, 54-56; attacks Vincennes, 57-60; captures Vincennes, 61-63; re-inforced, 64, 65; returns to Louisville, 65; expedition of 1780, 66; fails to capture Detroit, 66; failure of powers, 67; proposed for Western exploration, 67, 68; plans filibustering expedition, 68-70; Indian campaigns of, 343; later years, 70, 71; manuscripts concerning, 345; *Biography of*, 350.
Clark, Maj. Jonathan, 62, 345.
—, William, 68; papers of, 345.
— (Ill.), 142.
Clarksville (Ind.), 70.
Clay, Henry, Draper sees, 344.
Cleveland, Moses, pioneer, 343.
Clinton, DeWitt, at Lockport, 337.
Company of the West, for Louisiana, 306.
Congregationalists, in Wisconsin, 267-269.
Congress of Confederation, plans Western States, 76-79, 82.
— of United States, adjusts territorial boundaries, 81-93, 96, 101, 104-109; sells lead mines, 331; *Annals*, 96; *Secret Journals*, 77.
Congressional *Documents*, 330.
Connecticut cedes Western territory, 80.
Cook, Samuel F., *Drummond Island*, 223.
Copper mines, early French, 234, 254-256, 303.
Cornstalk, Shawnee chief, 6, 7.
Cottage Grove (Wis.), 175.
Coureurs de bois, 204, 212, 215, 247, 257, 301, 305.
Crawford, William, Indian fighter, 343, 350.
Cree (Christino) Indians, 236, 248.
Creek, Boyd's (Wis.), 236.
—, Catfish (Mo.), 320.
—, Fish (West Va.), 11.
—, French (Ontario), 206, 225.
—, Indian (Ill.), 136, 157, 160.
—, Redstone (Pa.), 278, 280, 288.
—, Sycamore (Ill.), 140, 148, 197.
—, Turtle (Pa.), 279, 284, 294.
—, Vanderventer (Wis.) 243.
—, West Bureau (Ill.), 135, 136, 142.
—, Will's (Md.), 278, 279, 289.
Croghan, Col. George, in War of 1812-15, 222, 345.

Croghan, Dr. John, Kentucky pioneer, 340.
—, William, Kentucky pioneer, 345.
Crow Wing Reservation, 269.
Crozat, Sieur Anthony, granted Louisiana, 305, 306, 316.
Cruikshank, Ernest, "Black Hawk's record," 122.
Cumberland (Md.), 279, 283, 286.
— Gap, 6, 278.

"DAD JOE," Illinois pioneer, 135.
Dad Joe's Grove (Ill.), 135.
Dakota Indians. *See* Sioux.
Davenport, Col. George, early trader, 324.
Davidson, John Nelson, "Missions on Chequamegon Bay," 265, 267, 268; *Unnamed Wisconsin*, 266.
— and Struve, *History of Illinois*, 96.
Davis, Jefferson, in Black Hawk War, 144, 145, 194; at lead mines, 331.
— County (Iowa), 195.
— farm (Ill.), in Black Hawk War, 157, 160.
Decorah, One-eyed, Winnebago chief, 193, 194.
Defiance (Wis.), 142.
Delaware Indians, visited by Draper, 343.
De Leyba, Francisco, Spanish governor of Louisiana, 37.
De l'Isle, Guillaume, map of, 252, 305.
—, Le Gardeur, searches for mines, 306, 307.
De Louvigny, ——, at Mackinac, 217.
Delta County (Mich.), 93.
Dement, Maj. John, in Black Hawk War, 161, 167.
Denison University (Ohio), 338, 339.
Denny, William H., *Memoir of Maj. Ebenezer Denny*, 30.
De Pere (Wis.), 246, 247.
De Renault, Philippe François, in Illinois, 306, 307.
Detroit, founded, 305; French post, 216, 246, 251; British post, 8, 12–14, 27, 40, 63, 225; attack on, planned, 19, 35, 65, 66, 219; American city, 76, 85, 90, 97, 99, 126.
De Villiers, Louis Coulon, Sieur, French officer, 288.

Dewitt, Abraham B., in Black Hawk War, 144.
Diamond Grove (Wis.), 142.
D'Iberville, Pierre LeMoyne, Sieur, in Louisiana, 303.
Dixon, John, in Black Hawk War, 135.
— (Ill.), 105.
Dixon's Ferry, 135; rendezvous in Black Hawk War, 136, 142, 147, 152, 156, 162, 163, 166, 172, 194.
Doddridge, Joseph, border historian, 339.
Dodge, Henry, governor of Wisconsin, 106; in Black Hawk War, 160–169, 171–174, 179, 184, 189, 191.
— County (Wis.), 174.
Dodgeville (Wis.), 136, 142.
Dorr County (Wis.), 93.
Doughty, Major ——, built Fort Washington, 313.
Doty, James Duane, early Wisconsin leader, 97–101, 262; manuscripts of, 98.
Drake, Dr. Daniel, pioneer historian, 340.
—, S. G., American historian, 349.
Draper, Luke, 336, 339.
—, Lyman Copeland, ancestors, 335; early life, 335–338; interest in the Revolution, 336, 337; at Mobile, 338; in college, 338, 339; designs pioneer biographies, 339, 340; correspondence, 340, 341; itineraries, 341–343; interviews with pioneers, 342–344, 346; interviews Indian chiefs, 343, 344; in Mississippi, 346–348; in Baltimore and Philadelphia, 348, 349; a collector, not a writer, 348, 350, 351; founds Wisconsin Historical Society, 352–355; as author, 354; retirement, 355; death, 356; characterized, 356, 357; bequeaths collections, 358; Notes, 313; *King's Mountain*, 354; *Draper Manuscripts*, 27, 30, 60, 68; described, 335, 345, 346.
Drummond, Robert A., invents blast furnace, 308.
Duane, James, congressman from New York, 75, 77.
Du Bois, ——, works lead mines, 314.
Dubuque, Julien, works lead mines, 313–315, 317–320, 326; gets grant from Spaniards, 219, 331.

Dubuque (Ia.), 144, 300, 302, 313.
— County (Ia.), lead mines in, 300, 305.
Ducharme, Dominique, in War of 1812-15, 314.
Dufour, John James, Swiss emigrant, 313.
Du Luth, Daniel Greysolon, 247, 248, 301.
Duluth (Minn.), 247.
Dunbar, Col. Richard, in Braddock's campaign, 294.
Dunbar's Camp (Pa.), 294, 295.
Dunleith (Wis.), 314, 320.
Dunmore, Lord John Murray, governor of Virginia, 6, 7.
Duralde, Martin Miloney, applies for mining grant, 311.

EARLY, Capt. Jacob M., in Black Hawk War, 158.
East Meadow Run, 286.
Edwards, Ninian, governor of Illinois, 100, 325 ; *Papers*, 100.
Eldon (Ia.), 195.
Elizabeth (Ill.), mines near, 315.
Elk Grove (Wis.), 142.
Equaysayway, Chippewa woman, 261.
Ewing, Col. W. L. D, in Black Hawk War, 171, 177, 179, 189.

FACENBAKER, Geoffrey, Pennsylvania farmer, 286, 292.
Falls of Niagara, 225.
— of Ohio, *see* Louisville.
— of St. Anthony, 327.
Fayette County (Pa.), *History of*, 291.
Ferry, Rev. William M., Mackinac clergyman, 268.
Fifield, Sam. S., Wisconsin citizen, 236.
Fire-arms, Indians learn to use, 300, 315.
Flint, Timothy, border historian, 339.
Florida, expedition against, 69.
Floyd, Serj. Charles, *Journal*, 345.
Fonda, John H., "Reminiscences of Wisconsin," 186.
Ford, Thomas, *History of Illinois*, 96, 120, 121, 183, 184.
—, Worthington C., *Writings of Washington*, 75.
Forman, Maj. Samuel S., *Narrative*, 312.

Forsyth, Maj. Thomas, Wisconsin Indian agent, 327, 328.
Fort Armstrong (Rock Island), 125, 135, 141, 143, 145, 194, 195.
— Atkinson (Wis.), 172.
— Chartres (Ill.), 306.
— Clark (Ill.), location, 329.
— Crawford (Wis.), 133, 144, 146, 180, 181, 331.
— Cumberland (Md.), 289.
— Dearborn (Ill.), 137.
— Duquesne, 25, 288, 294.
— George (Mackinac), 222, **223**.
— Hamilton (Wis.), 142, 168, 172.
— Holmes (Mackinac), 223.
— Howard (Wis.), 136.
— Jefferson, on the Mississippi, 66.
— Madison (Ia.), 134, 139.
— Massac (Ill.), 25.
— Necessity, 279, 281, 282, 285, 286, 288–292.
— Pitt, 5, 22, 23.
— Plum River (Ill.), 162, 166.
— Recovery, 82, 84.
— Sackville (Vincennes), surprised, 57, 58 ; besieged, 58–60 ; surrendered, 61–63 ; re-named Patrick Henry, 62.
— Sumter, 145.
— Union (Wis.), 164.
— Wayne (Ind.), 42.
— Wilburn (Ill.), 165.
— William (Ont.), 253.
— Winnebago (Wis.), 136, 171, 172, 180, 182.
Fortress Monroe, 121, 194.
Four Lakes (Wis.), 168, 175, 176, 178, 199.
Fox Indians, 9, 39, 116, 118, 134, 143, 244, 245 ; habitat, 246, 249, 318 ; war with French, 249 ; with Chippewas, 253 ; treaty with, 325 ; own lead mines, 313, 318 ; work lead mines, 322–324, 326, 327 ; in War of 1812-15, 314. *See also* Sauk Indians.
Fox's Bluff (Wis.), 163.
Fox-Wisconsin portage, 136, 171, 232, 248.
Franciscans, at Chequamegon, 272.
Franklin, Benjamin, U. S. peace commissioner, 71, 72.
Franquelin, Johannes Ludovicus, map of New France, 235, 244, 252.
Freeport (Ill.), 105.
French, settlements in the Northwest, 12, 14 ; furnish firearms to Indians, 300 ; life of settlers, 14–

French (*continued*).
17, 58, 215, 216, 226, 228; size of grants, 311; favor Americans, 32, 33, 54, 56, 65; as lead traders, 323, 324, 328, 329.

Frontenac, Louis de Baude, Comte de, 252.

Frontiersmen, characteristics, 17, 20-22, 137, 321; Indian name for, 28; warfare with Indians, 7, 9, 10; French fear, 18, 219; seek new land, 4-7, 10, 11, 72.

Fry, Jacob, in Black Hawk War, 144.

Frye, Col. Henry, in Black Hawk War, 158, 165, 179.

Fur-trade, territory kept for, 3, 72; French in, 12-15, 27, 215, 216, 315; British in, 8, 72, 203, 204, 220-227, 256, 286, 305; in Wisconsin, 233, 234, 247-254, 259-265; rivalled by lead mining, 323. *See also* American Fur Company and Hudson's Bay Company.

GAINES, Gen. Edmund P., in Black Hawk War, 130, 131.

Galena (Ill.), 105; named, 331; rendezvous in Black Hawk War, 134-136, 142, 161, 164, 165, 167, 170; mines near, 301-309, 315, 318, 321-324, 326, 329; *Gazette*, 100.

Galissonière, Comte de la, governor of New France, 256.

Genet, Charles E., expedition of, 68-70.

Georgia, Genet's expedition in, 69; manuscript relating to, 346.

Gibault, Pierre, Kaskaskia priest, 33, 34.

Girty, Mike, British agent, 141, 159, 160.

—, Simon, British scout, 66.

Gist, Christopher, pioneer scout, 279.

Gordon, Capt. Harry, *Journal*, 310.

Gosselin, A. H., *Jean Nicolet*, 207.

Grand Portage (Minn.), 225, 226, 248.

Grant County (Wis.), lead mines in, 300; *History of*, 316.

Gratiot, Henry, Wisconsin pioneer, 144, 160, 163.

Gratiot's Grove (Wis.), 142.

Gravier, Father Jacques, Jesuit missionary, 304, 305.

Great Meadow Run (Pa.), 290.

— Meadows, 286, 288, 289, 292.

Green Bay (Wis.), 12, 15, 97, 101, 181, 210, 213, 225, 311, 328; Jesuit mission at, 233, 245-247; *Advocate*, 214; *Sunday Messenger*, 214.

Greenville (Ohio), 83, 84; treaty of, 84, 224.

Groseilliers, Médard Chouart, Sieur de, French explorer, 207, 209, 213, 300; on Lake Superior, 234-239, 247; in Minnesota, 239, 240; returns to Canada, 241; deserts to English, 242. *See also* Radisson.

Guis, Monsieur le, describes lead mines, 307-309.

Gulf of Mexico, 212, 232.

— of St. Lawrence, 232, 240.

HALDIMAND, Gen. Frederick, governor of Canada, 314.

Hall, Benjamin F., border historian, 339.

Hall, Rachel, captured by Indians, 160, 164.

—, Rev. Sherman, Wisconsin missionary, 265-269.

—, Sylvia, captured by Indians, 160, 164.

—, Gen. William, governor of Tennessee, 343.

—, William, Illinois pioneer, 160.

Hamilton, Henry, governor at Detroit, 8, 40; councils with Indians, 9; recaptures Vincennes, 40-42; attempts capture of Clark, 42-44; suspects Vigo, 45; surprised by Clark, 51, 54-59; besieged by Clark, 58-60; treats with Clark, 60, 61; surrenders, 61; prisoner, 62, 63; lieutenant-governor of Quebec, 63; governor of Dominica, 63.

—, William S., early lead miner, 142, 168.

Hampshire County (Va.), 23.

Hand, Gen. Edward, Revolutionary officer, 23.

Hanks, Lieut. Porter, commandant at Mackinac, 221, 224.

Harmar, Gen. Josiah, pioneer soldier, 345, 350.

Harney, Maj. William S., in Black Hawk War, 146.

Harrison, William Henry, 82, 344, 346.

Harrodsburg (Ky.), 10.
Hebberd, S. S., *Wisconsin under French Dominion*, 249.
Helena (Wis.), 183.
Helm, Leonard, Clark's captain, 20, 34, 38, 41, 60, 63.
Hennepin, Louis, French explorer, 248; map of, 301.
— (Ill.), 142.
Henry, ——, at Vincennes, 41.
—, Alexander, fur-trader, 255, 258–260; *Travels and Adventures*, 246, 258, 259.
—, Daniel, describes Clark's campaign, 30.
—, Maj. James D., in Black Hawk War, 144, 158, 165, 166, 169, 171–174, 182–184, 189–191.
—, Patrick, governor of Virginia, 18, 22, 23, 26, 36, 62–64.
Herculaneum (Mo.), shot tower at, 322.
Hermitage, Jackson's home, 346.
Hildreth, Richard, commends Draper, 349.
—, S. P., pioneer, 340.
Holderman's Grove (Ill.), 136.
Holmes, Maj. Andrew H., killed at Mackinac, 222.
—, Lieut. Reuben, in Black Hawk War, 187.
—, W. H., explores Lake Superior, 234.
Hopwood (Pa.), 281.
Hough, Franklin B., *American Constitutions*, 91.
Houghton Point (Wis.), 240.
Hudson's Bay Company, 208, 235, 242, 255.
Hulbert, Archer Butler, *Historic Highways*, 135.
Hunt, ——, fur-trader, 227.
Hunt's Merchants' Magazine, 302.
Huron, proposed territory of, 100.
— Indians, 258; Jesuit mission to, 208–210, 235, 239, 241–246; visited by Draper, 343.
Hustisford (Wis.), 169, 173.
Hutchins, Thomas, chart of, 85.

ILES, Capt. Elijah, in Black Hawk War, 158.
Illinoia, proposed State of, 77, 78.
Illinois, under French regime, 17, 207, 306; under British regime, 3, 21, 32; captured by Americans, 28–42; erected into a county, 64, 65; made a territory, 92, 93;

Illinois (*continued*).
made a State, 92, 95, 96; boundaries of, 99–101, 104–107, 110, 166; lead mines in, 162, 300, 302, 306–310, 329; in Black Hawk War, 130, 135-166, 193, 198-200; manuscripts relating to, 346.
Illinois Indians, 213, 245; learn use of firearms, 300.
Indiana, under British regime, 3, 40–42, 54–62; made a territory, 83, 84, 95; territory divided, 86, 92, 93; admitted as State, 93; settlers of, 137.
Indians, hunting grounds of, 3, 6; harry the border, 6, 8, 10, 17, 22, 28, 65, 66; incited by British, 119, 120, 223, 323, 344; relation to French, 17, 34, 38, 320, 321; Clark's methods with, 38–40, 54–59, 65, 219. *See also* the separate tribes.
Iowa, included in Illinois, 306; made a territory, 107, 110, 195; historical archives of, 194, 195.
— City, capital of State, 195.
— County (Wis.), lead mines in, 300.
— Indians, 39.
Iroquois Indians, enemies of New France, 216, 234; war with Hurons, 208–211, 239, 245, 246.
Irvine, William, Revolutionary soldier, 346.
Irving, Washington, *Astoria*, 226.
Island, Basswood, in Chequamegon Bay, 252.
—, Bois Blanc, 99, 219.
—, Corn, Clark's rendezvous, 24, 70.
—, Drummond's, 99, 223.
—, La Pointe. *See* Madelaine.
—, Mackinac, 204, 210, 217, 219, 220.
—, Madelaine, 240, 241, 249, 252, 257, 260, 262, 266, 274; early names for, 252, 256.
Islands, Manitoulin, 206, 208, 210, 246.
—, Twelve Apostles, 239, 244.
Isle La Grosse. *See* Mackinac.
— Ronde. *See* Madelaine.
— Royale, in Lake Superior, 234.
— St. Josephs, 220, 222.

JACKER, Edward, Mackinac missionary, 214.
Jackson, Andrew, in Creek War, 343; message on admission of

Jackson, Andrew (*continued*). Michigan, 90; visited by Draper, 344, 347.
— George E., Missouri miner, 320-322.
— (Wis.), 142.
James, Maj. Thomas, in Black Hawk War, 144.
James, Rev. Woodbridge L., Wisconsin missionary, 268.
Jay, John, American peace commissioner, 71, 72.
Jefferson, Thomas, addresses Clark, 67, 68; proposes Western States, 77, 78.
— (Wis.), 174.
— Barracks (St. Louis), 144, 194.
— Junction (Wis.), 175.
Jesuit missions, 12, 28, 34, 204, 207-211, 213, 216, 219, 220, 233, 240, 242-247, 272.
Jesuit Relations, 208, 235, 243, 244.
Jobin, ——, Frenchman killed, 252.
Jo Daviess County (Ill.), 101, 106; lead mines in, 300, 308 ; *History of*, 316, 333.
Jogues, Isaac, Jesuit missionary, 207, 209.
Johnson, Benjamin, in lead trade, 328.
—, Col. James, 147 ; in lead mines, 326, 329.
—, Col. Richard M., of Kentucky, 326, 340, 344.
Johnston, John, at Chequamegon Bay, 259, 260.
Jolliet, Louis, 212, 213, 235, 300.
Jones, Col. Gabriel, in Black Hawk War, 179.
Jouan, Henri, " Interprète voyageur au Canada," 207.
Joutel, Henri, early French traveller, 301.
Jumonville, Joseph Coulon, Sieur de, French officer, 288, 293-295 ; camp of, 282, 293, 294.
Juneau, Solomon, Milwaukee pioneer, 137.

KAMINISTIQUA (Ont.), 253.
Kansas City (Mo.), 97.
Kaskaskia (Ill.), early French settlement, 12-14, 306, 309 ; captured by Americans, 24-32, 58, 64, 219; habitants aid Americans, 33-36, 44, 47; made county seat, 65 ; lead market, 313.

Kellogg's Grove (Ill.), 135, 142, 161, 166-168.
— trail, 135, 329.
Kenton, Simon, Indian fighter, 343, 346, 350.
Kentucky, settlement of, 6-8, 11 ; raided, 10, 17, 18, 42, 46 ; protection for, 66, 289 ; pioneers of, 24, 28, 137, 340, 342 ; Genet's expedition in, 69, 70; manuscripts relating to, 346.
Keokuk, Fox chief, 119, 124, 125, 134, 192, 195.
Keweenaw Point (Mich.), 236, 253.
Kickapoo Indians, 57, 244, 245.
Kilbourn City (Wis.), 193.
Kingsbury, Lieut. Gaines P., in Black Hawk War, 187.
King's Mountain, manuscripts relating to, 346 ; Draper's book on, 354.
Kinzie, Mrs. John H., *Wau Bun*, 180.

LABUXIÈRE, Joseph, attorney at St. Louis, 311.
Lacassangue, Michael, Louisville merchant, 313.
Lac Courte Oreille (Wis.), 12, 241, 262, 264.
— Flambeau (Wis.), 12, 264.
Lachine Rapids, 206, 213.
La Fayette, Marquis de, visits United States, 337.
— County (Wis.), 160 ; lead mines in, 300, 320 ; *History of*, 320, 322, 326, 328.
La Hontan, Armand Louis de Delondarce, Baron de, early French traveller, 301.
Lake Assiniboin, 226, 241.
— Chetek (Wis.), 12.
— of the Desert, 102.
— Erie, 6, 12, 74, 85, 86, 95, 216.
— Geneva (Wis.), 136.
— Great Slave, 225.
— Horicon (Cranberry Lake, Wis.), 174.
— Huron, 12, 76, 95, 99, 203, 205, 214, 216, 246.
— Kegonsa (First Lake, Wis.), 196.
— Koshkonong (Wis.), Black Hawk at, 154, 159, 160, 168-172, 183.
— Mendota (Fourth Lake, Wis.), 163, 164, 177.

Lake Michigan 203, 214, 219, 301 ; explored, 207, 231 ; Indians near, 9 ; trails from, 136, 137 ; as a boundary, 76, 81, 84-89, 92, 93, 96-102, 105, 232.
— Mills (Wis.), 175.
— Monona (Third Lake, Wis.), 176, 177.
— Nipissing, 206.
— Ontario, 216.
— Peoria (Ill.), lead purchased at, 302.
— Pepin (Wis.), 303.
— St. Clair, 76, 95.
— Sandy, 247.
— Shawano (Wis.), 9.
— Superior, as a boundary, 103, 110, 232 ; Indians of, 8, 240-247, 250 ; explored, 206-209, 235-239 ; copper mines near, 234, 254-256 ; missions on, 242-247 ; commerce of, 203, 214, 226, 247-256 ; map of, 252, 264.
— Waubesa (Second Lake, Wis.), 176.
— Winnipeg, 226.
Lallemant, Jerome, Jesuit missionary, 235.
La Mothe. *See* Cadillac.
La Motte, Monsieur de, finds lead mines, 306, 309.
Langlade, Charles, early Wisconsin settler, 12.
La Pointe, Story of, 231-274; origin of name, 243, 261 ; locations, 273. *See also* Bay, Chequamegon.
La Potherie, Bacqueville de, French historian, 302.
La Prairie-du Rocher, 43.
La Ronde, Denys de, junior, 254-256.
—, Louis Denys, Sieur de, 252, 254-256.
Larrabee, Charles H., Wisconsin citizen, 347, 348, 352.
La Salle, Robert Cavelier, Sieur de, 247.
— (Ill.), 136.
Laurel Hills (Pa.), 280, 281.
Law, John, grantee of Louisiana, 306.
—, John, *Colonial History of Vincennes*, 52.
Lead mines, 124, 136, 142, 144, 162, 299-332.
Le Font, Dr. ——, Jesuit, at Kaskaskia, 34.
Lena (Ill.), 161.

Le Sueur, Pierre Charles, early French explorer, 248-252, 303-305.
Lewis, Freeman, surveyed Fort Necessity, 290.
Lewis and Clark's expedition, 68, 345.
Libby, Orin G., "Chronicle of Helena Shot Tower," 184.
Lincoln, Abraham, in Black Hawk War, 144, 158.
Linctot, Sieur de, French commandant, 253.
—, Godefroy, aids Americans, 40.
Little Meadows (Pa.), 286.
Little Thunder, Winnebago chief, 174.
Lodge, Henry Cabot, *Story of Revolution*, 30.
Logan, Benjamin, Kentucky pioneer, 11.
Logan's Station (Ky.), 10.
Long, Maj. Thomas, in Black Hawk War, 144.
Lossing, Benson J., American historian, 349-352.
Louisiana, under French regime, 80, 299-309 ; under Spanish regime, 37, 41, 45, 309-314, 319 ; retroceded to France, 320 ; purchased by United States, 96, 320 ; map of, 305 ; mines in, 299-331.
Louisville (Ky.), 20, 23, 35, 36, 64, 65, 71, 313.
Louvigny. *See* De Louvigny.
Lucas, Robert, governor of Iowa, 195.
Lynn, Capt. ——, Revolutionary soldier, 23.

McBRIDE, David, "Capture of Black Hawk," 193.
McCarty, Capt. Richard, in Clark's campaign, 61.
McDonald, John, pioneer, 340.
McDouall, Col. Robert, commandant at Mackinac, 223.
McDowell, John, Indian fighter, 345.
McHenry County (Ill.), 106.
McKee, Alexander, border renegade, 66.
McKenney, Thomas L., *History of Indian Tribes*, 252, 260.
Mackenzie, Alexander, explorer, 232.
Mackinac, Story of, 203-228 ; meridian of, 86, 92, 100 ; French post, 203, 214, 216-218, 248, 255 ;

Mackinac, Story of (*continued*).
British, 12-14, 203, 218-220, 314;
American, 203, 220-224, 262; missions at, 246, 247, 265, 268; fur-trade, 211, 215, 224-227, 251.
— boats, 146.
— County (Mich.), 93, 102.
— Strait, 207, 217
Mackinaw City (Mich.), 204, 217.
Macklot, J., early shot-maker, 322.
Madison (Wis.), 107, 163, 168, 175, 177-179.
Malden, British at, 120, 123, 126, 129, 132, 136.
Margry, Pierre, *Découvertes et établissements des Français*, 246, 304.
Marquette, Jacques, Jesuit missionary, 210-214, 235, 245-247, 270, 271, 300; journal of, 213, 301.
Martin, Col. William, pioneer, 340, 350.
"Martin Manuscripts," Canadian Archives, 256.
Mason, George, governor of Virginia, 90; Clark's letter to, 19, 22, 30, 50, 64.
Massachusetts, cedes Western lands, 80.
Matson, Nehemiah, *Memories of Shaubena*, 141.
Mecklenburg (N. C.), Declaration of Independence, 346.
Meeker, Dr. Moses, establishes mining colony, 330.
Ménard, Réné, Jesuit missionary, 209, 242.
Menominee Indians, 9 : in War of 1812-1815, 314; in Black Hawk War, 131, 132, 141, 181; mission to, 272.
Merriam, Adj. ——, in Black Hawk War, 174.
Metropotamia, proposed State of, 77, 78.
Miami Indians, 39, 75, 245, 302.
Michillimackinac. *See* Mackinac.
Michigan, under British regime, 3, 40; as territory, 86, 87, 95-98, 108, 136, 142, 154, 157; State proposed, 76; State erected, 91; upper peninsula of, 90-94, 100, 102, 104; boundaries of, 88-104, 236; Indians of, 227; *Herald*, 100; *Pioneer Collections*, 312.
Michigania, proposed State of, 77, 78.
Middleport (Wis.), 270, 274.

Mille Lac region, 236, 240, 248.
Miller, John S., early lead miner, 321, 322.
Mills, David, *Report on Boundaries of Ontario*, 301.
Milwaukee, 12, 133.
Mineral Point (Wis.), 134, 136, 142.
Minnesota, explored, 239, 240; as a territory, 109-111; boundaries of, 235, 247, 248; Indians of, 8, 18 , 188, 250; *Historical Collections*, 233, 240, 241, 243, 249, 250, 252, 253, 256, 258, 259, 261, 262, 264, 265.
Missions, Jesuit, 233, 240-247; Protestant, 265-270.
Missouri, belongs to Illinois, 306; lead mines in, 300, 305, 312, 314, 320, 328, 330; boundaries of, 96, 99, 104, 110; Indian purchase in, 116.
Mitchell, John, map, 84, 85.
Mohawk Indians, visited by Draper, 343, 344.
Monroe County (Ill), De Renault's grant in, 307.
Montreal, 15, 225, 234, 241, 242, 251, 252, 256, 261.
Moore, Charles, "Discoveries of Lake Superior," 209.
Morgan, Indian chief, 119.
Moundsville (Ill.), 25.
Mount Braddock (Pa.), 279.
Mountraille County (Dak.), 96.
Muir, Samuel C., in lead mines, 326.
Mullamphy, John, early Missouri settler, 331.

NASHVILLE (Tenn.), 347.
Natchez (Miss.), 66.
Neapope, Sauk chief, 132, 133, 139, 178, 179, 182, 194, 197.
Neill, Edward, *History of Minnesota*, 303, 305; "History of Ojibways," 243, 249, 256, 267.
Nemacolin, Delaware Indian, 279; his path, 279, 280, 286, 288, 289, 294.
Neville and Martin, *Historic Green Bay*, 233.
Newark (Ill.), 136.
New France. *See* Canada.
New Orleans, 27, 310, 344.
New York, pioneers, 342; manuscripts relating to, 346; *Colonial Documents*, 255, 256; *Nation*, 226.
Niagara, fort at, 251.

Nicolay and Hay, *Abraham Lincoln*, 138.
Nicolet, Jean, French explorer, 206, 207, 231, 233, 234, 253, 300.
Northwest, discovered, 206; taken for France, 208, 249 ; British control in, 224-226 ; conquest of, 3-72.
North West Fur Company, 224, 225, 255, 262.
Northwest Territory, boundaries, 75, 76; organized, 76-82; divided into States, 82-111.
Noüe, Robertel de la, French commandant, 253.

O'BAIL, Maj. Henry, Seneca chief, 337.
Odanah Reservation (Wis.), 269, 273.
Ogden, George W., *Letters from the West*, 312.
Ogle County (Ill.), 106.
Ohio, part of Quebec, 3 ; Indian raids from, 65-67 ; State organized, 76, 84-86; boundaries of, 88-92, 95, 101, 104, 105 ; pioneers of, 137, 340, 342 ; manuscripts relating to, 346.
— Company, 278, 279.
Old Mackinaw. *See* Mackinaw City.
Oneida Indians, visited by Draper, 343.
Onontio, Indian name for French governor, 252.
Ordinance of 1787, 79-82, 84-87, 93, 95, 101-106.
Oregon (Ill.), 105.
Osage Indians, 39.
Ottawa Indians, 39, 132, 209, 210, 234, 240, 241, 244-246 ; reservation for, 325.
— (Ill.), 157, 158, 160, 165, 318.

PAQUETTE, Pierre, Wisconsin pioneer, 172, 173, 182.
Parish, Thomas J., in Black Hawk War, 142.
Parish's (Wis.), 142.
Parkinson, Col. Daniel L., in Black Hawk War, 142.
Parkman, Francis, commends Draper, 349; *Conspiracy of Pontiac*, 218; *Half Century of Conflict*, 249; *Jesuits*, 208.
— Club *Publications*, 209.
Patterson, J. B., edits Black Hawk's *Autobiography*, 120.

Patterson, Robert, pioneer, 346.
Payne, ——, in lead trade, 328.
Pearson, Philippe, Jesuit missionary, 212.
Pelisipia, proposed State of, 77, 78.
Pénicaut, ——, journal of, 303, 304.
Pennsylvania, 5, 19, 137; as a boundary, 76, 79, 81 ; manuscripts relating to, 346; Historical Society *Publications*, 30.
Peoria (Ill.), 135, 142, 329; De Renault's grant near, 307.
Peosta, Fox warrior, 313.
Perrot, Nicholas, early French explorer, 301 ; lead mines of, 302, 304.
Perry (N. Y.), *Democrat*, 347.
Peru (Ill.), 136, 142, 165.
Pheasant Branch (Wis.), 177.
Philadelphia, 79.
Piankeshaw Indians, 57.
Pickaway Plains (Ohio), 7.
Pickens, Andrew, South Carolina pioneer, 343.
Pictured Rocks of Lake Superior, 236.
Pike, Maj. Zebulon M., *Expedition*, 319, 320.
Pirtle, Alfred, *Clark's Campaign*, 47, 55.
Pittman, Capt. Philip, *Settlements on the Mississippi*, 311, 312.
Pittsburg, 277, 288, 313.
Platteville (Wis.), 101, 142.
Point aux Pins, Lake Superior, 255.
— St. Ignace. *See* Mackinac.
Polypotamia, proposed State of, 77, 78.
Pope, Nathaniel, Illinois congressman, 96.
Portage des Sioux, 125.
Posey, Gen. Alexander, in Black Hawk War, 161, 165-172, 184, 189.
Potawatomi Indians, 9, 39, 244-246 ; in Black Hawk War, 122, 127, 132, 136, 139, 140, 148-154, 159, 160, 166 ; treaty with, 325 ; visited by Draper, 343.
Potosi (Mo.), mines near, 306, 309.
— (Wis.), mines near, 304.
Potter, James, pioneer, 346.
Pownall, Thomas, chart by, 85 ; *Topographical Description*, 310.
Prairie du Chien (Wis.), 9, 40 ; French trading post, 12, 15, 40 ; in Black Hawk War, 126, 132,

Prairie du Chien (*continued*). 144, 146, 181, 186, 188, 193; lead market, 313, 322, 323, 328.
Prairie du Sac (Wis.), 180, 310.
Presbyterians, in Wisconsin, 265–269.
Preston, Senator, arranges Northwest boundaries, 102.
—, William C., pioneer, 340, 346.
Price's station (Ky.), 10.
Prince Society *Publications*, 209.
Prophet. *See* White Cloud.

QUASHQUAME, Indian chief, 125.
Québec, founded, 205; early explorers start from, 212, 231; Indians trade at, 250; province of, 3.

RADISSON, Pierre d'Esprit, Sieur de, French explorer, 207, 209, 213, 247; in Wisconsin, 234, 300; on Lake Superior, 235–239, 243, 244, 273; in Minnesota, 239, 240; returns to Canada, 241; deserts to British, 242; *Journal*, 209, 235, 236, 240. *See also* Groseilliers.
Randall, Henry Stephen, *Life of Jefferson*, 78.
Raudin, Sieur de, in fur-trade, 247.
Raymbault, Charles, Jesuit missionary, 207, 209.
Red Cliff (Wis.), 248.
Redstone. *See* Brownsville.
Red Wing (Minn.), 250.
Remsen, Peter A., cotton merchant, aids Draper, 338–340, 348, 349; death, 352.
Reynolds, Gov. John, in Black Hawk War, 130, 131, 141, 142, 145, 157, 158, 162, 165, 170; *My Own Times*, 121, 131, 146, 151, 157, 163, 171, 172, 182, 191.
Ritner, Lieut. Joseph, in Black Hawk War, 181.
River, Apple (Ill.), 135, 142, 161; mines on, 314, 328.
—, Arkansas, 225.
—, Athabasca, 204, 232.
—, Bad (Wis.), 269.
—, Bad Axe (Wis.), 186–190.
—, Bark (Wis.), 169, 170, 172.
—, Big Miami, 66, 75, 81.
—, Black (Wis.), 209, 304.
—, Blue (Minn.), 304.
—, Bois Brulé (Wis.), 248, 249, 254, 255.

River, Buffalo (Wis.), 304.
—, Catfish (Wis.), 177.
—, Chicago, 249.
—, Chippewa (Wis.), 304.
—, Columbia, 204.
—, Des Moines, 134, 195.
—, Embarrass, 49, 50.
—, Fever. *See* Galena.
—, Fox (Ill.), 116.
—, — (Wis.), 39, 136, 234, 235, 246. *See also* Fox-Wisconsin portage.
—, Galena, lead mines of, 299, 302, 304, 305, 308, 309, 315, 322–326, 329–331.
—, Grant (Wis.), lead mine on, 304.
—, Great Kanawha, 23.
—, Holston, settlement at, 24.
—, Illinois, 40, 116, 135, 136, 141, 142, 154, 306; mines on, 307.
—, Iron (Mich.), 255.
—, Iroquois (Ill.), 155.
—, James (Va.), 66.
—, Joachim (Mo.), 322.
—, Kaskaskia (Ill.), 26, 28.
—, Kentucky, 82, 313.
—, Kishwaukee (Ill.), 149, 154, 156, 157, 167, 199.
—, Mad, 75.
—, Maumee, 40, 75, 76, 85, 86, 89.
—, Menominee (Wis.), 102, 103.
—, Meramec (Mo.), lead mines on, 306.
—, Milwaukee, 9, 137.
—, Mississippi, explored, 207, 212, 213, 235, 247, 248, 300, 304, 305; French control, 233; French posts on, 250, 303; Spanish settlements on, 69; Indians on, 9, 39, 65, 118, 123, 131, 134, 139, 140, 166, 174, 180, 185, 197; battle upon, 186, 188; fugitives cross, 191–193; Clark on, 25, 66; as a boundary, 79, 80, 95–97, 107–110, 116, 232; lead-mining on, 299–332; commerce in, 143.
—, Missouri, 96, 97, 99, 104, 118.
—, Monongahela, 277, 278, 288.
—, Montreal, 102, 103, 236.
—, Muskingum, 71.
—, Ohio, as a boundary, 3, 5, 6, 17, 18, 76, 79, 81, 82, 92; settlements on, 8, 12; Clark on, 23, 25, 46, 47; voyage down, 278; lead transported on, 313.
—, Ottawa, 206, 216, 225.
—, Ozark, 23.
—, Peckatonica (Wis.), battle near, 160.

River, Pigeon, 226, 232, 251, 253; early name for, 235.
—, Platte, 204, 225.
—, Platte (Wis.), lead mine on 304.
—, Potomac, 278.
—, Raisin, battle near, 85.
—, Rock, 9, 135, 139, 154, 199; Black Hawk's village on, 118, 128, 196; Winnebago village, 127, 140, 143; settlements, 141, 165; pursuit of Black Hawk, 145, 156-159, 162, 171-175.
—, Rum, 248.
—, St. Croix, 108, 110, 248, 249, 254, 264, 303, 304.
—, St. François (Mo.), mines near, 306.
—, St. Josephs (Mich.), 76, 249.
—, St. Lawrence, 206, 215, 241, 257.
—, St. Louis, 110, 247, 248, 251.
—, St. Mary, 99, 223.
—, Sugar (Wis.), 168.
—, Thames, battle on, 122.
—, Wabash, 12, 40, 46, 47, 51, 65, 66, 80, 81, 126; drowned lands of, 48, 49.
—, White Earth, 96, 97, 104.
—, Whitewater (Wis.), 170.
—, Wisconsin (Ouisconsin), 9, 154, 199, 234; Dalles of, 188, 193; survey of, 304; Indians on, 116, 118; Ménard, 242; French post, 302; Black Hawk, 170, 177, 180, 183; territory named for, 99.
—, Youghiogheny, 286.
Rivière à la Mine. *See* Galena.
Roads, National (Pa.), 279, 281, 283, 285.
Robertson, James, Tennessee pioneer, 343, 350.
Rocheblave, Philippe de, commandant at Kaskaskia, 27, 30, 31, 33, 36.
Rochester (N. Y.), *Gem*, 338.
Rockford (Ill.), 105, 106.
Rock Island (Ill.), 99, 118, 131, 135, 193, 303, 322; settled, 324.
— Island County (Ill.), 106.
Rogers, Lieut. John, in Clark's campaign, 46, 62.
Royal India Company of Illinois, 306.

ST. ANGE, Louis de Bellerive, Sieur de, commandant of Illinois, 311.
St. Clair, Gen. Arthur, governor of

St. Clair, Gen. Arthur (*continued*). Northwest Territory, 82, 350; *Papers*, 82.
Ste. Genevieve (Mo.), lead market, 312.
St. Francis Xavier mission, Green Bay, 246, 247.
St. Ignace (Mich.), 211, 214, 217; mission, 247. *See also* Mackinac.
St. Louis (Mo.), 37, 45, 46, 125, 126, 143, 194, 311-313, 319, 322-327; *Pastoral Blatt*, 214.
Saint-Lusson, Sieur de, takes possession of Northwest, 208, 249, 259.
St. Paul (Minn.), 110.
St. Philippe, early Illinois settlement, 307.
St. Pierre, Paul le Gardeur, Sieur de, French explorer, 253.
Sarp, ——, fur-trader, 312.
Saratoga, proposed State of, 77, 78
Sauk Indians, habitat, 9, 39, 40, 118, 119, 128, 136, 244-246, 310, 318; in War of 1812-15, 314; own lead mines, 313-318, 322-324, 326, 327; treaty with, 325; encroached upon, 124, 128, 131, 197; massacre Menominees, 131, 132; raid the border, 166-178; battle with, 179, 180; seek peace, 182, 183; retreat, 183-188; last battle of, 188-192. *See also* Black Hawk and Fox Indians.
Sauk trail, 136.
Sault Ste. Marie, 206-208, 225, 235, 245, 249, 251, 253, 255, 256, 259, 260.
Scharf, J. T., *St. Louis*, 311, 312.
Schoolcraft, Henry B., *Narrative*, 244, 252, 262; *Discovery of Sources of Mississippi River*, 313; *View of Lead Mines of Missouri*, 314.
— County (Mich.), 93.
Scotch, in fur-trade, 225.
Scott, Gen. Winfield, in Black Hawk War, 158, 193.
Seneca Indians, visited by Draper, 343.
Sevier, John, Tennessee pioneer, 343, 350.
Shaubena, Potawatomi chief, 122, 141, 148, 155.
Shaw, Capt. John, lead trader, 323.
Shawnee Indians, 6, 122, 343.
Shea, John Gilmary, *Early Mississippi Voyages*, 303; *Charlevoix's Histoire*, 307.

Shelburne, Lord, on fur-trade, 72.
Shelby, Isaac, Western pioneer, 343.
Shepherd, David, pioneer, 346.
Shore's Landing (Wis.), 236.
Shot manufacture, 322.
Shreeve, Henry, lead trader, 323.
Shull, Jesse W., in lead mines, 326.
Shullsburg (Wis.), 142.
Sinclair, Patrick, British officer, 218, 219, 223, 314.
Sinsiniwa Mound (Wis.), 162.
Sire, Joseph A., lead merchant, 312.
Sioux Indians, habitat, 8, 187, 210, 240; war with Chippewas, 244–248, 253; in Black Hawk War, 131, 187, 192, 197; lead mines among, 300.
Smith, William R., *History of Wisconsin*, 163.
Smithsonian Institution, 234.
Soulard, James G., early traveller, 326.
South Carolina, pioneers of, 340; manuscripts relating to, 346.
— Ottawa (Ill.), 136, 142.
South West Fur Company, 224, 225
Spafford's Farm (Wis.), 160.
Spaniards, on Mississippi, 69; work mines, 314; grant land to Dubuque, 319, 331; befriend Clark, 36–38.
Sparks, Jared, American historian, 291, 349.
"Speedwell," Lake Superior vessel, 255.
Spooner, Abigail, Wisconsin missionary, 268.
Stambaugh, Col. S. C., in Black Hawk War, 181.
Stephenson, Capt. J. W., in Black Hawk War, 164, 168.
— County (Ill.), 106, 161.
Stillman, Maj. Isaiah, in Black Hawk War, 147–153, 156, 163, 165.
Stillman's Run. *See* Creek, Sycamore.
Stoddard, Maj. Amos, *Sketches of Louisiana*, 312.
Street, Gen. Joseph, Wisconsin Indian agent, 132, 181, 193, 194.
Suggett, ——, in lead trade, 328.
Sully, R. M., paints Black Hawk's portrait, 121.

Sulte, Benjamin, *Mélanges*, 270.
Sumter, Gen. Thomas, pioneer, 343, 346.
Sylvania, proposed State of, 77, 78.
Symmes, John Cleves, Ohio pioneer, 346.

TALCOTT, Capt. A., surveyor, 85, 89.
Tawanears (Governor Blacksnake), Seneca chief, 344.
Taylor, Col. Zachary, in Black Hawk War, 146, 169.
Tecumseh, 122, 127; death of, 326, 344; papers concerning, 346.
Tennessee, 66, 329, 340, 342; manuscripts relating to, 346.
Thomas, Henry, early Illinois settler, 135.
—, Col. John, in Black Hawk War, 144.
—, Lieut. M., superintendent of lead mines, 319.
Thompson, Samuel M., in Black Hawk War, 144.
Throckmorton, John, captain of the "Warrior," 186.
Thwaites, Reuben Gold, "Boundaries of Wisconsin," 111; *Hennepin's New Discovery*, 248; *Father Marquette*, 214; *Story of Wisconsin*, 303.
Timms's Grove (Ill.), 161.
Todd, Andrew, trader in Upper Louisiana, 319.
—, Charles S., pioneer, 340.
—, John, county-lieutenant of Illinois, 64, 65.
Toledo (Ohio), 89.
Tommy Jimmy, Seneca chief, 337.
Treaties, Ghent, 122, 222, 224; Jay, 220, 224, 225; Paris, 71, 80, 220.
Turner, Frederick Jackson, "Clark Manuscripts," 27; "Correspondence of Clark and Genet," 69; "Fur Trade in Wisconsin," 225.
Tuscarora Indians, visited by Draper, 343.
Two Rivers (Wis.), 12.

UNDERWOOD, Joseph R., pioneer, 340.
Union (Wis.), 142.
Uniontown (Pa.), 279–281, 284, 295.
United States, supreme court on lead-mining claims, 331, 332.

VAN METRE, A. P., in lead mines, 326.
Vaudreuil, Marquis de, governor of Canada, 217.
Venango, Washington visits, 279.
Verwyst, Rev. Chrysostom, "Historic Sites on Chequamegon Bay," 236, 240, 243; *Missionary Labors of Fathers Marquette, Ménard, and Allouez*, 244, 270-272.
Vevay (Ind.), founded, 313.
Vigo, Francis, French trader, 45, 46, 313.
Vincennes, 12-14, 18; surrenders to Americans, 34; captured by Hamilton, 40-42; re-taken by Clark, 45-63, 67, 219; garrisoned, 65; seat of government, 83; meridian of, 81, 93.
Virginia, 5, 6, 10, 70, 71, 342; Clark in, 18, 19, 66, 67; captures Northwest, 33, 34, 44, 45; Hamilton sent to, 62-64; cedes territory, 80, 89; occupies forks of Ohio, 288; manuscripts relating to, 346.

WABASHA, Sioux chief, 187, 192.
Waddam's Grove (Ill.), 161.
Wakefield, John A., *History of Black Hawk War*, 144, 155, 176, 180, 183, 191, 193.
Walker, Gov. William, Wyandot chief, 344.
Wallace, J., *Illinois and Louisiana*, 305, 308.
Wapello, Fox chief, 119.
Ward, Capt. James, Kentucky pioneer, 343.
Warren, Hooper, early editor, 100.
—, Lyman Marcus, early Wisconsin settler, 263-265, 267, 270.
—, Richard, 263.
—, Truman Abraham, early Wisconsin settler, 263, 264.
—, William Whipple, 264, 265; "History of Ojibways," 233, 240, 258, 259, 261, 262.
"Warrior," Mississippi steamer, 186-188, 191, 197.
Wars, French and Fox, 249; French and Indian, 288; Pontiac's, 259; Lord Dunmore's, 6, 7, 11, 71; Revolutionary, 3, 5, 7, 14, 65, 66, 219, 336, 337, 354; with

Wars, French and Fox (*continued*). Creeks, 343; of 1812-15, 119, 122, 131, 141, 221, 224, 262, 314, 337, 345; Black Hawk, 115-200.
Washburn (Wis.), 236, 273.
Washburne, E. B., 100, 101, 164, 307; *Edwards Papers*, 325.
Washington, George, 11; in French and Indian War, 279, 280, 285, 286, 288, 292, 293, 295; scores Hamilton, 63; ends Genet's expedition, 70; proposes Western States, 75, 76.
—, proposed State of, 77, 78.
— City, 69, 78, 120, 194.
— Springs (Pa.), 282, 293
Watertown (Wis.), 174.
Waubojeeg, Chippewa chief, 260.
Wayne, Anthony, 224, 350.
Weatherford, Creek chief, 338.
West Augusta (Va.), Clark recruits in, 20
Wetzels, Kentucky pioneers, 28, 343, 345, 350.
Wheeler, Edward P., authority on La Pointe, 233, 236.
—, Rev. Leonard Hemenway, Wisconsin missionary, 268, 269.
Wheeling (W. Va.), 22, 28.
White, Hugh L., pioneer, 340.
— Cloud (Prophet), Winnebago chief, 126-129, 132, 133, 139, 140, 143, 193; village of, 140, 144, 147, 188, 194.
— Crane, Chippewa chief, 261.
— Crow (Kaukishkaka), Winnebago chief, 160, 163, 164, 168-170, 172.
— Fisher. *See* Waubojeeg.
Whiteman, Gen. Benjamin, Ohio pioneer, 343.
White Oak Springs (Wis.), 142.
Whiteside, Gen. Samuel, in Black Hawk War, 145-147, 156, 158.
Whitesides County (Ill.), 106.
Whitley, William, Kentucky pioneer, 350.
Whittlesey's Creek (Wis.), 236.
Wilburn (Ill.), 142, 165.
Williams, Capt. John, in Clark's campaign, 61.
—, M. C., *Old Mission Church of Mackinac Island*, 228.
Williamsburg (Va.), 34, 63.
"Willing," Clark's galley, 46, 47, 51.
Wilson, ——, fur-trader, 227.
Winchell, Newton H., *Geological Survey of Minnesota*, 301.

Wingville (Wis.), 142.
Winnebago County (Ill.), 106.
— Indians, habitat, 9, 39, 127, 173, 318; language of, 182, 197; in War of 1812-15, 314; in Black Hawk War, 128, 129, 139, 148, 154, 159, 163, 166-175, 180, 182, 187, 188, 199, 200; capture Black Hawk, 193, 194; agency of, 322; claims of, 325.
Winnipeg country, 232.
Winona (Minn.), 187.
Winsor, Justin, criticises Draper, 354; *Cartier to Frontenac*, 305; *History of America*, 306.
Winter, ——, early Illinois settler, 135.
Wiota (Wis.), 142, 168.
Wisconsin, topography, 232; Indians of, 8, 65, 209, 210, 227, 244, 245, 250, 256, 300; under French regime, 12, 207, 231, 233; under British regime, 3, 39, 40, 219; organized as territory, 99, 101, 105, 110; State formed, 108; legislature of, 106-110; boundaries of, 92, 93, 98, 102, 104,

Wisconsin (*continued*.)
105, 107-110, 236, 247; in Black Hawk War, 136, 142, 162-200; missions in, 242-247, 249, 265-273; University of, 177, 354; Historical Society, 121, 194, 235, 352, 353; library of, 335, 345, 353; *Collections*, 4, 78, 101, 111, 122, 135, 136, 144, 159, 161, 163, 164, 172, 175, 181, 184, 186, 193, 207-209, 226, 233, 234, 236, 249, 253, 258, 265, 268, 272, 300, 302, 303, 314, 316, 322, 323, 326, 327, 329, 330, 353; *Proceedings*, 225, 255.
— Heights, battle of, 179-181, 184, 197, 199.
Withers, Alexander S., border historian, 339.
Worthington, Capt. Edward, in Clark's campaign, 61, 62.
Woodbridge, Adj. W. W., in Black Hawk War, 174.
Wyandot Indians. *See* Hurons.

YELLOW BANKS, 139, 155, 162, 192.

Companion volume to " Down Historic Waterways "

On the Storied Ohio

AN HISTORICAL PILGRIMAGE OF A THOUSAND
MILES IN A SKIFF, FROM REDSTONE TO CAIRO

*Being a new and revised edition of " Afloat on the Ohio,"
with new Preface and full-page illustrations from photographs*

THIS trip was undertaken by Mr. Thwaites some years ago, with the idea of gathering local color for his studies of Western history. The Ohio River was an important factor in the development of the West. He therefore wished to know intimately the great waterway in its various phases, and there seemed no better way than to make the pilgrimage as nearly as possible in the manner of the pioneer canoeist or flat-boatman himself. The voyage is described with much charm and humor, and with a constant realization of the historical traditions on every side.

For the better understanding of these references the author has added a brief sketch of the settlement of the Ohio Valley.

A selected list of journals of previous travellers has also been added.

Uniform with " Down Historic Waterways" and " How George Rogers Clark Won the Northwest"

12mo.   300 pages, $1.20 net

A. C. McCLURG & CO., *Publishers*